THE

EPOCH OF THE MAMMOTH.

AVEBURY.

THE
EPOCH OF THE MAMMOTH
AND
THE APPARITION OF MAN UPON THE EARTH.

BY

JAMES C. SOUTHALL, A.M., LL.D.,

AUTHOR OF THE "RECENT ORIGIN OF MAN."

With Illustrations.

PHILADELPHIA:

J. B. LIPPINCOTT & CO.

1878.

PREFACE.

THE question of the antiquity of man is intimately connected with the truth or falsity of the theories of evolution which colour so materially all current scientific investigations. If traces of man shall be carried back to the Glacial Age, and if the date of this epoch in the geological history of the earth can be fixed at one or several hundred thousand years ago; and if, moreover, it shall prove true also, on examination, that man is *pre-glacial*, and that his remains may be found even in the strata of the Pliocene and Miocene periods, then, undoubtedly, a powerful accession is made to the testimony from the lower world adduced in favour of the gradual development of animal life from earlier and more simple forms. If, on the other hand, these traces of man fail in the glacial and pre-glacial deposits, and the glacial epoch should prove, in addition, to be removed from us by no considerable lapse of time; and much more, if introduced recently and since the glacial epoch, man should appear in the beginning, in the words of M. Pruner-Bey, " constituted man in the full force of the term "—*the man* in all respects of the present day;—

then it is impossible, so far at least as man is concerned, for the evolution theory to be true.

The ultimate decision of these great questions must rest on *the facts;* and the active exploration of the post-tertiary (and tertiary) strata in most parts of the world within the past thirty years has accumulated a mass of evidence on the subject which must very soon put an end, one way or the other, to the discussion.

The object of the present volume is to give in a compact form all that the investigations of the students of geology and pre-historic archæology have brought to light with regard to "man's age in the world." It is a question which should be decided apart from all theological prepossessions, and in no way prejudged by any supposed interpretations of a biblical revelation on the subject. It is purely as a question of science that I propose to discuss it; and if we arrive at a conclusion out of harmony with religion, let it be squarely recognised, and let the adjustment constitute a separate task.

If, on the other hand, the two records agree, it is only another wonderful testimony to the endurance and vitality of the Hebrew books.

It is very certain that at some undefined period in the past man was to be found all over Europe, *south of the Baltic and the line of* 54° *lat. in England,* living in caves, and that elephants and rhinoceroses, lions and hyænas, reindeer and hippopotami, abounded in all this region at that time.

It is equally certain that some time after the race had been thus spread over Europe, *a great flood* covered a large portion of the continent with water, and that the same deluge submerged large districts of country in America and in Asia. This was the *Flood of the Loess*, which closed the Palæolithic Age. It was probably subsequent to the Noachian Deluge, which was probably local in its character and more serious in its effects, within its range. It is extremely doubtful whether, previous to this—the Biblical Deluge—the human race had left their original home. They were probably up to that time shut in by the ice and the sea to a very limited area. There was an African Mediterranean Sea covering the space now occupied by the Northern Sahara, and an Asiatic Mediterranean, of which the Caspian and the Aral and the Black Seas are the shrunken relics. Far to the south the reign of ice prevailed in Europe, and the Northern Ocean rolled far over Russia and Siberia. The Arabian and Nubian deserts, with the snow-capped mountains of Abyssinia and the east coast of Africa, formed, it is not unlikely, a barrier in that direction. There were glaciers in the Lebanon; glaciers in the Atlas; glaciers in Anatolia. The Himalaya Mountains constituted a barrier towards India, and the elevated plâteau of Central Asia shut out China on the east, a great portion of which was probably under water—as was North-western India—Central India (like the western part of North America) being at the same time the theatre of terrific volcanic convulsions.

Such was the geology and zoology of the earth when man appeared. The crust of the earth was still in an unstable condition, although that strange episode in the geological history of the earth, the Glacial Age, had nearly done its work—the work of consolidating this surface-crust for the reign of MAN.

Man did not penetrate at once into the North of Europe — he was unquestionably pre-glacial in that sense; for the ice had not retired from Scandinavia and Denmark and Scotland. Man never entered these countries until the Polished Stone Age, and we shall find herein in the sequel a clue to the date of the Glacial Age.

The Chevalier Bunsen in his work on Egypt, and M. Lenormant in his "Ancient History of the East," both recognise in the Zend-Avesta an allusion to the Glacial Age, and both think that, according to the tradition of the Aryan race, that primeval people "were frozen out of their paradise."

The earliest traces of the human race ought to be found in Central or Western Asia, amongst these very Aryans, or amongst the early population of the Chaldæan Valley, or in Egypt. For it is admitted that Central or Western Asia was the point of departure. It is a startling fact, however, that the Chaldæans, the primitive Aryans, the Egyptians, the Assyrians, the South Arabian Cushites, the Phœnicians, the Phrygians, the "Pelasgi" (and probably the Chinese)—all set out as builders of cities and acquainted with the arts of civilised life; while we are told that there are no traces of a Stone Age among the great Uralo-Altaic race [the primitive Asiatic Scythians] from Lake Baikal to the Kama river in Russia.

The presence of the mammoth and the other great extinct animals in the bone-caves and river-gravels in association with human remains, carried with it a very strong suggestion of the antiquity of the palæolithic tribes of Western Europe; but when it is remembered that the elephant roamed in herds on the north-western coast of Africa at the beginning of the Christian Era, and now that it is ascertained that he was hunted in the Tigris Valley by the Assyrian monarchs in the twelfth century before the same era, the existence of the palæolithic fauna in Europe along with man does not appear so remarkable.

Mr. Boyd Dawkins identifies the cave-dwellers of the Palæolithic Age with the modern Eskimo, and these, we know from their language, are related to the Finns and the tribes of the Altai, whose tongue, on the other hand, philology now connects with the primitive language of Chaldæa (the Accadian), thus bringing together "the artisans of the drift," whose remains are found in the Somme Valley, and the tenants of those ancient tombs in the Southern Tetrapolis of Babylonia, in which we find mingled implements of stone and bronze and iron.

It is the endeavour of the following pages to construct a picture of these pre-historic times, uncoloured by the pencil of fancy—a map or a chart rather than a picture of the post-glacial world; to discern the human shadows that begin to flit in the dissolving darkness of the glacial night, or rather the struggling dawn of what geologists denominate the Recent Period—before the earth had been laved with the partial baptism of the Loess Flood, or the gigantic fauna of the quaternary epoch had vanished from Europe; to correlate the abrupt civilisation on the Lower Euphrates and at the mouth of the Nile—or the restless movements of the Aryan tribes—with the rock-shelters and caves of the Western Troglodytes, living in the primeval wilderness, and battling with their rude implements against the elements, and the wild beasts who almost shared their habitations with them. What changes have occurred since then—not only in the shifting scenes of human life, but in the brute creation, and in the climate and physical geography of the earth! When was it?

CONTENTS.

CHAPTER I.

CHAPTER II.

CHAPTER III.

CHAPTER IV.

CHAPTER V.

CHAPTER VI.

CHAPTER VII.

THE

EPOCH OF THE MAMMOTH.

CHAPTER I.

THE FIRST GLIMPSES OF THE HUMAN RACE.

Evolution—No traces of Tertiary man—Quaternary man—Identified with Eskimo race—The first glimpses of man in the East—Egypt, Chaldæa, Arabia, Persia—No Stone Age in these countries—Began as civilised races—Central Asia the primeval centre—The loss of the memory of the metals by the palæolithic tribes of Europe—These stone-using tribes no older than the primitive Aryans, Chaldæans, and Egyptians—That the theory of Mr. Darwin fails as to man, if man began life in the East as a civilised race.

WHEN we observe the stages of evolution through which the earth has passed as revealed by geology and astronomy, we are naturally led to inquire whether the animated beings which move upon it are not also the products of similar processes of development through a long lapse of ages. If a solar system is the result of a gradually-unfolding development—and if a planet acquires its present shape by evolution, the vegetation which covers it may have been a further step in the process; and another succeeding to it may have been the appearance of the humblest forms of animal life—

from which, in turn, the highest forms may have gradually proceeded—until we come to MAN.

This is the beautiful theory of some of the most gifted minds of the present day, supported by a great number of facts and analogies, and in illustration of these views we find many of our most eminent palæontologists and naturalists engaged at the present time in tracing the pedigree of particular animals.

If this theory be true, we must carry back the beginnings of the human race to some remote and undefined period in the Tertiary Age, when the first incipient human forms emerged from the earlier pithecoid types. The human organism at this stage of transition would only be slightly differentiated from that of the higher apes, and man would hardly have commenced to help himself with implements of even the rudest kind. Miocene man would be a being far lower in the stage of existence than the men whose uncouth flint "axes" have been found in the river-gravels of Europe and India, and, associated with extinct animals, in the bone-caverns of France, England, Germany, Italy, and other countries.

The evidences for the antiquity of man on this hypothesis—the evolution theory—are purely speculative; no human remains having as yet been actually found in either the Miocene or Pliocene strata.

Quaternary man—the creation of the new science of Pre-historic Archæology—has very different credentials. His bones have been obtained in various instances, and the tools with which he worked, lying side by side with the remains of the hippopotamus, the elephant, the rhinoceros, the reindeer, the hyæna, have been found in many of the river-valleys and caves of all the countries of Middle, Western, and Southern Europe; or, if one is still unconvinced, we can produce from Southern France the horns of the reindeer carved into implements, and delineations on bone and horn and stone of the reindeer, the mammoth, the cave-bear, and other animals belonging to the so-called Palæolithic period.

This Quaternary or Palæolithic man is identified by some of the highest authorities on the subject with the Eskimo race, whose manner of life bears the most striking resemblance to that of which there are traces in the caves, and whose implements so much resemble those of stone and bone which were in use among the Cave-men.

Such is the state of the case in Western Europe.

The best opinion among ethnologists is that the migrations of the human race (supposing one original centre) commenced from Central (or Western) Asia.

If we turn to the East, the teachings of history and archæology indicate that in Egypt, in Babylonia, in Southern Arabia, as well as among the Aryan tribes of ancient Bactria, the primitive condition of mankind was one of civilisation. The first glimpse that we catch of the race in Egypt and Babylonia, presents it as engaged in erecting pyramids and great temple-towers, as acquainted with bronze and even iron, as possessing a written language, and already deeply absorbed in the study of astronomy and medicine. The farther we go back in Egypt, the more perfect is the art—as the statue of Kephren (the builder of the second pyramid at Ghizeh), the wooden statue in the Museum of Boulaq, the celebrated sphinx, and the seated scribe in the Louvre.

Professor Owen, of England, speaking of the statue of King Kephren (which is a seated figure cut in diorite, a stone harder than granite or serpentine), says of it: "The head is plainly a portrait; the trunk, or torso, is soberly modelled, but in anatomical truth equal to any work by Michael Angelo." And to the same purport M. Renan exclaims: "When we think of this civilisation, that it had known no infancy; that this art, of which there remain innumerable monuments, had no archaic epoch; that the Egypt of Cheops and Kephren is superior, in a sense, to all that followed, *on est pris de vertige.*"

These statues and the pyramids were of course worked with metal tools—possibly with iron; and iron has been found, along with bronze and stone implements, in the oldest tombs of Babylonia.

There was no Stone Age in Egypt or in Chaldæa. Stone implements occur in the Babylonian tombs, as we have said, but bronze and iron also occur at the same time; in Egypt the stone adze is figured in the Third Dynasty, and continues as a hieroglyphic character to the time of the Fifth; while the flint knives have been repeatedly found in the Egyptian tombs by the side of the mummies. The flint arrow-heads, according to Sir Gardiner Wilkinson, continued in use as late as the Eighteenth Dynasty—about 1500 B.C.

There is nothing in either Egypt or Babylonia *prior* to this—*not a trace* of man or his implements.

It is not maintained in any quarter that the date of Menes, the first king of the First Dynasty of Egypt, is earlier than some 5000 years B.C. Lepsius fixes it at 3892.[1] Sir Gardiner Wilkinson and the English Egyptologists (Stuart Pool, Birch, &c.) place it about 2700 B.C.

If, then, MAN, as geologists and archæologists affirm, has been on the earth several hundred thousand years, why are there no traces of him anterior to the organised and civilised communities which we have referred to, in Egypt and Babylonia? If tribes, savage, barbarous, and half-civilised, had been inhabiting the valley of the Nile a hundred and fifty thousand, still more a million, years before Menes, we ought to find, if not their bones, at least their implements; and in the case of the more advanced tribes—as we approach the period of Egyptian civilisation—we ought to find some traces of their *habitations* and *tombs.* We find rude monuments or remains in other countries—the round towers and cromlechs of Ireland, the sculptured stones and weems and burghs of Scotland, the lake-dwellings of Switzerland, the kjökken-möddings of Denmark. In Italy we find the flint implements in the gravel of the valley of the Tiber, the traces of the Polished Stone Age, the Pelasgic walls, the tombs of the Etruscans with their vessels and implements of bronze, the pile-villages and *terramares* of Parma and Modena, and then the *Cloaca Maxima* and the beginnings of Rome, down to the Circus Maximus and the Coliseum. In Egypt and in

[1] Sayce, Smith, and others claim about the same antiquity for the First Dynasty of Babylonia.

the valleys of the Euphrates and the Tigris—prior to the great monuments we have referred to—there is nothing which human hands have touched.

It is a remarkable fact that the Book of Genesis makes a precisely similar representation with regard to the beginnings of the human race. We find, before the Flood, Cain *building a city:* in the eighth generation Jubal is mentioned as "the father of all such as handle the harp and the organ," and Tubal-cain, his brother, as "an instructer of every artificer in brass and iron;" while, after the Flood, Nimrod, the great-grandson of Noah, is associated with the cities of "Babel, and Erech, and Accad, and Calneh;" and Abraham, in the tenth generation from Noah, goes down to Egypt, and finds an organised state.

If we turn to another branch of the human family—the Aryans, in their primeval seats in Central Asia—we find them settled in villages; working in gold, silver, and bronze; in possession of the domestic animals; harnessing horses and oxen to carriages; worshipping the "holy" Ahuramazda, "creator of existing worlds, truth-telling," from whom proceeded "the creative Word, which existed before all things, . . . having its germ in truth."

The Cushite cities of Southern Arabia and the primeval civilisation of China tell the same story.

Civilisation in Asia and North-Eastern Africa, savage tribes in Southern (?) and Western Europe, such is the presentation with regard to the first glimpses which we catch of the human race. All the evidences for the antiquity of man are found in Europe or in the river-valleys of India, but none such in Egypt, nor in Middle or Western Asia, which has been generally accepted as the primeval centre of the families of man.

When we leave these *origines gentium*—when the primitive tribes (if it be so) wander off from the seats of civilisation into the forests of Europe and India, they leave the metals behind them, and we find their rude stone implements in the gravel deposits of the river-valleys.[1]

[1] The question has been asked (see the "Westminster Review" for July 1876, article entitled "Phases of Civilisation"), How, if the post-diluvians set out with a knowledge of the arts of life, and were dispersed over the face of the earth, it happened that the palæolithic tribes of Western Europe "forgot so soon the use of the metals"?

But the Reviewer is oblivious of the remarkable revelations as to the primitive life of mankind in the relic-beds at Troy. Why is there no trace of iron there? Why did these people, 2000 or 2500 years, according to the Reviewer's chronology, after iron and bronze were used in Babylonia and Egypt, continue to use stone, and that as late as 700 B.C.? Now, if in the Troad 50 per cent. of the implements, 1000 or 1200 B.C., were of stone, is it astonishing that, 2000 or 2500 B.C., 100 per cent. of the implements should have been of stone, in the forest solitudes of what is now France and England?

The stone implements, we are told, occur in all the early Chaldæan tombs (along with metal—iron being very rare): a family or a tribe wandering into the wilderness of Europe—perhaps inferior to that great family of *builders* who settled on the Euphrates—would find itself compelled to use stone, and perhaps unable to procure metal, even if it remembered it. In a few generations, no mines having been opened, no metal perhaps discovered, they would have actually forgotten it. It is important also, as hinted above, to bear in mind that the primitive races exhibit different capacities and different characters. The Hamites were the first builders. There are peculiarities marking the Japhetic, the Shemitic, and the Hamitic races—just as the Bedouin Arabs and the Hebrews exhibit indestructible types of character, derived from their original progenitors. We see the same fixed temperament in the Gypsies and the American Indians; and, these last being mentioned, we may remark on the difference between the Village and the Roving Indians, who are the same people, and yet the latter cannot be tamed nor held down to any permanent settlements.

Another illustration is afforded by the people called the Icthyophagi, who, living on the coast of the Arabian Sea, between Persia and India—

Did the first inhabitants of India and Italy and France proceed from the Mesopotamian valley or the shores of the Caspian and the Persian Gulf?

One division of the Aryan family, we know, did cross the Hindoo Koosh, and occupy the valley of the Indus and its tributaries (*Scinde* and the *Punjab*); and this migration, we know, had been preceded by a Cushite occupation of the same region.

The probability is that the primeval stone-using tribes of Central and Western Europe (identified, as stated, with the Arctic races) moved from the same centres; and this is in correspondence with the known history of the movements from Asia to Europe from

at the mouth of the Persian Gulf—in the time of Strabo are described as "having no iron and using arrows and darts hardened in the fire." Why had they never learned to use metal?

Why had the Massagetæ, the powerful Scythian tribe which defeated Cyrus the Great, never learned the use of iron, even as late as the time of the history of Herodotus—and, indeed, in the days of Strabo? Why do the Bojos of Northern Abyssinia at the present day—inhabiting a region where flourished the ancient civilisation of Ethiopia, and where as late as the Christian era the arts of Greece and Egypt were practised in the cities of the powerful Auxumitæ—make use of tools and weapons of stone along with tools and implements of iron?

It is only necessary to refer further to the South Sea Islanders (who originally had the metals)—to the American Indians—the Mound-Builders—the Mexicans—the Peruvians.

We would just add to this note, in connection with the remarks offered in reply to the "Westminster Review" touching the absence of metal among the palæolithic kinsmen of the more civilised Turanian tribes of Western Asia, that the Swiss lake-dwellings illustrate our position. We remarked that even if the first wanderers from the primeval centre should preserve a remembrance of the metals, this memory would soon pass away. Now Dr. Keller tells us that at the oldest pile-villages in Switzerland "traces of copper and bronze have been met with in the lower beds before the appearance of nephrite."

Now this is at the Stone-Age settlements, and seems to indicate that the original settlers had some few implements of metal; while their descendants possessed only stone. The *nephrite* referred to shows where these lake-dwellers came from—for it is not found in Europe.

very early periods, and with the fact that out of thirty-five domestic animals possessed by Europe, thirty-one appear to have originated in Central Asia or Northern Africa.

If it be true that the first population of Europe came from Central Asia, the men of the European river-gravels and bone-caves are no older than the earliest inhabitants of the Chaldæan plain and the table-land of Iran; and if these latter, as well as the Egyptians, appeared in a civilised condition abruptly on the scene some 6000 or 10,000 years ago, Palæolithic Man, as he is called by writers on pre-historic archæology, cannot claim any higher antiquity.

And if, again, it be true that man did appear in a civilised condition abruptly on the scene some 6000 or 10,000 years ago—and there are no traces of such a being prior to this—then, so far as man is concerned, the theory of Mr. Darwin, and all theories of evolution as applied to man, are negatived.

CHAPTER II.

THE UNITY OF THE HUMAN RACE.

The establishment of the unity of the race simplifies the inquiry as to man's age in the world—Proof of this unity derived from the prevalence of certain traditions and customs in all parts of the world—The pre-Christian cross—The Deluge—The Terrestrial Paradise—The megalithic monuments and tumuli—The practice of distorting the human skull—The practice of scalping—The boomerang and the womera—The custom of depositing flint implements with the dead—The Lingham or Phallus—Serpent-worship—That if the Chaldæans and Egyptians were of the same race with the palæolithic tribes of Europe, then the latter are no older than the former.

THE consideration of the question of the antiquity or the recent origin of the human race is very much simplified if the unity of the race is established. We cannot go into this discussion here, and must refer our readers to the formal treatises on the subject, such as Prichard's, De Quatrefages', or Carpenter's. We desire, however, to call attention to certain common traditions and customs among the scattered families of mankind which suggest almost irresistibly that these races were originally one, and that they have proceeded from a common centre.

1. The "pre-Christian cross" is a symbol which is traced in almost every part of the world, and among nearly all the nations of antiquity—either in the form of the *crux ansata,* or handle-cross, of Egypt, Chaldæa, and

Phœnicia, or as the *swastika* of the Buddhists and the *leo-tseu* of China.

The *crux ansata*—the mystical *Tau* (so named from its resemblance to the letter T)—has been called the "key of the Nile," from its universal presence on Egyptian and Coptic monuments. It was figured on the gigantic emerald or glass statue of Serapis, which was transported by order of Ptolemy Soter from Sinope, on the southern shores of the Black Sea, and re-erected in the famous labyrinth which encompassed the banks of Lake Mœris. M. Mariette has recently discovered it in a niche of the holy of holies in the temple of Dendera. It is seen on the breast of a mummy in the museum of the London University. It was the symbol of "life;" of immortality; of creative energy. We encounter it on the cross-cakes of Egypt as the emblem of the supreme content of "the better land."

On a Babylonian cylinder in Munter's Paris Cabinet of Antiquities it is upheld in the presence of a king or a god. It is held in the hand of an eagle-headed man represented on a stele from Khorsabad.

In the south of Asia the kiakra or tschakra, commonly found in the hands of Brahma, Vishnu, and Siva, is only a modification of it; and it is said to be the oldest sign of majesty in India. It is represented in a Mexican manuscript; and Istar, the Assyrian Venus, is figured standing upon a lion, and holding the same sacred emblem in her left hand.

The *swastika* of India—another form of the cross—was a symbol among the Buddhists, and served as the monogram of Vishnu and Siva. But at a far earlier date it was known in China, where it is portrayed on the walls of their pagodas, and upon the lanterns used to illumine their most sacred precincts. It was one of the most important religious symbols in Bactria and in the villages of the Oxus in primitive times. It is represented again in the great temple of Rameses II. at Thebes—the symbol here, as in China, of heaven. It is the principal ornament on the crowns and sceptres of the Bompa deities of Thibet, who dispute the palm of antiquity with all other deities. It was a religious sign among the Etruscans, and appears on the urns exhumed from the ancient lake-beds between Parma and Placentia. It is impressed on the terra-cotta vases from Alba Longa, where it symbolised Persephone, the awful queen of the shades, the "arbiter of mortal fate," and appears again in the catacombs of Rome and on the roll of the Roman soldiery, where it is the symbol of "life." It is found on the Runic monuments of Scandinavia, on the sculptured stones of Scotland, on the ivories from Nimrud, on the ancient coins of Gaul, among the sect of Xaca Japonicus in Japan, on the pottery from all the relic-beds at Troy, in the tombs alike of Cyprus and Mycenæ, on the temples of Mexico, and near Bahia, in Brazil.

The occurrence of these two symbols—and we might add a third form of them, the Maltese cross, which is found among the Phœnicians, at Nineveh, on the garments of the Etruscan priests, in Cyprus, in Sicily, in Asia Minor, at Troy, in Mexico, in Peru—is thus recognised in all parts of the world; and the fact that we find them on the monuments or relics of the oldest communities—the Chaldæans, the Egyptians, the primitive Bactrians, the Hindoos, the Chinese, the Etruscans, and the primitive inhabitants of America—shows that all these nations derived them from a common centre. The idea and the sign were the common property of the race.

2. Let the attention be now directed to the nearly universal legend of *The Deluge*. If all the families of mankind have this tradition, it will prove, first, the fact of the Deluge, and, secondly, the unity of the existing races—especially if the catastrophe was confined to a small and limited area.

The Mosaic account shows that the legend belonged to the Shemitic race. The pages of Berosus, confirmed by the discoveries of Mr. George Smith, show that it was one of the traditions of the Chaldæans. Among the Aryans of India we find it associated, as in the foregoing instances, with the story of the ark, which, as their sacred books represent, was landed on Mount Himarat (Himalaya). The traditions of China represent that Fuh-he, the founder of Chinese civilisation, escaped from a deluge, with his wife, his three daughters, and his three sons; and this, according to the Jesuit M. Martinius, they affirm to have taken place four thousand years before the Christian era. We meet with the same story among the myths of Persia—"The world having been corrupted by Ahriman, it was necessary to bring over it a universal flood of water, that all impurity might be washed away. The rain came down in drops as big as the head of a bull." The same event is referred to by Lucian, Apollodorus, and Ovid. In the reign of Septimius Severus, it was commemorated by a medal struck at Apamæa, on which is delineated an ark or chest floating on the waters, and two birds, one perched on the top of the ark, and another flying towards it bearing a branch in its feet. On some specimens of this medal or coin are found the letters *NΩ* or *NΩE.* This city of Apamæa was indeed originally called "Kibotos," or "The Ark." The Phrygian account (Apamæa was a city of Phrygia) represents that King Annakos (Enoch), who reigned in Iconium, and who reached the age of three hundred years, foretold the Flood.

Humboldt informs us that the Aztecs, the Zapotecs, the Tlascoltecs, and the Mechoacans, in Mexico, had paintings of the Deluge. The Noah, Xisuthrus, or Manu of these nations, is termed Coxcox, Teo-Cipactli, and Tezpi. He saved himself with his wife, Xochiquetzatl, on a raft. Ararat in the tradition is represented by the mountain of Colhuacan. The "dove" also appears in the picture. According to the Mechoacan tradition, when the Great Spirit ordered the waters to withdraw, Tezpi sent out from his bark a vulture, and subsequently a humming-bird, which returned holding in its beak a branch. Humboldt likewise found the tradition of the Deluge among the wild Indians on the Orinoco in South America. It has been found also in Brazil, in Peru, and in Cuba. We find it again among the Cherokee Indians, and among the Fijis of the Pacific Ocean—the tradition of these last making mention of *eight* persons. Another account of the Deluge is found in the Sibylline oracles, where it is represented that after that catastrophe the world was ruled by Kronos, Titan, and Japetus.

It has been said that the recollection of the Flood is confined to the Shemitic and Aryan races, but is not found among the Turanian family nor the Hamites. This is contradicted as to the former by the legends of the Chinese, of the natives of Polynesia, of the American Indians, and, we may add, of the Tatars; for we are told by M. Malte-Brun that "the tradition of the Deluge is found very distinctly among the Calmucs."[1]

Is there any escape, then, from the conclusion that (1) there was a flood, and (2) that these races derived their memory of it from a common source?

3. Another singular tradition, which is the common property of most of the nations of the world, is that of *a Terrestrial Paradise.* We read of the gardens of Alcinous and Laertes; of the Omphalium of the Cretans; of the sacred Asgard of the Scandinavians, springing from the centre of a fruitful land, which was watered by the four primeval rivers of milk. Arab legends tell of a garden in the East, on the summit of a mountain of jacinth, abounding with trees and flowers of rare colours and fragrance. The Zend-Avesta mentions a region which it calls *Heden;* and Zoroaster, we are told in the same ancient books, is said to have been at a place called *Hedenèsh.* The Vishnu Purána tells us that in the centre of Jambu-dwípa is the golden mountain Méru, which stands like the seed-cup of the lotos of the earth. On its summit is the vast city of Brahmá, encircled by the Ganges, which, issuing from the foot of

[1] Précis de Géographie, vol. lx.

Vishnu, *is divided into four streams*, that flow to the four quarters of the earth. Here is the grove of Indra, and here too is the *Jambu-tree*, from whose fruit are fed the Jambu waters, which bestow immortal life on all who drink of them. The Chinese, too, have their "enchanted gardens" in the midst of the summits of the Houanlun, where is the fountain of immortality dividing off into *four streams;* and so we read again of the Harâmberezaitím of the Parsí, of the Ilá of the Singhalese and the Thibetans, and of the Sinéru of the Buddhist, with its four-limbed D'amba-tree and never-fading blossoms, from between whose roots issue the four sacred streams that water the garden of the supreme god, Sekrá.

4. The megalithic monuments (the menhirs, dolmens, tumuli, circles, &c.), which we observe in such widely-separated countries, imply, of course, a connection between the races by whom they were constructed. At Carnac, in Brittany, we find long avenues of stones that seem to have been copied from the menhirs on the Khassia Hills. In Algiers and the north of Europe we see the same dolmens. The circle near Peshawur, in Afghanistan, is the counterpart of the standing stones of Stennis, in the Orkneys. The trilithons at Stonehenge are precisely like those at Ksaca and Elkeb, in Tripoli, and those described by Mr. Gifford Palgrave in Central Arabia. And the great serpent-mound of Loch Nell, in Argyleshire, strangely recalls the serpent-mounds of Wisconsin and Ohio. The chambered tumuli of the Etruscans are repeated in Scandinavia, in Britain, in Asia Minor, and in China; while the

same vast sepulchres, chambered and unchambered, are found in Madagascar and Siberia, and scattered throughout North America, from the Great Lakes and the Rocky Mountains to Georgia and Mexico.

5. The custom of *distorting the human skull* prevailed in ancient times among the *Macrocephali*, referred to by Hippocrates, in the fifth century before our era, as living on the shores of the Euxine. Strabo refers to the practice as common among the migratory tribes of Western Asia. Stephanus Byzantinus, nearly a thousand years after Hippocrates, speaks of macrocephalic Scythians, in Colchis, on the eastern shore of the Euxine Sea.

A number of skulls, greatly elongated by artificial compression, have been found in Austria, at St. Romain, in Savoy, and in the valley of the Doubs, near Mandeuse. Dr. Fitzinger, who investigated the subject, mentions the interesting fact, in a memoir before the Imperial Academy of Vienna, that an ancient medal had been discovered, which was struck to commemorate the destruction of Aquileia by Attila, the Hun, in 452, and that on one side of it is an effigy of this famous chieftain, presenting the macrocephalic form of the skull.

The prevalence of this custom among the ancient Peruvians is attested by the crania found in the Peruvian tombs, and Garcilasso de la Vega and Torquemada both mention the fact.

The same custom prevailed among the Flat-head Indians along the Columbia River and on the Pacific coast, who represent some twenty different tribes—the

Chinooks, the Klatsaps, the Cowlitz, the Songas, the Chartays, &c.

The Natchez Indians, on the Lower Mississippi, had the same practice. The custom existed also in Central America, as well as among the Malays of the Sandwich Islands. And it has been affirmed that it was not unknown among the ancient inhabitants of Caledonia and Scandinavia.

6. The custom of *scalping* is not peculiar to the American Indians. Herodotus mentions that it was one of the most characteristic practices of the Scythian tribes; and we are told that to-day the wild tribes of the frontier, in the north-eastern district of Bengal, "use the scalping-knife with a ferocity that is only equalled by the American Indians, and the scalps are carefully preserved as evidences of their prowess and vengeance over their enemies."

7. The *boomerang* is so remarkable a weapon that we should not expect to find it except among kindred races. It had never, until recently, been met with by Europeans, except in Australia. But it has now been ascertained to be in use among the Moqui Indians of Northern Arizona and New Mexico, the Indians of California, the Eskimo, the Furus Indians of South America, the Dravidian races of India, and, as we learn from an address by Colonel Lane Fox before the Anthropological Sub-section of the British Association, among the ancient Egyptians.[1] In this last-named country it is seen in the hands of hunters in a basso-relievo at Thebes.

[1] Nature, August 22, 1872.

It has also been discovered in the hands of the sculptured Nimrod at Khorsabad; and we are told by a writer in the 'Ulster Journal of Archæology' that it was known in ancient times to the Gauls, and to the Lybian tribes who accompanied Hannibal into Italy.

There is also another very peculiar implement common to the Australians, the Eskimo, the New Caledonians, and some Brazilian tribes—the *womera*, or throwing-stick, for propelling spears. "It seems most unlikely," says the 'Westminster Review,'[1] "that two such peculiar implements as the boomerang and the womera should have been independently invented by Australians, Esquimaux, and North American Indians; we are therefore forced to the conclusion that these peoples were branches from a common stock, which had attained to the use of these implements, as well as those of stone, before those branches spread over distant lands."

8. The custom of depositing flint implements in the grave has been observed in many parts of the world—in all parts of Europe, on the shores of the Black Sea, in the Egyptian mummy cases, in the tombs of Babylonia, in Algiers, among the mound-builders of North America. One common sentiment with regard to the stone celts seems to have existed among all the nations of the world—that they were *thunderbolts.* This belief prevailed in Cornwall, Ireland, Scotland, Norway, Denmark, Brittany, Germany, Portugal, Italy, China, Japan, Burmah, Assam, and Western Africa. And it is finally to be remarked, that archæologists have expressed their

[1] July 1876, p. 52. A review of "The Recent Origin of Man."

astonishment at *the identity of form* of these implements all over the world.[1]

9. The lingham, or phallus, worship prevailed in Egypt, in Assyria, among the Scythians, among the Greeks, in Rome, in Central America and Mexico, and in the southern parts of the United States.

10. The universal prevalence of serpent-worship among the nations of antiquity (and its survival to the present day in some parts of the world), in analogy with the facts above mentioned, point to a common source for this sentiment.

[1] Nilsson on the Stone Age, p. 103; British Quarterly Review, October 1872 ("Present Phase of Pre-historic Archæology"); Year-Book of Facts, 1871, p. 174.

See also Mr. Boyd Dawkins' work on "Cave-Hunting," p. 358. This author remarks that "the implements found in Belgium, France, or Britain differ scarcely more from those now used in West Georgia, than the latter do from those now in use in Greenland or Melville Peninsula." He concludes from this that the Eskimo are the descendants of the ancient European cave-men. "There are," he says, "no two savage tribes now living which use the same *set* of implements, without being connected by blood."

Professor Nilsson observes that "the great resemblance which exists among the stone implements of nations of different tribes, during very different periods and in most different countries, . . . is remarkable."

The opinion expressed by Mr. Boyd Dawkins, that the Eskimo are of the same race with the ancient cave-men, is very important in view of the fact that the Eskimo are admitted to be a branch of the great Turanian family, "and," says a writer in the 'Quarterly Review' for October 1876, "carry in their speech the best evidence of their origin, in the affinity which their language bears to the Lapp, Bask, Hungarian, and Turkish dialects of their common race."

We trace this race again in the Accad of the south of Chaldæa—the dominant caste at Babylon—who brought to Babylon and Assyria the cuneiform writing, and to whom belonged the primitive national language of Chaldæa, which has been ascertained to be an idiom of the Uralo-Finnish group of languages.

M. Broca believes that there is a connection between the Guanches of Teneriffe (who a few centuries ago were in their stone age) and the Cro-Magnon race of M. Quatrefages (palæolithic), and of both with the Berbers and the Basques.

There are various other practices and traditions common to many of the races which we find widely separated in time, and inhabiting different continents. Those which we have selected seem to us to prove the unity of the race almost without any other argument on the subject. They do certainly create a *strong presumption.*

The application which we propose to make of the fact has been already indicated. If the human race is one, the Egyptian, the Hindoo, the Babylonian, and the Palæolithic tribes of the Somme valley were one; and if Kephren and Cheops were near of kin to the fossil man of Mentone or the savage who owned the Neanderthal skull; and if, moreover, the antiquity of man in Egypt and Babylonia does not go farther back than some ten thousand years—*then* the men of the French and English river-gravels cannot be more than ten thousand years old. The reverse would only be possible on the hypothesis that the Egyptians were the descendants of the men of the Somme valley. But this is excluded by the fact that the Egyptians appear at once as a civilised race; and, as we have stated, there are no earlier remains of any kind in Egypt.

CHAPTER III.

PREMATURE ANNOUNCEMENTS OF THE ANTIQUITY OF MAN.

The argument of the last chapter not absolutely conclusive—Opinions of scientific men with regard to the antiquity of man—Errors fallen into on this subject in past years—The zodiacs of Dendera and Esne—The fossil men of Guadaloupe—The fossil man of Denise—The fossil human bones from the coral formation of Florida—The rock-cut temples of India—Perforated sharks' teeth from the English "crag"—Tombs under the peperino near Albano—The cone of the Tinière—The date of the Stone Age at the Pont de Thièle—Incised bones from the Pliocene and Miocene beds of France and Italy—The Miocene man of the Dardanelles—The Newton stone.

THE argument of the foregoing chapter is not *conclusive of the question*, for two reasons: 1. It is *possible* that men originated on the earth at different centres, and that the race *is not one*—palæolithic man in the regions now called France and India *may* have been unrelated to the races which dwelt between the Caspian Sea and the Indian Ocean, and those which occupied the valleys of the Euphrates and the Nile. 2. Palæolithic remains may be found in Egypt and Babylonia or in Central Asia *hereafter*.

It is necessary for us, therefore, to consider the positive evidence for the antiquity of man in Europe. This may prove so clear and weighty that it cannot be rejected. Indeed it has appeared so weighty and conclusive that a decided majority of our scientific men in all the countries of Europe and in America believe the fact to be established—such men as M. de Quatrefages, M. de Mortillet, M. Cartailhac, Dr. Broca, the Abbé Bourgeois, Professor Nilsson, Professor Worsaae, M. Dupont, M. Desor, Mr. Darwin, Mr. Wallace, Mr. Huxley, Professor Busk, Mr. Prestwich, Mr. Boyd Dawkins, Mr. John Evans, Sir John Lubbock, Professor Owen, Mr. James Geikie, Colonel Fox Talbot, Carl Vogt, Virchow, Fraas, Gastaldi, Ponzi, Ceselli, Wilson, Cope, Whitney; and among the dead, Sir C. Lyell, M. Lartet, M. Morlot, Dr. Falconer, Agassiz, Dr. Foster. Indeed it cannot be denied that it is the prevailing scientific opinion at present, as is indicated by the fact that the doctrine has been incorporated in our advanced text-books of geology, such as Lyell's and Page's; and in our standard historical works, such as Lenormant's "Ancient History of the East."

Chevalier Bunsen, in his work on Egypt, fixed the beginning of the human period at 20,000 years B.C. Mr. Jukes, one of the highest geological authorities in England, has, we believe, assigned 100,000 years as the probable antiquity of our race. Professor Fuhlrott, of Germany, who writes a work on the Neanderthal skull, fixed the age of that fossil at 200,000 or 300,000 years. Mr. Hunt, formerly President of the British Anthropological Society, goes back as far as 9,000,000 years. Mr. A. R. Wallace has suggested 500,000 years. Professor Huxley believes that man existed "when a tropical fauna and flora flourished in our northern clime." Sir Charles Lyell was converted some twenty years before his death to a belief in the existence of Quaternary man, and it was his opinion that human remains will yet be found in the Pliocene strata; while Sir John Lubbock expects that they will be found to occur even in the Miocene strata.

Mr. James Geikie, in his work entitled "The Great Ice Age," contends that man is pre-glacial, and this opinion is concurred in by Mr. Boyd Dawkins in his learned and pleasant volume on "Cave-Hunting."

Authorities like these are well calculated to shake our preconceived ideas with regard to human chronology; at the same time we must bear in mind, on the other hand, that physical science has its fashions like metaphysics, that theories are ever changing, and that Darwinism and pre-historic archæology twenty years from to-day may be both forgotten. Geological science especially is far from being settled, and we are, even at this very juncture, probably on the eve of important modifications of pre-existing theories. With regard to the antiquity of man, we have been prematurely advised so often of discoveries in this direction, that we must receive such announcements with peculiar caution, for eminent men of science have been more than once deceived on the subject. We may instance Professor Playfair and M. Bailly, and their articles on the Hindoo astronomy about the close of the last century, and Professor Playfair's article in 1811 in the 'Edinburgh Review' on the zodiacs of Dendera and Esne, figures of which had been published by M. Denon in his work on Egypt, and which had created so much excitement in Paris. Professor Playfair—we pass by the tables of

Tirvalore — by astronomical calculations, ascertained that the zodiac of Dendera was about 3800 years old, while that of Esne was "much more ancient." "We must assign it," says the writer in the 'Edinburgh,' "an antiquity of *more than five thousand three hundred years.*" Champollion, the younger, however, who had just previously assisted in solving the secret of the Egyptian hieroglyphics, happened, about this time, to examine the planisphere of Dendera, before it had been removed to Paris, and deciphered on it in Greek letters the word for *emperor*, and on the walls of the temple he discovered the names, titles, and surnames of *Tiberius, Claudius, Nero,* and *Domitian.* Upon the portico of Esne, which had been pronounced "the more ancient," he read the names of *Claudius* and *Antoninus Pius.* This, of course, put an end to the antiquity of the Egyptian zodiacs.

Nott and Gliddon in their "Types of Mankind" suggested a great antiquity for "the fossil men of Guadaloupe" found embedded in rock in the West Indies; but it is well ascertained now that the skeletons belonged to the Carib Indians, and are not more than a few centuries old.

So the "fossil man of Denise," being found buried under the lava in Auvergne, in a region where it was believed that there had been no volcanic activity for many ages—certainly not since the days of Julius Cæsar, who encamped on the spot—was supposed to imply a much greater antiquity for our race than had generally been assigned it. But it has been ascertained from an old Gaulish history, re-edited some years since, that there were volcanic eruptions in this district from A.D. 458 to 460, and that the Rogation days were appointed by Mamercus, Bishop of Vienne at this time, for the purpose of chanting litanies to stay the devastations which were visiting his diocese. It is evident, therefore, that the mere position of the skull in the lava is no proof of its antiquity.

We may refer also to the supposed fossil human bones found (as was alleged on the authority of Professor Agassiz) in the coral formation of Florida. Nott and Gliddon give prominence to this discovery, and it is cited among the evidences of the antiquity of man by Sir Charles Lyell in the last edition of his work on this subject (1873); but Count L. F. Pourtalès, the original discoverer of these bones, has in the last few years declared that the remains "were not found in the coral formation, but in a fresh-water sandstone on the shores of Lake Monroe, associated with fresh-water shells of species still living in the lake," and "that no date can be assigned to the formation of that deposit."[1]

Another example may be taken from the rock-cut temples of India, which were pronounced to be "ante-Sanskrit," and the work of a "Cushite race" which occupied India before the Aryan invasion. These works are now believed to have been Buddhist temples, not older than some 200 or 300 years B.C., and some of them as recent as A.D. 1100.

A few years since, Professor Owen and other scientific men expressed the opinion that certain perforated sharks' teeth, found in the "crag" formation in Eng-

[1] American Naturalist, vol. ii. p. 434.

land (referred to the Pliocene period), had been bored by human agency; but a writer in the 'Geological Magazine' for June 1872 declares that "there is not the slightest reason for attributing the phenomena in question to the agency of man."

In 1817 a number of ancient tombs were alleged to have been found at Marino, near Albano, in Italy, under an intact layer of peperino or consolidated volcanic ash, and the place was re-examined by Sir John Lubbock and Professor Pigorini in 1869, the former of whom in his "Pre-historic Times" refers the tombs to "the close of the Bronze Age," and "a period when the volcanoes near Rome were still in a state of activity." This, according to the date usually assigned by archæologists to the close of the Bronze Age in the south of Europe, would make the tombs and the relics contained in them some 3500 or 4000 years old. But since the examination of Sir John Lubbock, M. Ponzi has discovered in the same region a coin (the "rude" *œs,* which belongs to about 700 B.C.) beneath this same volcanic ash, and he is of opinion that this deposit was made during an eruption which gave birth to the little crater of *Monte Pila,* and that this occurred after the establishment of the kingly government at Rome.[1] It may be added that frequent shocks of earthquakes were felt at Rome A.U.C. 319, and that many houses in the city were then thrown down.

[1] Matériaux pour l'Histoire de l'Homme, Janvier 1872, p. 25.

See farther Dr. Henry Schliemann, in the 'Academy,' 1875, who has examined the spot, and declares that the relics alleged to have been found at Albano under the peperino were never in fact found in that position.

In so recent a work as Sir John Lubbock's "Pre-historic Times," and in the last edition of Lyell's "Antiquity of Man," the calculation derived from the "cone of the Tinière," first presented by M. Morlot, is repeated, and we are encouraged to believe that we have here the approximate data for fixing the epoch of the Neolithic Age at about 6000 years ago.

The cone of the Tinière is a deposit of gravel, in the shape of a half-cone, on a plateau on the border of the Lake of Geneva, brought down from the mountains by the torrent of the Tinière, at the city of Villeneuve. A railroad cut has exposed a section through this cone nearly to its base. Four feet from the top (as we are told) were Roman relics; at ten feet were found bronze implements; and at nineteen feet stone implements. The entire depth of the cone is thirty-two feet six inches. Some two hundred years ago the increase of this deposit was stopped by confining the torrent between stone walls. This leaves some 1400 or 1500 years for the lapse of time since the Roman period. In this time (as the calculation runs) about four feet of gravel were deposited, or about three and a half inches in a century. From this datum M. Morlot calculated that the antiquity of the bronze relics is about 3800 years, that of the stone relics about 6000 years, and that of the whole cone about 10,000 years.

Very nearly the same figures were obtained by another calculation, based on the silting up of the Lake of Bienne, by M. Gilliéron, professor at the College of Neuveville.[1] There are remains of a lake-village at the

[1] See Pre-historic Times, p. 171.

Pont de Thièle, on the stream which connects the lakes of Neufchâtel and Bienne. "It is evident," says Sir John Lubbock, "that the valley, as far as the bridge over the Thièle, was once occupied by the lake, which has gradually been silted up by the action of the forces still in operation, and, if we could ascertain how long it would have taken to effect this change, we should then know approximately the date of the remains found at the Pont de Thièle. . . . The Abbey of St. Jean, which stands in the valley, about 375 metres from the present shore of the lake, . . . is about 750 years old. . . . Even if the abbey were built on the edge of the lake, the gain of land will only have been 375 metres in 750 years." Without going into the details, this gain of 375 metres in 750 years is compared with the distance of 3375 metres from the lake to the lake-dwelling, and it would appear that the latter must have "a minimum antiquity of 6700 years."

Now, with regard to the cone of the Tinière, Professor Andrews of Chicago has shown that there is a grave fallacy in the computation. "On the supposition," says Professor Andrews,[1] "that the torrent brings down about the same amount of gravel every year, it will readily be seen that the first year's deposit will lie upon the plateau in a conical heap of no great breadth, but of considerable height. The second year's gravel, however, will be spread over the entire surface of the first, and, extending wider, it must be much thinner. The third year's accretion will be broader and thinner still; and so on to the last. It follows that the superficial

[1] American Journal of Science, October 1868.

annual layers are always the thinnest, because the broadest. Now, if Morlot is correctly quoted, he first derives his scale of from $3\frac{3}{10}$ to 4 inches increase per century from the superficial layers where they are thinnest, and then applies it without modification to the interior, where the annual accretions were much thicker. His unit of measure is therefore too small, and exaggerates the total age. It is perfectly plain that the true method is to take the cubic contents of the whole cone; or, in plain language, if the annual rainfall and gravel-wash has been uniform, then as the quantity of gravel in the layers deposited since the Roman Conquest is to the quantity in the whole cone, so is the time required for the deposit of these layers to the time required for the formation of the whole cone."

Dr. Andrews then ascertains the cubic feet in the strata deposited since the Roman period to be 5,283,205; time of deposition, 1300 to 1500 years; and the cubic contents of the entire cone to be 16,116,408 feet; and therefore the time for the formation of the whole cone to have been 3965 to 4576 years. This is less than half the time (10,000 years) ascertained by M. Morlot, and would fix the date of the stone relics at about 3000 years ago.[1]

As regards the lake-dwelling at the Pont de Thièle, it is sufficient to say that we learn from Dr. Keller's work that *Roman pottery and tiles* were

[1] We may observe that if the volume of the Tinière was greater two thousand years ago (as is by no means unlikely), the amount of the gravel brought down would be proportionally greater.

And again, the *supply* of gravel may have been greater formerly than it is now.

found at this station; and these cannot be older than 1900 years.

It may be added that M. Desor informs us (in another connection) that landslips have been distinguished at the mouth of the Thièle.[1]

Various announcements from very high authority have been made within a few years of the discovery of traces of both Pliocene and Miocene man. In 1869 we believe it was, M. Delaunay stated that he had found certain human cuttings or markings on a rib belonging to the *Halitherium fossile*, a well-known Miocene species. It was also represented about the same time that M. Desnoyers had discovered in the Pliocene beds of Saint-Prest certain bones belonging to the *Elephas meridionalis*, *Rhinoceros leptorhinus*, &c., which contained incisions or hackings, "tout à fait analogues à celles que produiraient les outils de silex tranchants à point plus ou moins aiguë, à bords plus ou moins dentelés."

Similarly notched bones from the Pliocene beds of the Val d'Arno, "said to bear marks of knives," were exhibited by Professor Ramorino to the Italian Society of Natural Sciences.

It is now conceded on all hands that these announcements were premature; precisely similar striæ or cuts are made on bones which have been gnawed by the porcupine, and in the beds at Saint-Prest the remains of an extinct rodent of the beaver family (*Trogontherium*) were found with the bones of the *Elephas meridionalis.*

[1] See Smithsonian Report for 1865, p. 351.

By way of farther illustration, we may mention that in 1873 Mr. Frank Calvert announced, in one of the English literary or scientific journals, that he had discovered manifest proofs of the existence of man in the Miocene age in a formation, at the depth of 800 feet below the surface, in the face of a cliff near the Dardanelles. He represented that he had encountered in this bed the bone of a dinotherium or a mastodon on which was graven "the unmistakable figure of an animal with horns;" and that near this engraved bone he had found a flint implement, and the bones of animals, "evidently broken by man, according to the custom of the primitive races." The statement seemed the more important from the fact that Sir John Lubbock, noticing the discovery, commended Mr. Calvert as a conscientious geologist. The matter was subsequently investigated by Professor George Washburn of Roberts College, Constantinople, who sent a paper on the subject to the American Association which met at Portland in 1873. Mr. Washburn stated that there is not the slightest trace of human workmanship on the specimens; that the scratches on the bones do not appear to be artificial, and represent nothing; that the flints (Mr. Calvert found a number of these at another point) are mere natural fragments; and that the bones alleged to be split by the hands of man are a delusion, he having himself found at the locality old bones, which, on being dropped, split open of themselves in the same way.

Very extravagant statements were at one time indulged in with regard to the antiquity of the round towers of Ireland, and the weems, beehive-houses, burghs, and pillar stones of Scotland. Dr. Mill, the well-known Sanskrit scholar, read the inscription on the famous Newton stone backwards, and pronounced it *Phœnician*, explaining that it commemorated "the escape from shipwreck of a high magistrate of the city of Tyre, while on a voyage to the north of Scotland." He read a paper to this effect before the British Association at Cambridge in 1862. In a work written since by Dr. George Moore, M.R.C.P., entitled "The Ancient Pillar Stones of Scotland," the interpretation of Dr. Mill is rejected, and the inscription pronounced to be "Arian." Dr. Moore represents that "Arian" missionaries, when the whole "Arian" people were still located at one central spot in Central Asia, speaking the primal "Arian" language, made their way across Asia and Europe, to plant in North Scotland this pure monument of Buddhism—which system they are supposed to have established there. But the inscription is in fact probably not older than the fifth century of our era—these pillar stones ranging from about that time to the eighth century.

A group of "beehive-houses" on the shore of Loch Resort, in Long Island, was occupied until 1823; and the Burgh of Moussa, in the Shetlands, was the refuge of Erling in 1150, who carried off the beautiful Margaret, mother of Harold, Earl of Orkney.

Mistakes like these, we remark, suggest caution; and if a more formidable array of evidences for the antiquity of man is now adduced, warned by previous miscalculations, we should subject the facts presented to the most careful and searching scrutiny before abandoning opinions which do not refer alone to mere matters of curiosity, but also bear upon some of the gravest questions which concern us.

The evidence for the antiquity of man, as presented by pre-historic archæology, is usually marshalled under the heads of the Megalithic Monuments, the Lake-Dwellings, the Danish Shell-Mounds, the Peat Deposits, the Bone-Caves, and the River-Gravel.

We do not consider it necessary to detain the reader with the megalithic monuments and tumuli, which are found throughout Europe, in North Africa, in Asia, America, and Australia. The subject is fully discussed in "The Recent Origin of Man," if special information is desired with regard to it. It is sufficient here merely to say that these monuments are, in most instances, later than the beginning of our era.

Kit's Cotty House.

The stones of the most celebrated of the great stone circles—Stonehenge—are hewn, and tenoned and mor-

'tised, which of course could only have been accomplished with the aid of metal tools.

Countless Stones, Aylesford. (Fergusson.)

Dolmen, near Mettray. (Fergusson.)

Metal tools have also evidently shaped the great stones represented in the preceding cuts.

The same is true of the grand Dol ar Marchant and Gavr Innis in Brittany, and the superb battle-axe here

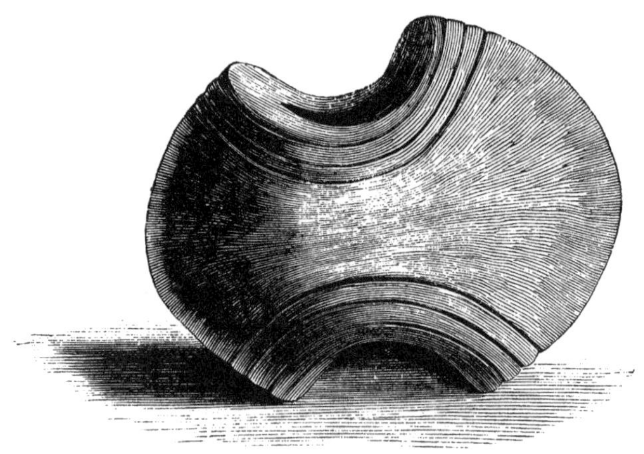

Battle-axe from Crichie, Aberdeenshire. (Evans.)

represented was obtained from a "Druidical" circle at Crichie, near Inverury.

Holed Dolmen, at Trie. (Fergusson.)

The age of these monuments, in most instances, is to be derived, however, from their contents, and it is only necessary to remark that objects of metal or relics of the Roman period constantly occur in them. Iron has been frequently found in those which are considered the oldest—the great chambered tumuli or passage-graves, which are regarded by the archæologists as specially characteristic of the Stone Age.

Dolmen of Grandmont. (Fergusson.)

CHAPTER IV.

THE LAKE-DWELLINGS.

Implements of stone in use among the barbarians of Europe prior to the advance of the Roman arms—Numbers of them lived in pile-villages over water—These lake-dwellings assigned by the archæologists to a remote antiquity—But are mentioned by Herodotus and other ancient writers—Delineated on Trajan's Column—Are referred to different ages—The lake-dwellings of Switzerland—Objects found at these stations: grain, bread, cloth, dried fruits, metal, glass, &c.—Traces of metal in the very oldest—Stone, bronze, and iron often found at them together, and frequently, along with these, Roman relics—Unter-Uhldingen, Sipplingen, Nidau, Möringen, Ile des Lapins, La Tène, Estavayer, &c. &c.—Similar settlements on land, where again stone and metal occur together—Pile-dwellings of Italy, Prussia (Lubtow), France, &c.—Pile-villages of the sixth century—Continued to the Carlovingian epoch in France, and to the eleventh century in the north of Europe—Crannoges of Ireland—Pile-villages still to be found in various parts of the world.

SINCE the curtain has been lifted, we realise now that over the most of Europe, at some time prior to the advance of the Romans beyond the Alps, the barbarous or semi-civilised tribes which were in possession of the country, had little or no acquaintance with the metals, and served themselves with tools and weapons made of stone. Their knives, their hammers, their chisels, their saws, their spear-heads, their battle-axes, were of stone. The savages of America, when that continent was discovered, were living in precisely the same way; but it had not occurred to anybody, it would seem, that the ancient Britons and Germans and Gauls were not supplied with less primitive implements.

Another remarkable feature of the rude society which existed in Europe at this period, has been brought to light by the labours of the archæologists: it is ascertained that the whole continent (Spain and Russia have not been explored) was dotted over with villages constructed over water, on piles—some of them, like those of Robenhausen, Morges,[1] and Wangen, in Switzerland, of considerable extent. Within the past twenty years these "lake-dwellings" have been discovered in Switzerland, Italy, France, Austria, Prussia, Poland, England, Scotland, Ireland, and Sweden. As many as fifty have been recognised on the Lake of Neufchâtel alone. The archæologists inform us that some of these settlements belong to the Stone Age, some to the Bronze Age, and some to the Iron Age, and that the first have an antiquity of at least 6000 or 7000 years. They appeared to the late Professor Agassiz so ancient that in 1866, in an address before the Boston Society of Natural History, referring to the discoveries of Dr. Ferdinand Keller, he exclaimed, "Humanity is now connected with geological phenomena."

Even in those which are regarded as the very oldest of the lake-dwellings, indications are observed of considerable social progress—relics implying the enjoyment of many of the comforts and conveniences of domestic life—and the antiquity of the people who lived on the

[1] This settlement covered an area of 70,000 square yards, while at Robenhausen there are 100,000 piles.

bosom of these lakes was inferred from the fact that history seemed to be silent with regard to them, and that their implements were all of stone (or bone). But, in regard to the first, it ought to have been remembered that, except an occasional reference in a Greek or Roman writer, history does not begin in Middle and Northern Europe until the dawn of the Christian era; and, more than this, it is not true that the ancient records are entirely silent on this subject. The lake-dwellings are delineated on the celebrated historical column of Trajan in Rome, which was erected A.D. 114 to commemorate his victories over the Dacians. This single fact divests these remains of that illusion of antiquity which has been too frequently associated with objects and practices of which we are merely ignorant. If the army of Trajan, in the second century, encountered the pile-dwellers on the Danube or the lakes of Austria, it results that, while this method of life may extend back to very remote times, it certainly prevailed at a comparatively recent period, and has no bearing one way or the other on the question of the antiquity of man.

The lake-dwellers are also expressly mentioned by Herodotus and Hippocrates. The former describes a pile-village as existing in his day on Lake Prasias, at the head of the Ægean Sea, in Eastern Macedonia—not thirty miles from the city of Philippi. "Beams fastened together are fixed," he says, "on lofty piles in the middle of the lake, having a narrow approach from the shore by a single bridge. And all the citizens in common have been wont from some very ancient time to plant the piles which support the beams. And this is the custom followed as to planting the piles," &c.[1] These people had "horses and cattle" which they fed on fish—as was the custom formerly, according to Torfæus, in Norway and Sweden. Hippocrates, writing about the same time as Herodotus, describes a similar settlement on the Phasis (in Colchis, Asia Minor), where the inhabitants, as he tells us, "sailed up and down in boats made of a single trunk of a tree."[2]

The geographer Abulfeda, in the beginning of the fourteenth century, mentions a pile-settlement on the Apamæan Lake, in Syria—his native country. This lake, he says, "is commonly called the lake of the Christians, because it is inhabited by Christian fishermen who live here on the lake in wooden huts built on piles."[3]

The evidence for the antiquity of the older lake-dwellings must be based, therefore, exclusively on the fact of the absence of metal, and the presence of stone implements. Of this we shall speak more particularly hereafter. For the matter in hand we simply observe that this state of things—the Stone Age—exists at the present day on the Pacific coasts of North America, in Australia, and in Africa, as it did at a very recent period among the Fijians, who dwelt at the same time in fortified towns, and were acquainted with agriculture and navigation, worshipped in temples, and lived under

[1] Book v. 16.

[2] De Aeribus, chap. xxxvii.

[3] Supplem. Tab. Syriæ, cap. ii.

a complicated and carefully-administered political system. So, as will hereafter appear, the site of Troy was occupied in the seventh century before our era by a population who used stone implements, and had little or no metal, while in the relic-bed referred by Dr. Schliemann to the Trojans of the Homeric poems stone implements also occur in great abundance. This circumstance, therefore, of the employment of stone for tools and weapons also fails to constitute an evidence of a high antiquity.

There is no other evidence whatever of a high antiquity for any of the lake-dwellings, and the case might terminate here, and be dismissed. As so much, however, has been written on the subject, and so much emphasis laid on the remains found in this connection, it will be more satisfactory to examine in greater detail into this branch of the evidence for the antiquity of man. We shall therefore proceed to notice a number of the pile-village stations which have been explored in Switzerland and in other parts of Europe.

It is necessary to premise that the lake-dwellings assigned to the Stone Age belong to the *Polished Stone Period*, and do not go back to the Palæolithic or First Stone Age; they are, in other words, much more recent than the human remains found in the river-gravel and the earliest bone-caves. Their age, according to the archæologists, corresponds with that of the peat of the Somme Valley and of Denmark. The flint implements of the Palæolithic Age were never polished; the finer implements of the Neolithic Period are elaborately finished, and, it is alleged, indicate a great advance in the lapidary art.[1]

For the purpose of comparison we reproduce the following implements of the Palæolithic Age from the gravels of the Somme Valley and the caves of Périgord.

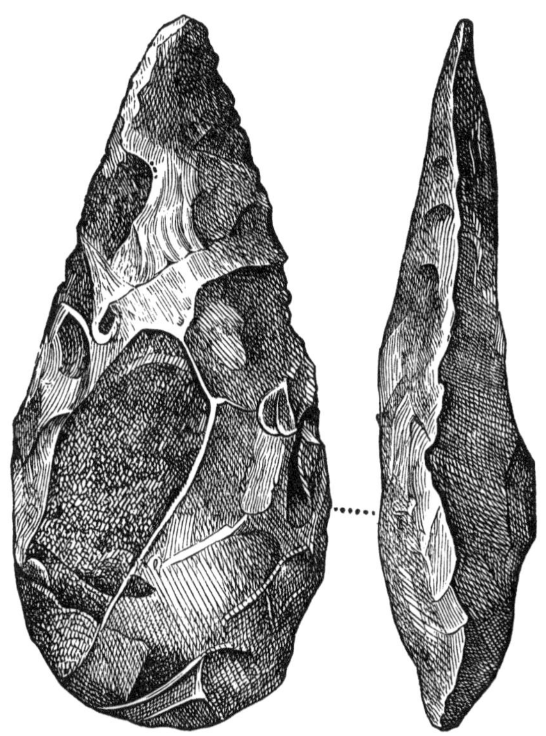

Flint Hatchet from Saint-Acheul.

[1] But it must not be supposed that all of the implements of the Neolithic Age were polished; in a majority of instances they are as rude as those of the First Stone Age.

Wrought Flint.

Worked Flint from Périgord (Knife).

Worked Flint from Périgord (Hatchet).

And the following specimens of the Neolithic Age.

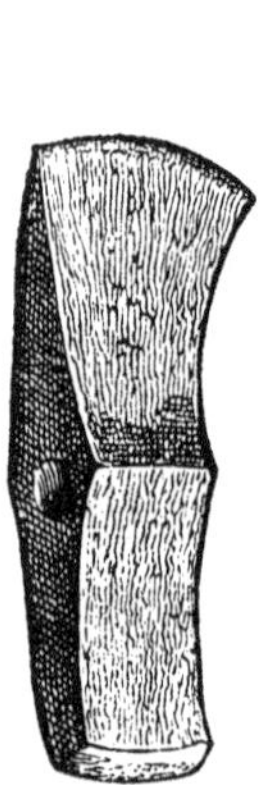

Perforated Axe.

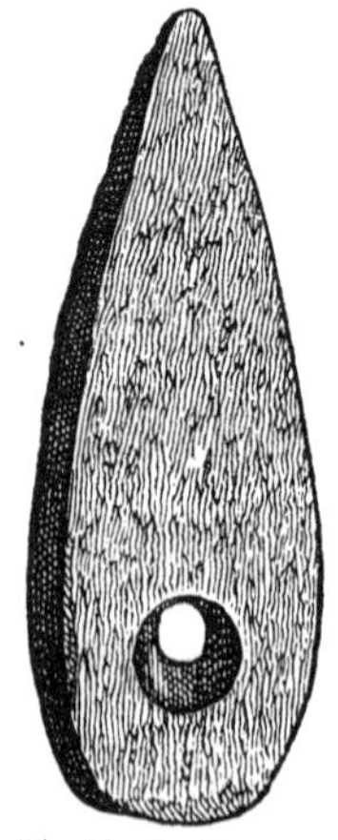

Danish Axe-hammer, drilled for handle.

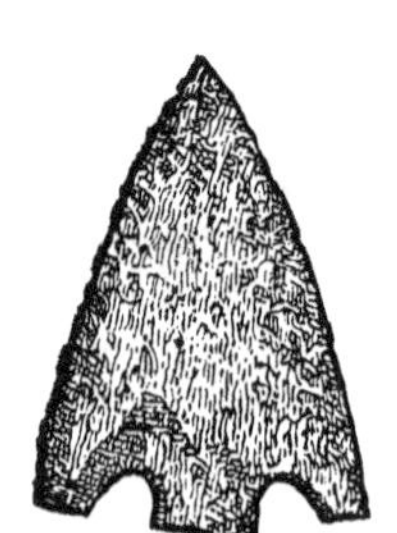

Arrow-head.

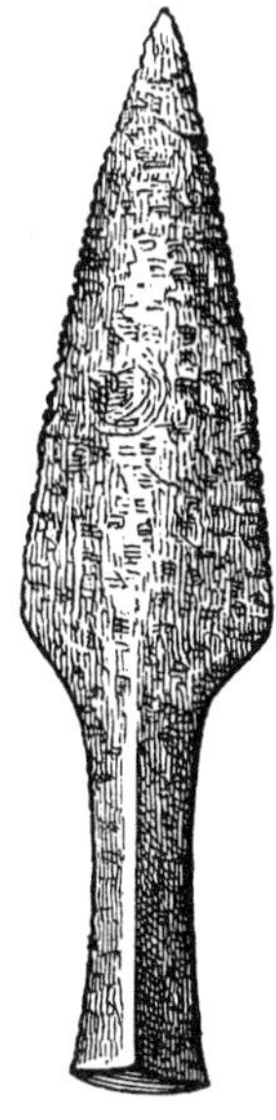

Flint Poniard from Denmark.

Harpoon made of stag's horn, from the lacustrine habitations of Switzerland.

SWITZERLAND.

According to the character of the relics, the lake-settlements, as we have remarked, are assigned by the archæologists to the Stone, the Bronze, or the Iron Age; in some instances, it is alleged, there has been *a succession* of the three ages at the same station.

In the Stone-Age lake-stations, pottery (hand-made) is found in abundance, as are also the remains of spinning-wheels of stone and clay, and fragments of thread, ropes, mats, coverlets, &c., made of flax. The oldest lake-dwellers were, therefore, potters and weavers. They had also domesticated the ox, the goat, the sheep, and the dog. They were also an agricultural people, as is proved by the discovery of three varieties of wheat, two of barley, and two of millet. Bread, in the shape of flat round cakes, apples dried and put away for winter use, seeds of the raspberry and blackberry, have also been found, and indicate that the appetites of the earliest lake-folk were not wholly unrefined. The occurrence of the Cretan catch-fly and the corn-blue-bottle, which are found in the Mediterranean, but never in Switzerland or Germany, points to a communication with Southern Europe, as do fragments of Mediterranean coral found at Concise, on the Lake of Neufchâtel.

Vessels and utensils in wood, showing, in the words of Dr. Keller, "astonishing skill in carving," were obtained at the ancient station of Robenhausen—ladles very similar to those now in use in the Swiss milk-chalets, yew-wood combs, a threshing-flail, a yoke of hazel-wood, a shoemaker's last, a great tub cut out of maple-wood, &c. At the Stone-Age station of Irgenhausen, near to Robenhausen, were found specimens of embroidered cloth. Now, the sole evidence for the remote antiquity of these relics is the presence along with them of axes, arrow-heads, and other implements of stone—precisely similar to those which are found in numerous instances associated with Roman remains in various parts of Europe, and even in Merovingian graves.

It must not be presumed, however, that the inhabitants of the very oldest (or most primitive) lake-stations, those situated in the most secluded valleys of the Alps, were entirely unacquainted with the metals. This impression has been created, but it is not true; for Dr. Keller informs us that "*traces of copper and bronze have been met with in the lower beds of the Stone-Age settlements, before the appearance of nephrite.*" [1]

Nor are the remains of any of the extinct animals, such as the mammoth, the reindeer, the megaceros, &c., found here, excepting only the urus, which only became extinct in Germany in the sixteenth century.

The oldest, so regarded, of the lake-settlements of importance are those of Robenhausen, Lake of Pfäffikon; Wangen, Lake of Constance; Nussdorf, Lake of Constance; Wauwyl (occupying the bed of a former lake, which is now a peat-moss), in the canton of Lucerne; Moosseedorf, another peat-moss station, near Berne; Locras, Lake of Bienne; Concise, Lake of Neufchâtel; and Meilen, Lake of Zurich.

With regard to Robenhausen, already spoken of, we may state that Dr. Heer believes the fæces of goats which occur here in regular beds were manure-heaps, hoarded for agricultural purposes; [2] while Dr. Keller gives us a picture of some cloth found here, "betraying," as he says, "a certain refinement of life, and a tendency to luxury."

At Wangen great quantities of corn, baked cakes of bread, and abundant remains of flax were found; and we are told that "the inhabitants were pre-eminent as agriculturists and handicraftsmen." Perforated stone

[1] Dr. Keller's work, trans., p. 57. Earthen crucibles, containing melted bronze, were found at Robenhausen, Quarterly Review, October 1868.

[2] Dr. Keller, p. 46.

axes were also found here. Of these Sir John Lubbock remarks: "The pierced axes are generally found in the graves of the Bronze Period, and it is most probable that this mode of attaching the handle was used very rarely, if at all, until the discovery of metal had rendered the process far more easy than could have been the case previously."

Axes of *nephrite* were found also at Wangen — a material which does not occur in Europe, and could have come only from Turkestan or the region of Lake Baikal; in other words, the axes of nephrite found in the Swiss lake-dwellings were brought there by immigrants from Asia.

The third ancient station which we have specified is Nussdorf. Fifty perforated axes and fifty axes of nephrite were obtained here.

At Wauwyl an axe of nephrite and a glass bead were found.

At Moosseedorf we have nephrite reported, and wheat, barley, linseed, with the remains of the dog, the sheep, the hog, the goat, and the cow.

At Locras, which was explored by Dr. V. Gross, axes of nephrite and jadeite—one of the latter measuring eight inches in length—were obtained, and also two perforated stone hammers.[1]

At Concise eighty stone celts, flint arrow-heads, perforated stone hammers, amber, tin, bronze hair-pins and bracelets, and two beautiful bronze swords were found.

At Meilen the relics were chiefly of stone, but we

[1] Matériaux pour l'Histoire de l'Homme, 5e et 6e livraisons, 1873, p. 209.

are told that a perforated stone hammer, a bronze armilla, and a bronze celt were also found; and, at one point, a number of piles which had been sharpened by "a sharply-ground bronze celt."

These are the oldest stations, and yet it is obvious that they were inhabited by an intelligent and thrifty population, who, moreover, were not entirely ignorant of the metals.

That they did not *abandon* the use of stone, and supply themselves abundantly with tools and weapons of metal, is by no means a proof that they lived four or five thousand years before our era, since we know that obsidian swords and knives were used in Mexico by the subjects of Montezuma three centuries ago, and that in the relic-bed at Troy third from the bottom the implements are almost entirely of stone.

But the evidence on this subject in favour of the recent date of these settlements is far more specific than the above meagre statements would indicate.

We shall proceed to show that at many of these lake-stations, stone, bronze, and iron are all *found together* (just as they often are in the tumuli and dolmens). We shall also show that in many of them Roman relics occur. And finally we shall prove that the pile-dwellings were occupied in Switzerland down to the sixth century of our era; in France, down to the eighth century; and in Sweden and Pomerania, down to the eleventh century.

Where stone implements alone seem to have been used in a particular locality, and there is no trace of metal, the impression may be natural that they must belong to a very remote period. But this, as we have already suggested, does not necessarily follow. Cæsar found the inhabitants of the south-eastern coasts of Britain much more advanced than those in the interior. Metal is rare in the Yorkshire barrows, but Yorkshire was a very inaccessible point before the Romans got into Britain. So we should naturally expect the lake-dwellers in the west of Switzerland, on the lakes of Geneva and Neufchâtel—150 or 200 miles distant from Lugdunum and Massilia, and also, no doubt, in communication with Northern Italy—to be in advance of the population on the Lake of Constance, in the extreme east. In other words, the stone implements from the solitary valleys of Zurich and Pfäffikon, and the Bavarian Alps, may not be older than the bronze implements from Möringen or Nidau on the Lake of Bienne.

If, however, we concede that the "Stone-Age" settlements are older than those assigned to the "Bronze Age" or the "Iron Age," the fact that stone implements occur, mingled with bronze and iron implements, in the stations of the Bronze and the Iron Ages, shows *that stone implements were used down to the period represented by the bronze and the iron.* But if stone was used in this way down to the Roman period (or, if preferred, some centuries earlier), the presence of the stone implements in the "Stone-Age" stations fails to create a presumption of any great antiquity.

The usual method of evading the natural inference from the finding of stone and metal implements together is the suggestion that the use of stone *lapped* from the Stone Age over into the Bronze Age. But from this theory an awkward circumstance arises when we observe the flints in association with *iron*—for then the Stone Age must have lapped entirely across the Bronze Age (some 1500 years), and continued after the introduction of iron. And without going any farther, it will be seen that we shall find the stone implements in these lake-dwellings, associated with objects of Roman manufacture.

We shall proceed to notice (in addition to those already referred to) a number of the principal of these stations. Want of space compels us to be brief.

LAKE OF CONSTANCE.

On the western shore of the Ueberlinger See there is a station which is assigned to the Bronze Age. At it were found bronze celts, an iron knife, two iron arrow-heads, a fragment of an iron fish-hook, and flint flakes—all three ages.

On the eastern shore of this same sheet of water is the important station of

Unter-Uhldingen.—This is classed as a Bronze-Age station (and, being 1000 feet from the shore, must have been constructed with the aid of metal tools). The articles obtained here consisted of stone, bronze, and iron—three hundred stone axes and chisels, flint saws, stone hammers, &c.; a number of bronze celts, bronze lance-heads, twenty-five bronze knives, bronze sickles, bronze armlets, &c.; and of iron, one lance-head, five arrow-points, one axe, two chisels, fourteen knives, a ring, a fibula, and the remains of two swords.

Roman pottery, the fragments of twelve glass goblets, and a glass slab were also found.

Dr. Keller refers this station to the Bronze Age; and yet the stone implements are far the most numerous of all; and there are various objects of iron, along with Roman pottery and glass goblets. It will hardly do to say that the bronze-using people *succeeded* the stone-using settlers, because the Stone-Age settlements are always in shallow water near the shore.

Sipplingen.—Is only a half-hour's walk from Unter-Uhldingen, and is more than a quarter of a mile from the shore. Two hundred unperforated and twenty perforated stone axes were found here, besides many other implements of stone. Also one copper celt and sixteen objects of iron, including a sword and a Roman key, and five pieces of glass. There was not one object of bronze—and therefore the settlement, according to the theory, must have passed at once from the Stone to the Iron Age.

LAKE OF BIENNE.

Nidau.—There were found here thirty-three stone axes (some of them perforated), twenty-three bronze axes, iron spear-heads and various other objects of iron, glass beads, and two pieces of pottery believed by Dr. Keller to be Roman.

Sutz.—Yielded perforated stone axes, flint chippings, bronze celts, bronze pins, a bronze sword, two iron lance-heads, and a Roman millstone.

Möringen.—Called a bronze station. It yielded many articles of bronze, such as celts, knives, sickles, bracelets, &c., and also glass and amber beads. Re-explored by Dr. Gross, there were also obtained here a dozen stone axes, three bronze swords, one iron sword, and a bronze bridle-bit (showing the domestication of the horse). Dr. Gross observes: "This sword-blade of iron, with its handle of bronze, associated with other objects in bronze, and even some stone axes, leads us to conclude that the station of Möringen was constructed at an epoch when, concurrently with bronze, stone was still in use, and that it has existed during the age of bronze, and was destroyed after the appearance of iron in our countries." The objects appear to have been all found together.[1]

Little Island.—Colonel Schwab "found here objects of the stone, bronze, and Gallo-Roman periods, all mixed together."

Ile des Lapins.—"The remains of all the ages here," says Dr. Gross, "from the epoch of polished stone to the Gallo-Roman epoch, seem to testify that this station served as *a place of re-union where the merchants of different countries met together.*" But if the men of the Stone Age lived from four to six thousand years before the Christian era, we do not see how this accounts for the association of stone implements with relics of the Gallo-Roman period.

LAKE OF NEUFCHÂTEL.

La Tène or *Marin.*—This is called an iron station. Flint flakes, however, occur in great abundance. A dozen or more bronze objects were also found. Of iron implements there were found, in addition to many other articles, fifty swords, similar to those found at Alise.

[1] Matériaux pour l'Histoire de l'Homme, livraisons 5ᵉ et 6ᵉ, 1873, p.p. 221, 280, 281.

There were found also fragments of glass, Roman pottery, and Gallic and Roman coins.

Colombier.—Flint implements, stone celts, and Roman tiles.

Chez les Moines.—Stone chisels and Roman tiles.

Forel.—Roman tiles.

Near Chevroux.—Stone celts, bronze swords, sickles, &c., and a great iron fork.

Gletterens.—Roman tiles.

Pont de Thièle.—Stone celts and Roman tiles.

Estavayer.—Bronze and stone.

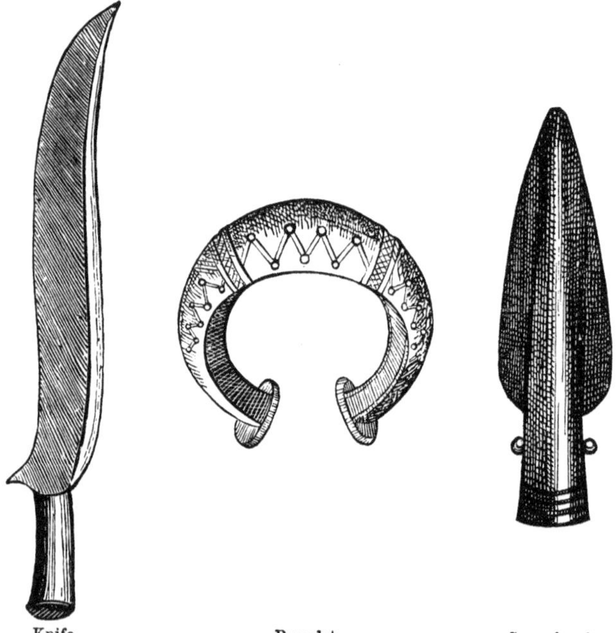

Knife. Bracelet. Spear-head.

We may introduce here the preceding samples of the bronze implements and ornaments found at these stations.

Corcelettes.—Great numbers of articles in bronze were found here, but none of iron, and not a great many of stone. A Roman amphora, however, was found; which indicates either that the iron had perished, or that after this region was known to the Romans iron was not in use.

LAKE OF MORAT.

Greng.—Near the shore we find only implements of stone, while farther in the lake we find stone and bronze mingled together, and also some objects of iron.

Montellier.—Stone and bronze.

Station No. 6.—Roman tiles.

Station No. 14.—A stone celt, an iron javelin, and Roman tiles.

LAKE OF GENEVA.

Les Roseaux.—The piles here were sharpened with bronze axes, and the station yielded implements of stone, bronze, and iron. Dr. Keller remarks that the spot was not occupied long. But we have all the *three ages.*

Remains resembling in all respects, and evidently contemporary with, the lake-dwellings, are found on land. Thus, in front of Vorbourg, in the Bernese Alps, M. Quiquerez informs us that a number of pre-historic objects—representative of all the three ages—were found. Among them was wheel-made pottery. At Windisch, the Roman Vindonissa, were found Celtic pottery, bronze clasps, iron implements, a flint knife, a flint scraper, a stone celt, &c. At Ebersburg, M. G. von Escher, at the depth of five feet, found stone implements mingled with a number of bronze implements and ornaments, and a glass bead exactly like those found in the Roman settlements.

ITALY, FRANCE, ETC.

The lake-dwellings seem to have been numerous in Northern Italy. They are most generally assigned by the archæologists to the Bronze Age. At Mercurago, near Arona, in a peat-moor, which was formerly a lake, M. Gastaldi and M. Moro found among the piles a great number of objects "in flint, bronze, and clay, and a canoe." In the neighbouring moor of Conturbia, a number of piles were found in the peat, which are said to have had the lower ends furnished with iron points.

Traces of a lake-village, we are told, have been found in the marshy soil along the course of the river Chiana, in Tuscany. The relics consisted of utensils of copper [bronze ?], lances of iron, statuettes in metal, &c., and *a copper coin.*

The bronze which is conspicuous in the lake-dwellings and *terramares* of Italy, is doubtless to be attributed to the Etruscan influence—bronze having been in great requisition among that people, as appears from the relics which are found in their tombs. No doubt the lake-dwellers of Italy were well supplied with bronze when stone constituted in Switzerland the chief material for tools and weapons.

Near Olmütz, in Moravia, on the March, a pile-village has been recognised, from which were obtained a stone knife, a bone hatchet, bronze rings, and other objects.

A drinking-cup is described "as exactly similar to those which we often find in the burial-mounds of the Helvetic era (two hundred years before and until Christ)."[1]

Roman relics have been obtained from a lake-station in Bavaria.

In Prussia, the traces of pile-dwellings have been recognised in Pomerania, near Lubtow, which are referred to by M. Desor in his paper on the "Palafittes of the Lake of Neufchâtel." Two distinct beds occur. In the lower were found fragments of pottery, axes of serpentine, flint, and amphibole, a bronze chisel, carbonised wheat, barley, and peas. In the upper bed were found similar objects, and also utensils of iron.[2] M. Figuier, referring to the same station, makes the statement that in the lower of the two beds bronze and stone implements were found "all mingled together."[3] The upper bed, he says, belongs to the Iron Age. There occurs, therefore, here, under the most unequivocal circumstances, a coexistence of the three ages. In the lower bed we have, first, bronze and stone "mingled together." Another occupation supervenes, and having now fully entered—as the archæologists would represent it—upon the Bronze Age, the employment of stone continues, and mingled with the stone and bronze we have iron.

Numerous traces of pile-villages have been met with in France—as in the Lake of Bourget (Savoy), and in the departments of Ariège, Aude, Haute-Garonne, and the Pyrénées-Orientales. They extend over the whole

[1] Smiths. Report for 1865. [2] Ibid., p. 402.
[3] Primitive Man, trans., p. 229.

of South-western France, from the Mediterranean to the ocean, from Bayonne and Dax to the eastern limits of the Pyrenees.

Relics of bronze and iron, superior pottery—resembling the Greek—and at Chatillon a Roman vase, were obtained from the Lake of Bourget.

In a paper from M. F. Garrigou, presented to the French Academy of Sciences by M. de Quatrefages, an account is given of one of these stations (near Saint-Dos) in the Basses-Pyrénées. Like most of the others in this region, it is assigned not only to the Metal Age, but to the age of *iron*.[1]

From these examples in Switzerland, Italy, Austria, Prussia, and France, it is plain that we have fulfilled our promise to show that stone, bronze, and iron are constantly found together at these stations, and that in many of them we find Roman relics: it appears, at the same time, that even these Roman objects are associated with implements of bronze and stone.

PILE-VILLAGES IN THE MIDDLE AGES.

There is evidence that the lake-dwellers were to be found in Europe down to a yet more recent period than this. In Switzerland, at Noville and Chavannes (Canton de Vaud), such stations were inhabited as late as the sixth century; and on the Lake of Bienne, as we are told by Dr. Gross, there exist at various places sites covered with pile-work which belong to an epoch "much less ancient than the Iron Age"—two of which he mentions as having been recognised by him in the vicinity

[1] Comptes Rendus, 1871, p. 476.

of Neuveville and Landeron.[1] In France, it is ascertained through the discoveries of M. Chantre in the Lake of Paladru, in the department of Isère, that (in the words of M. de Quatrefages) "there existed lacustrine habitations down to the Carlovingian epoch." At the Grands Roseaux, one of the stations which he examined on this lake, M. Chantre obtained axes, lance-heads, keys, spurs, &c., all of iron, and with them *a Carlovingian coin.*[2] The Lake of Paladru is about seventy-five miles from Geneva.

But, in the north of Europe, as was stated by M. Virchow at the Stockholm meeting of the International Anthropological Congress in 1874, it appears that these settlements were in existence *in the tenth or the eleventh century.* One of these was at Björkö, in Sweden; another in Pomerania, at Julin, the modern Wollin, on the island of Wollin, at the mouth of the Oder.[3]

In Ireland the lake-dwellings were known as *Crannoges,* and were constructed (like the *steinbergs* or *ténevières* of the Swiss lakes) with heaps of stones, held together by piles or frameworks of wood. These crannoges are said by Sir William Wilde to date from the ninth to the sixteenth century. The implements found in them are mostly of iron or bronze. Occasionally stone implements occur.

[1] Matériaux pour l'Histoire de l'Homme, 5e et 6e livraisons, 1873, p. 206.

[2] Comptes Rendus, Acad. des Sciences, 1872, p. 204.

[3] Matériaux, 8e, 9e, et 10e livraisons, 1874, p. 320.

At the meeting of the Berlin Anthropological Society in 1874, M. Virchow described another pile-dwelling at Potzlow, in Poland, which he referred to a period when that region was visited by Byzantine traders—probably about the seventh or eighth century. — Archiv für Anthrop., August 1875.

It is not strange, however, that we recognise the existence of the pile-villages in the tenth and eleventh centuries; for they may be found even at this day in various parts of the world. The city of Borneo is altogether built on piles; the city of Tcherkask is built over the Don; similar dwellings occur in Venezuela, in the Caroline Islands, in New Guinea, Celebes, Ceram, Mindanao, and Solo; and *the fishermen of Lake Prasias still inhabit wooden cottages over water as in the days of Herodotus.*

From these facts it is obvious that there is no warrant whatever for assigning to any of these structures an antiquity of six or seven thousand years, as Sir John Lubbock attempts to do, or connecting them, as Professor Agassiz did, with "geological phenomena." Of course, some of them *may be* four thousand years old; but there is no *evidence* to prove that the oldest are older than three thousand years.

CHAPTER V.

THE DANISH KJÖKKEN-MÖDDINGS.

Fauna of the Shell-Mounds—Antiquity inferred from the absence of metal, and rudeness of flints—Fallacy of this reasoning—Shell-mound of the Roman period on the island of Herm—Loch Spynie—Shell-mound at Newhaven, Sussex, of Roman date, and also in the Isle of Thanet—Recent discovery of bronze in Danish shell-mound—Similar accumulations on the coasts of the United States.

ARCHÆOLOGISTS appeal next, in proof of the antiquity of man, to the Danish "kitchen-middens" or shell-mounds on the eastern coasts of Denmark. In these shell-heaps, which are the remains of the repasts of the rude fishermen who anciently dwelt upon these shores, are found implements of flint, pottery, and the bones of the stag, the roedeer, the wild boar, the urus, the dog, the fox, the bear, the wolf, &c. The musk-ox, the domestic ox, the reindeer, the elk, the hare, the sheep, and the domestic hog are absent. The flint implements are unpolished and extremely rude, insomuch that Professor Worsaae assigns them to the Palæolithic Age, and Lubbock to the "early part" of the Neolithic Age.

The antiquity of the Danish shell-mounds is deduced entirely from the presence of these rude flints, and the absence of metal.

We learn, however, from M. Morlot that "some rare

specimens of flints of fine workmanship have been found in the kjökken-möddings," which is corroborated by Sir John Lubbock.

The very rudest implements, moreover, are found in the dolmens and tumuli; and are constantly found in the United States and Canada on the surface of the ground, in association with the most highly-finished specimens, showing that the Indians to a very great extent made use of flints of very inferior workmanship. The rudeness of most of those found in the shell-mounds, where the dog is the only domesticated animal represented, only proves the primitive condition of these Danish fishermen. If the mere rudeness of the stone implement proves antiquity, the Australian of the present day would be assigned by some future archæologist to the Palæolithic Period.

With regard to the absence of metal, the Danish antiquaries admit that iron was not known in that country until some centuries after the Christian era; and if bronze was to be found there some centuries earlier, it is hardly to be presumed that it would be found among a wretched population like this. In the Shetland and Orkney Islands stone knives were in use "at no distant period," and Mr. Evans informs us that "there are traditions extant of their having been in use in the present century." [1]

The fauna of the shell-mounds by no means implies a high antiquity—there being no extinct animals except the urus, and this, as we shall see, was living in Europe a few centuries ago. The aurochs and the reindeer are

[1] Ancient Stone Implements, on authority of Sir W. R. Wilde, p. 11.

both absent, the former of which occurs in the Swiss lake-dwellings, and the latter in the Danish peat. It is, therefore, not easy to comprehend the grounds on which Professor Worsaae refers these refuse-heaps to the Palæolithic Age, and more difficult to understand the Rev. Dunbar Heath, F.R.S.L., who speaks of kitchen-middens occupied at the close of the Tertiary Age by a race of mutes.[1]

It is proverbially difficult to prove a negative, and, therefore, as with the lake-dwellings, we may not produce a demonstration that the shell-mounds are not six or ten thousand years old; but we are not called upon to do this; the burden of proof is with those who assert the great antiquity of these remains. The mere presence of stone arrow-heads and scrapers does not by any means establish this fact.

We are guided somewhat in fixing the probable date of the Danish shell-mounds by some explorations which have taken place in other, though not very distant, localities. In the "Anthropological Review" for 1869,[2] Mr. J. W. Flower, F.G.S., gives an account of a shell-mound examined by him on the west coast of the island of Herm—one of the Channel Islands, between Guernsey and Sark. He found the bones of the horse, ox, sheep, pig, goat, &c., and, strange to say, no remains of the dog; also small cylindrical bricks, pottery, hand-mills, rude stone mullers or chisels, rude stone hammers, a bronze pin, an instrument of iron, and a fragment of

[1] Paper read before the Anthropological Society in 1867. See Anthropological Review, April 1867.

[2] Page 115.

glass. Some of the pottery, says Mr. Flower, "is clearly of Roman workmanship," several pieces being "undoubted Samian ware."

We have thus a post-Roman kjökken-mödding, and with the Roman relics we find implements of stone.

Sir John Lubbock examined another shell-mound on Loch Spynie (near the coast), in Scotland. He did not find any implements or pottery, but a labourer, we are told, had previously found "some fragments of rude pottery and a bronze pin." Mr. Franks, to whom the pin was submitted, gave it as his opinion that it is probably "not older than 800 or 900 A.D."

Hugh Miller mentions that articles of bronze along with rude implements of bone and flint were found in some shell-mounds on the Scottish coast.[1]

A kjökken-mödding has also been discovered at Newhaven, in Sussex, containing, along with bones, shells, pottery, and flint flakes, two or three objects of metal, including a leaden hook and a small *coin*. Some of the pottery (found *below* the flint flakes) was recognised as Roman.[2]

Colonel Lane Fox, commenting on Mr. Flower's account of the shell-mound (above referred to) on the island of Herm, states that he had found a shell-mound in the Isle of Thanet, in which finger-bricks (used probably for baking pottery) like those described by Mr. Flower, were obtained along with Roman pottery.

But that Professor Worsaae and Sir John Lubbock spoke unadvisedly in connecting the kjökken-möddings

[1] Journal of the Anthropological Society, 1865, vol. iii. p. 21.
[2] Intellectual Observer, vol. vii. p. 233.

with the Palæolithic or the Post-Palæolithic Age, appears further from the fact that within the last few years objects of bronze have been found in a kjökken-mödding near the city of Kallundborg, in Seeland, associated with stone implements and the remains of the domesticated ox and sheep.[1] M. Valdemar Schmidt, in view of the presence of the objects of bronze, refers the kjökken-mödding of Samsingerbanken, as it is called, to the *transition period* from stone to bronze; but, if this were the case, as Dr. Schliemann remarks, "then there ought to be found here only polished stone weapons and implements; but such is not the case; on the contrary, in *no other* 'kjökken-mödding' are the stone weapons and implements so rudely made as in this."

Such being the condition of the facts, the shell-mounds seem, as in the case of the lake-dwellings, to be taken out of the category of the evidences for the antiquity of man.

We may add that shell-mounds (some of them of vast proportions) occur on all the coasts of the United States —from Maine to Florida, and from Oregon to California. Professor Leidy examined some of these near the town of Lewes, on Delaware Bay. All of them contained "fragments of pottery, chips of jasper, and stone arrow-heads. A few copper rings were also found, and in one heap Mr. Canby found several *English* coins." [2]

[1] Matériaux, livraisons 8e et 9e, 1875, p. 350. Academy, August 28, 1875, Letter from Dr. Schliemann.

[2] Proc. Phil. Acad. Nat. Sci., 1866, p. 291.

CHAPTER VI.

THE BONE-CAVES.

Involve a more difficult inquiry—Human remains found with the bones of extinct animals, as the elephant, hippopotamus, &c.—Sometimes under floors of stalagmite—Changes in the physical geography of the cave-districts—Kent's Cavern—Caves of the Dordogne—Facts which tend to negative a high antiquity for the relics found in the caves—Carefully-worked implements of stone and bone—Art amongst the Troglodytes; their drawings and carvings—Manufactured pottery—Palæolithic flint factories—Extensive traffic of the cave-men—Nephrite at Chaleux—The skulls of the cave-men—Burial of the dead—No gap between the First and Second Stone Ages—Gourdan—Thäyngen—Hohlefels—The stalagmitic floors considered.

THE evidence for the antiquity of the Bronze Age and the Polished Stone Age, derivable from the megalithic monuments, the lake-dwellings, and the shell-mounds, breaks down completely, and is readily disposed of; but in entering upon the Palæolithic Age, represented by the bone-caves and the river-gravel, much more difficult questions present themselves. The river-gravel we shall consider hereafter; in the present chapter we shall pass under review the bone-caves. In these, implements of bone and horn and flint, and in some instances human bones, are found (often buried deep in the soil of the caves) in association with the remains of extinct animals—such as the mammoth (*Elephas primigenius*), the rhinoceros (*tichorinus*), the hippopotamus (*major*), the reindeer, the cave-bear, the cave-lion, the cave-hyæna, &c. This does not occur once or occasionally, but in a great multitude of instances, and that not in one country or district, but in many parts of France, England, Germany, Italy, and Spain; so often, that the association cannot be regarded as accidental, or as attributable to the disturbing effects of water or any other agency, but is only to be explained on the hypothesis that man and these animals occupied these districts in the same age, and were familiar objects the one to the other. Moreover (in Southern France, for example), bones and horns of the reindeer are constantly obtained from these caves, which have been fashioned into weapons and tools; and the bones or teeth of the great carnivores present also frequently traces of human workmanship or handling. Nor is this all: the reindeer, the cave-bear, the cave-lion, the mammoth (?), the bison, &c., are more or less faithfully delineated by the palæolithic savages on bone, horn, ivory, and stone.

In some of the caves (the instances are the exception) these remains, all mingled together, are found under solid floors of stalagmite, which Sir Charles Lyell and other advocates of the antiquity of man believe to have required long ages for their formation.

In some instances, moreover, as at Brixham Cave and Kent's Hole, the physical geography of the locality of the caves has been greatly altered since they were inhabited by man, the streams in the neighbourhood running now one hundred feet below the position of the caves, which give evidence of having been formerly swept by water.

It was not strange that such facts as these should suggest the idea that a vast period had elapsed since Europe was first occupied by the human race; and if this opinion is erroneous, it has to be shown that the reindeer and the mammoth were in Southern France in recent times; that the rate of formation of the stalagmitic rock is much more rapid than has been generally supposed; and that great alterations in the crust of the earth have occurred within a few thousand years.

Kent's Hole.—For the purposes of illustration we may briefly indicate one of the most celebrated of these caves. Perhaps the most famous in England is that of Kent's Hole, on the coast of Devonshire. According to Mr. Evans, the beds here consist of (1) large blocks of limestone which have fallen from the roof, sometimes cemented by stalagmite; (2) a layer of black, muddy mould, three to twelve inches thick; (3) stalagmite, one to three feet thick, almost continuous; (4) red cave-earth, containing flint implements and bones of extinct animals. Above the stalagmite, chiefly in bed 2, objects of bronze, Roman pottery, bone instruments, and numbers of flint flakes, cores, and chips occur. In bed 4, below the stalagmite, occur flint implements, bone implements, and the bones of extinct (and existing) animals—such as the cave-lion, cave-hyæna, wolf, fox, glutton, cave-bear, grizzly bear, brown bear, mammoth, woolly rhinoceros, horse, urus, bison, Irish elk, reindeer, &c. The animals above the stalagmitic floor were the dog, short-horn ox, roedeer, sheep, goat, pig, and rabbit.

Certain caves of the Dordogne, in France, were very thoroughly explored by M. Lartet and Mr. Christy, and are among the best known in connection with the subject under discussion—among them those of Laugerie-Basse, Laugerie-Haute, La Madelaine, Les Eyzies, Le Moustier, Badegoule, &c.

No remains which in the opinion of M. Lartet and Mr. Christy could be referred to the domestic animals have been found in these caves. The bones of the reindeer, which are numerous, are all broken for the marrow. The flint implements procured consist of scrapers, cores, awls, lance-heads, knives, hammers, &c., &c. With these are found numerous implements of horn and bone.

FINELY-WROUGHT IMPLEMENTS FROM THE CAVES.

The first fact which awakens a feeling of distrust with regard to the antiquity of these remains is *the perfection of the work* observable in some instances, as at Laugerie-Haute and Badegoule, where, as we are told by Sir John Lubbock, "fragments of leaf-shaped lance-heads, almost as well worked as some of those from Denmark, are far from uncommon." This fact, observable also at Gourdan, Solutré, and several other localities where the remains of the great extinct animals exist in association with the flint implements, tends to destroy the argument derived for the antiquity of the palæolithic caves from the extreme rudeness of the implements in general, and to break down the distinction usually drawn between the First and the Second Stone Age, based on the form and finish of the stone weapons.

The elegance of some of the bone implements occasions also a suspicion that we are not removed by one or two hundred thousand years from the fabricators of thèse objects—such, for example, as the harpoon-shaped lance-heads and the finely-pointed polished needles, drilled with small, round eyes, "so small and regular" that some doubt was created as to their having been drilled with stone.

PALÆOLITHIC ART.

But it is the *palæolithic art,* as evinced by the drawings on bone and stone, which seems least of all to accord with the vast antiquity claimed for these relics. Some of these delineations are really astonishing, and far in advance of anything which can be accomplished among modern savages. It is impossible to admit the belief that the browsing reindeer in the cut on next page, from the grotto of Thäyngen, in Switzerland, is a hundred thousand years old.[1] Other examples

Drawing of a fish.

Staff of authority, on which are graven representations of a man, two horses, and a fish.

[1] The drawing, so elegant and accurate in its execution, speaks louder than all the facts presented to prove the antiquity of man. No imbecile hand guided that pencil, and the blood which coursed in its veins is not separated by any extravagant period from the blood which produces the same artistic representations to-day.

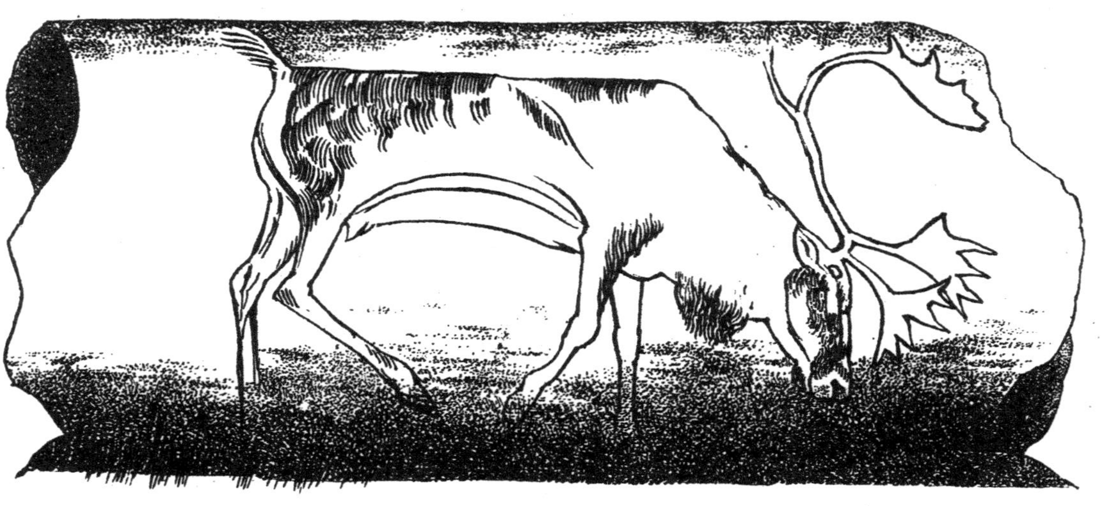

REINDEER ENGRAVED ON BONE, FROM THE GROTTO OF THÄYNGEN (SWITZERLAND).
(*Taken from "Matériaux pour l'Histoire de l'Homme,"* 1874).

(*Face p.* 70)

of the skill of the cave-dwellers of the Palæolithic Age in drawing and carving are presented in the two cuts preceding this, and in the three following cuts:—

Group of reindeer.

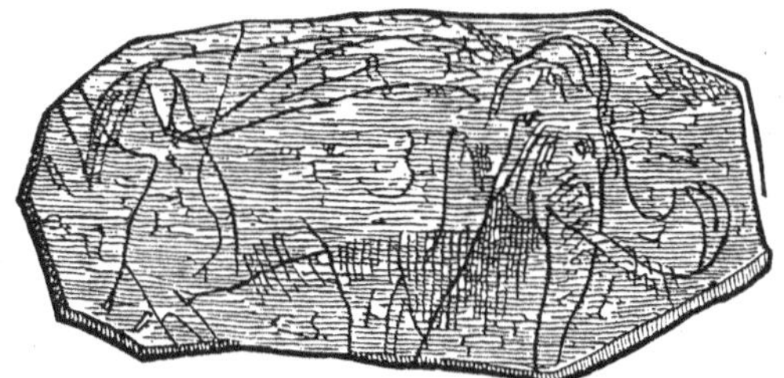

Sketch of a mammoth, graven on a slab of ivory.

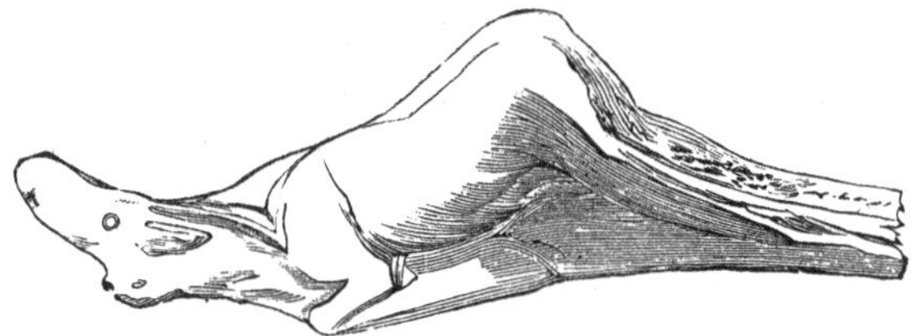

Handle of a poniard.

MANUFACTURE OF POTTERY.

If in addition it be found to be true that the palæolithic cave-men *manufactured pottery* (which among modern savages is true only of the Hottentots, the North American Indians, and the Fijians[1]), it would require very unequivocal evidence to convince us that one or two hundred thousand years have rolled by since these people prosecuted their primitive arts in the valley of the Lesse or the Rhine.

M. de Mortillet, Sir John Lubbock, Mr. Boyd Dawkins, and most of the archæologists, refuse to admit that pottery was manufactured earlier than the Neolithic Age. It has been found, however, in the French caves, in a number of instances, associated with palæolithic remains, as at Nabrigas, where M. Joly found the skull of a cave-bear, and "close by a fragment of pottery bearing the imprint of the fingers of the man who moulded it;"[2] at Vergisson (Saône-et-Loire), where M. Ferry found the bones of the cave-bear, mammoth, rhinoceros, reindeer, &c., mingled with wrought flints and rough pottery;[3] at Pondres (Hérault), where M. de Cristolles "discovered human bones, and pottery, mixed with the remains of the rhinoceros, bear, hyæna, and many other animals;" in the caverns of Bize; at the Trou du Renard, in the valley of the Rhone (Vivarais); at La Salpêtrière (Gard); and at the cavern of Rochebertier, in the valley of the Tardoire (Charente). We

[1] And is not true of the Eskimo, the New Zealanders, the Tahitians, the Australians, the Bushmen, or the Fuegians.

[2] Figuier, Primitive Man, trans., p. 8.

[3] Primitive Man, p. 73.

begin with the French caves, because M. Cartailhac, the editor of "Matériaux pour l'Histoire de l'Homme," has raised some plausible doubts with regard to them, affirming that at Nabrigas, Pondres, Bise, and Vergisson[1] the soil of the caves has been disturbed, and that the pottery obtained belongs to a second occupation thereof in the Neolithic Age. It is certainly a rare event to find pottery in the palæolithic caves of France, and sometimes the relics from different beds do get together. M. Cartailhac may, therefore, be right with regard to the instances mentioned; but there was no trace of disturbance at Rochebertier, and not a trace of polished stone or metal. The implements were "palæolithic;" the fauna, bear, hyæna, lion, reindeer, horse, &c.[2] M. Fermond, the explorer of this cave, assigns it to the epoch of La Madelaine, and remarks that "tout indique que ce sol n'a jamais été rémanié."

It would be a great point gained by the advocates of the antiquity of the Palæolithic Age, if it could be proved that the men of that period were unacquainted with pottery; for, as we have remarked, it is incredible that pottery was manufactured in these caves one or two or three (or, according to Mr. A. R. Wallace, five) hundred thousand years ago. The absence of pottery does not establish the remoteness of the period; but the presence of it creates a very strong presumption in favour of a recent date for the associated remains.

Now, however it be in France, it is not disputed (except by Mr. Boyd Dawkins) that pottery was manu-

[1] Matériaux, Avril et Mai 1872, pp. 206, 210.
[2] Ibid., 1e livraison, 1874, p. 7.

facturea in Belgium in the Palæolithic Age. This fact has been demonstrated by the researches of M. Ed. Dupont in the Belgian caves, and is admitted by both M. Cartailhac and Sir John Lubbock. Sir John merely has to say of it that it is "exceptional,"[1] while M. Cartailhac states that he declines to generalise on the subject, and confines his observations to France, "car nous ne pouvons aller contre les résultats des admirables fouilles de M. Ed. Dupont en Belgique."[2]

One of the caves in Belgium where pottery occurred was the celebrated cave of Engis, explored originally by Dr. Schmerling, and more recently by M. Dupont. It was in this cave that the Engis skull was obtained from a mass of breccia containing bones and teeth of the rhinoceros, mammoth, hyæna, bear, and horse, along with worked flints and a small fragment of coarse earthenware.

The little urn figured below comes from the Trou du

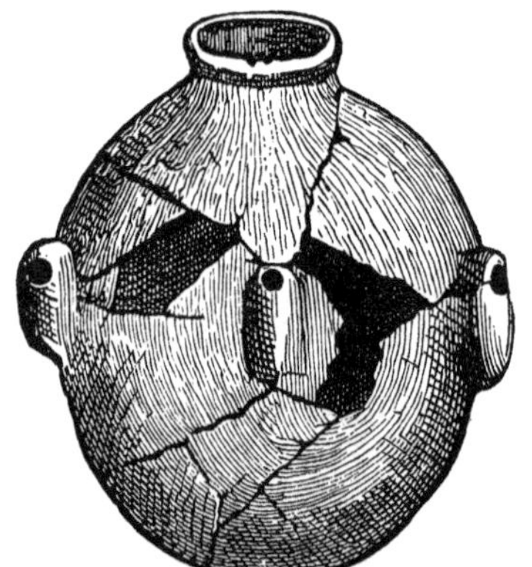

Earthen vase found in a cave at Furfooz (Belgium).

[1] Journal of Anthropological Institute, 1872, p. 383.
[2] Matériaux, Avril et Mai 1872, p. 210.

Frontal, near Furfooz, and was found with flint flakes, ornaments in fluorine, human skeletons, and bones of the reindeer, lagomys or tailless hare, urus, stag, chamois, &c. Mr. Dawkins questions the assignment by M. Dupont of this station to the Palæolithic Age, but the fauna is a palæolithic fauna. The pottery, it is true, has a neolithic look; and yet, on the other hand, there are no other neolithic relics, and the caves close by, the Trou des Nutons and the Trou Rosette, are of Palæolithic Age.

Pottery has also been found associated with the remains of the cave-bear in several of the caves of Italy, of which, however, we shall speak hereafter.

It was encountered also in some abundance by Dr. Fraas in the cavern or grotto of Hohlefels, near Blaubeuren, in Wurtemberg. Dr. Fraas found here more than fifty flint knives of the palæolithic type, numerous chippings of flint, many instruments in bone, and fragments of pottery. The animal remains belonged to the cave-bear, *Ursus priscus*, reindeer, horse, rhinoceros, mammoth, lion, fox, duck, heron, &c. Dr. Fraas is one of the most highly esteemed anthropologists of Europe. Speaking at the Congress of Brussels of the distinction made by M. de Mortillet and other French archæologists between the "age of the reindeer" and "the age of the mammoth," he said: "It may be that all this has been seen in France, but it is not so in Germany. There is there no age of the mammoth, no age of the bear, no age of the reindeer. All these animals lived, and were eaten by man, at the same epoch. These remains, in fine, are mingled in the grotto of Hohlefels, and the only thing missing there is the modern fauna, the stag, the sheep, &c. . . . One can see, in Belgium, that pottery existed with the reindeer and the mammoth, and that things passed in that country as in Germany and not as in France. They ought to be in France as in Germany."[1]

Dr. C. A. Jentzsch, in a paper "On the Quaternary Formations in the Neighbourhood of Dresden," speaking of the fresh-water limestone of Robschutz, in the Trebisch Valley, states that in this formation remains of the mammoth and rhinoceros "abound" along with human bones and pottery.[2]

Pottery was found again at the palæolithic station explored by M. von Ecker, near Munzingen, not far from Friburg, in the valley of the Rhine. The bones of the reindeer, and stone and bone implements, were found, in this instance, at the depth of from one to four feet in the loess. There were also hearths, giving evidence of a continued occupation. The settlement had been overwhelmed by the palæolithic flood, and buried beneath the sediments with which the Rhine was so heavily charged during that cataclysm.[3]

We may mention yet another example, which is reported from France, where, near La Bastide de Béarn, MM. Garrigou and Duparc discovered the traces of a very primitive lacustrine or palustrine village. There

[1] Matériaux, Août et Septembre 1872, p. 404. In the same discussion Mr. Franks (whose authority on such questions is so high) remarked that he believed that pottery of the age of the reindeer had been found in Southern France, but that in any case all doubt must disappear in view of the facts observed in Belgium.

[2] Academy, December 1, 1871.

[3] Archiv für Anthrop., August 1875, s. 87.

were no piles, but the settlement had been constructed with the trunks of trees worked by means of fire, the smaller end of the trunk being "worked," and planted in the mud. The interlaced roots above formed a sort of scaffolding. Chipped flints, remains of the reindeer, and rude pottery were found associated in this ancient settlement.[1]

FLINT-IMPLEMENT MANUFACTORIES, AND EXTENDED TRAFFIC OF THE CAVE-DWELLERS.

The cave-men not only fabricated pottery, and whiled away the tedium of their indoor hours by attempts, more or less successful, at delineating the abounding life of the palæolithic forests, but there are various stations which bear evidence to an active industry and commerce in the manufacture and barter of the utensils and implements which ministered to the supply of their daily wants. There were palæolithic manufactories of flint implements at Laugerie-Haute, in Périgord; at Chaleux, in Belgium; at Pressigny, in Touraine; at Hoxne, in Suffolk. In the last case the flints occur in the river-gravel deposits; at Pressigny they cover the surface of the ground over a superficies of twelve or fourteen acres. At the cave of Chaleux more than thirty thousand flints have been obtained; and the extended *traffic* of the cave-dwellers is evidenced by the fact that M. Dupont found here fifty-four fossil shells which are not found originally in this region, but only in Champagne, from whence they were brought to be manufactured into necklaces for the people of the

[1] Matériaux, 10e à 12e livraisons, 1873, p. 457.

valley of the Lesse. The dwellers in the cave of Chaleux travelled even to the west of France (some 300 miles) to gratify their fancy with the honey-coloured flints of Grand-Pressigny. And so at Thäyngen M. Mayer detected Miocene fossils from the Vienne basin in France; and at Barma, near Mentone, Dr. Rivière discovered shells that had been brought from the ocean. The most interesting discovery at Chaleux, however, was the *nephrite* from Asia, which we have already met with at the Swiss lake-dwellings. The cave of Chaleux had never been disturbed, the roof having fallen in, and in this manner sealed up the precious relics of the First Stone Age, and preserved them unmolested until the distinguished Belgian archæologist, in 1864, made his memorable examination of the Belgian caves. At the depth of eight feet below the compact detritus the original floor of the cavern was reached. Besides the immense number of flint implements discovered, there were others also of bone and reindeer's horn. In the middle of the cave was found the hearth, formed of flat stones, and on it lay the ashes and coals where the occupants of the cave had prepared their food. We learn from M. Dupont's report to the Belgian Government that they found among the relics "fragments of ammonite, fluorine from the Devonian limestone, shells from Champagne, flints from Pressigny, fragments of elephants' teeth, out of which they manufactured their beautiful needles, and nephrite from the East."[1] This nephrite, as we have previously remarked, is not found

[1] See this Report reprinted in the Memoirs of the Anthropological Society of London for 1867–69.

nearer than Turkestan, and seems to furnish conclusive evidence of the migration of the palæolithic tribes of Belgium *from Asia*, and of relations with the pile-dwellers of the Swiss lakes.[1]

If M. Dupont has made no mistake, the non-antiquity of these palæolithic caves is established at once by this discovery, for it would hardly be suggested that this nephrite was brought to Europe from Asia one hundred and fifty or two hundred thousand years ago.[2]

The facts we have mentioned—the skill exhibited by the cave-men in the manufacture of their implements of bone, horn, ivory, and flint; the wonderful examples which we find in the relic-beds of their taste and accuracy in delineating the animals around them; the workshops which they maintained for the regular production of flint weapons and tools; the extended traffic which was carried on between widely-separated tribes; and their manufacture of pottery—raise a strong presumption against the idea that these people were pre-glacial,

[1] M. Desor states that for twenty years this rock has been carefully sought for in Europe, but that it has never been found, and he suggests that the axes of nephrite and jade found in the Swiss lake-dwellings may have been brought to Europe during the original migrations to that continent from Asia. See paper by him in "Cong. d'Anthrop.," 1872, p. 351.

[2] In a paper published in "Matériaux," by M. Fischer (1876, p. 488), on the "Recent and Fossil Shells found in the Caverns of the South of France and Liguria," we are told that there was an active traffic kept up among these palæolithic tribes, as is evidenced by the shells found in the caverns. "The living shells, nevertheless," remarks M. Fischer, "belong to two faunas, that of the ocean, and that of the Mediterranean; none of them come from the Indian Ocean, which requires us to believe that the commercial communications were not very extended, and that the shells the most anciently used as a monetary sign in Asia and Africa (*Cypræa moneta*) were not known in the west of Europe."

But M. Fischer adds in a note: "This is not true of Thäyngen, where M. Mayer indicates a valve of *Ostrea cucullata—a species from the Red Sea or the Indian Ocean.*" See note at end of chapter.

or that they are removed from the present times by any such gap as pre-historic archæology asserts. The savages of Aquitaine or the basin of the Meuse, at the epoch of the reindeer and the mammoth, led precisely such a life as the Eskimo lead now, or as the North American Indians led a century ago. The modern Eskimo flint scrapers (a point already touched on) are identical in form with those from the river-gravel, and their fishing-spears and bone needles are identical in form with those from the Auvergne caves.

THE SKULLS OF THE CAVE-DWELLERS.

It was at one time regarded as not improbable that the crania of the "artisans of the drift" would exhibit a marked degradation as compared with the modern European skull; and a good deal of idle speculation was indulged in with regard to the *Neanderthal Skull.* A book was prepared on the subject by Professor Fuhlrott, who attributed to this relic an antiquity of two or three hundred thousand years. Professor Schaaffhausen read a paper on the subject before the Lower Rhine Medical and Natural History Society. Professor Huxley discussed it in "Man's Place in Nature," and assigned to it "a very high antiquity." Professor William King read a paper before the British Association, in which he referred it to the Glacial Period. It was described by Professor Huxley as "the most ape-like skull he ever beheld," and by Professor Busk and Professor Schaaffhausen as "the most brutal of all known human skulls, resembling those of the apes not only in the prodigious development of the superciliary prominences and the forward extension of the orbits, but still more in the depressed form of the brain-case, in the straightness of the squamosal suture, and in the complete retreat of the occiput forward and upward, from the superior occipital ridges."

But, in the first place, there is not a particle of evidence that the Neanderthal skull belongs to the Stone Age; and, secondly, its cranial capacity is seventy-five cubic inches, which is a fair average skull—equal to that of the Negro, and above the Malay. It has double the capacity of the largest gorilla skull known. It was found in 1857 in a cave near Düsseldorf, buried about five feet in the mud of the cave—not associated with either flint implements or the bones of extinct animals; and there is no warrant whatever to attribute to it a high antiquity.

The Engis skull found by Dr. Schmerling in a cave near Liége is admitted to be palæolithic, having been found in association with the bones of the mammoth, the cave-bear, and other extinct mammalia. But of this we are told that "there is no mark of degradation about any part of its structure"—"a fair average skull," says Professor Huxley, "which might have belonged to a philosopher, or might have contained the thoughtless brains of a savage."

The skulls from the rock-shelter of Bruniquel were pronounced by Professor Owen to exemplify "the distinct characteristics of the human genus and species as decidedly as do the corresponding parts of the present races"—and to "correspond in cranial capacity with that of the uneducated European of Celtic origin."

M. Broca, in a paper on "The Troglodytes of Les Eyzies," states that while the skulls exhibited traces of ferocity, they displayed also "a certain amount of superior development."[1]

The famous skeleton of Mentone possesses a very fine skull, and is a splendid specimen of humanity.

Thus again the evidence tends to rebut the assumption of the antiquity of these remains.[2]

The main point we have, of course, to consider—the presence of the extinct animals, or the fact that these cave-men were the contemporaries of the mammoth and the reindeer. This we shall discuss at the proper time—as well as the stalagmitic floors, and the changes in physical geography presented at the Gower caves in Glamorganshire, at Kent's Cavern, and in the cliffs of the Meuse Valley.

[1] Les Eyzies is a small village in Périgord, on the banks of the Vezère. The skeletons referred to were found in a cave near this village, called the cave of Cro-Magnon. M. de Quatrefages, describing these skulls before the French Academy of Sciences, on the occasion of the presentation of the second part of his "Crania Ethica," stated that the Cro-Magnon skull "is remarkable for its capacity"—"gauging, according to Dr. Broca, not less than 1590 cent. cubes, which is larger than the mean European skull of the present day."

It is in point, though he is speaking of the Neolithic Period, that Professor Rolleston, one of the leading British anthropologists, stated at the Bristol meeting of the British Association (1876), that an examination of the oldest barrows in Yorkshire proves that "the volume of brains contained in the most ancient skulls which have been found was much greater than that from modern European skulls."

[2] The fact that palæolithic man was (to use the words of M. Pruner Bey) "man in the full force of the term," appears inconsistent with the doctrine of evolution in a double aspect: first, we encounter man in a state of complete development without any earlier anthropoidal forms—for none such have been, nor are likely to be, discovered; secondly, we observe that man has not been modified in his mental or physical structure since. And if man has, as is contended, inhabited the earth for im-

If all of these were unexplained, to our mind it would still be hard to believe that the proprietor of a skull like that from Engis or Cro-Magnon, carrying in one hand a sketch like that of the reindeer of Thäyngen, and in the other the harpoons of La Madelaine (see cuts on p. 342 of Dawkins' "Cave-Hunting") or the spear-heads of Gourdan; making the journey from Dinant in Belgium to Tours in France to procure the flints of Touraine; provided with vessels of pottery; wearing skins which he himself had dressed and sewed together; decorated with paint and a necklace of shells,—had witnessed the setting-in of the Glacial Age or that excentricity of the earth's orbit which is described by Mr. Croll as having reached its last period of culmination some 200,000 years ago.

BURIAL OF THE DEAD.

There is, moreover, another impressive fact, now well established, in connection with these caves, which is hardly consistent with a pre-glacial date: *the burial of*

mense ages, and no change has taken place in his constitution and character, what ground can there be for supposing that such changes took place at any previous time?

No human remains so far have been found in the Tertiary strata. But "if man," says Sir John Lubbock, "constitutes a separate family of mammalia, . . . then, according to all palæontological analogies, he must have had representatives in Miocene times." He adds: "We need not, however, expect to find the proofs in Europe; our nearest relatives in the animal kingdom are confined to hot, almost to tropical climates, and it is in such countries that we are most likely to find the earliest traces of the human race." And so Lyell remarks that "the missing links" must be sought in the countries of the anthropomorphous apes—the tropical regions of Africa, and the islands of Borneo and Sumatra; which, he says, have not yet been explored (Antiq. Man, p. 538).

But the answer to this is, that in Miocene times the south of Europe had an almost tropical climate.

the dead. That this rite was practised among the palæolithic races is proved by various discoveries.

In a cavern near Mentone, in Italy, at the depth of six and a half metres, Dr. Rivière came upon a skeleton, around which were scattered a great number of flint implements of palæolithic type, and bones of the rhinoceros, mammoth, cave-bear, cave-lion, urus, and other animals. The skull (which was very large and extremely well formed) was covered with a head-dress of more than two hundred perforated shells. The thighs were of unusual length (eighteen inches), and, with the rest of the bones, indicated the subject to have belonged to a large race. The teeth and bones of the extinct animals occurred both above and below the skeleton, which lay in an attitude of repose, its legs crossed, and the arms folded. Mr. Boyd Dawkins doubts whether interment could have been practised so many ages ago, and suggests that the burial in this case and the animal remains which surround it are not of the same period. But Sir Charles Lyell, M. Cartailhac, and Mr. Pengelly deem the evidence conclusive. We would simply add, that it is hardly reasonable to conjecture, as Mr. Dawkins does, that it may be a neolithic burial in a palæolithic cave, for the reason that there are no neolithic implements, and the fauna is all palæolithic.

Several other skeletons have been found in these Mentone caverns since this first discovery in 1872.

Another palæolithic interment occurred at Laugerie-Basse. The caves of Cro-Magnon and Bruniquel, as well as some of the Belgian caves, have furnished additional examples. Mr. Dawkins raises doubts about all these (in opposition to the entire body of archæologists); but all inferences from the *a priori improbability* of such a fact are set aside by the numerous palæolithic sepultures which are presented at the station of Solutré in Eastern France, of which we shall speak more particularly in a future chapter. There is no doubt that palæolithic men practised burial.

NO GAP BETWEEN THE FIRST AND SECOND STONE AGES.

It is customary to assert that there was a great *lacuna* or *gap* between the Palæolithic and Neolithic Ages, and the difference in the finish and type of the implements used is cited as one evidence of this fact. The barbed and stemmed arrow-heads are said to have been unknown to the palæolithic people, and all the implements of this period are said to have been extremely rude in their character. On the latter point we have already made some remarks which contradict the declaration; with regard to the barbed arrow-heads, they have been detected at Badegoule, Laugerie-Haute, Excideuil, and Solutré—stations presenting a genuine palæolithic fauna, and of undoubted palæolithic date.

The finish of the flint implements at these stations, and these barbed specimens of arrow-points, and the beautiful bone implements found in the caves, destroy, as we have already said, the inference for a gap between the periods in question drawn from the rude type of most of the palæolithic implements. The forms at Solutré and the caves mentioned are essentially *transitional forms* from the palæolithic to the neolithic type.

Nor must it be forgotten that the great bulk of the implements in the Neolithic Period were just as rude as the rudest of the Palæolithic Period.

CAVE OF GOURDAN.

One of the caves most recently explored, and one of the most interesting, is that of Gourdan (Haute-Garonne), a detailed account of which has been published by the explorer, M. Piette. Great numbers of flint and bone implements, beautifully worked, were obtained from this cave, including some twenty or thirty barbed arrow-heads of bone. The animal remains included bear (*U. arctos*), beaver, wild boar, horse, wolf, lynx, chamois, ibex, reindeer, elk, and mammoth. The drawings executed on bone and horn were very numerous and extremely well done, the animals represented being rhinoceros (?), mammoth (?), reindeer, saiga, chamois, stag, goat, lynx, ox, horse, birds, &c.

Above this bed there is another bed, referred by M. Piette to the Neolithic Period. This bed rests in contact with and *immediately upon* the lower bed, and M. Piette observes: "On rémarquera qu'entre la couche qui représente l'âge du renne et celle qui correspond aux temps néolithiques, aucun dépôt formé par le débordement des eaux ou par l'effet d'autres causes naturelles ne se trouve intercallé. Les foyers d'une époque succèdent à ceux de l'époque précédente, sans qu'on puisse saisir entre eux la trace d'une perturbation géologique. Leur cendres n'ont été entraînées par aucun lavage; et si la présence d'une stalagmite epaisse annonce que certaines parties de la grotte ont été pendant longtemps inhabitées, dans les parties oú la stalagmite n'existe pas, on dirait que les pasteurs néolithiques sont venus s'installer le lendemain du jour où les chasseurs du renne l'ont quitté pour n'y plus revenir."[1]

Among the remains obtained here (in the lower bed) M. Piette is astonished to recognise those of the *hen*—a fact, however, which he observes has characterised the fauna of several other caves, and especially the cavern of Lherm.

THE KESSLERLOCH.

The cave of Thäyngen or the Kesslerloch, near Schaffhausen, Switzerland, from which was procured the remarkable drawing of the reindeer at p. 71, was discovered in 1873 by Mr. Conrad Merk, and an account of his explorations (in 1874) was published in the "Proceedings of the Society of Antiquaries of Zürich." A number of other drawings were found in this cavern, among them another sketch of a reindeer and a drawing of a horse, which, though not equal to that in question, are very well executed. There are carvings of the head of a horse and the musk-sheep, and some of the bone harpoons, needles, spear-heads, and other implements are not only exquisitely worked, but are ornamented with varying patterns of lines and dots. There are also ear-rings and neck-ornaments made of perforated teeth, bone, and *brown coal*.

The fauna at the Kesslerloch consisted in part

[1] Matériaux, 2e livraison, 1874.

of horse (*Equus caballus*), reindeer, mammoth, ibex, chamois, urus, aurochs, rhinoceros, lion, hyæna, glutton, common fox, ox (*Bos taurus*), pig, dog (?), and field-hare.

CAVE NEAR NUREMBERG.

We have spoken of the cave of Hohlefels (some eight or ten miles west of Ulm) in Wurtemberg; to the east of this in Bavaria, between Ratisbon and Nuremberg, a similar cave was explored in 1872. The lowermost layer, we are told, afforded no traces of man, but yielded only bones of the cave-bear, cave-hyæna, and cave-lion. Above this layer, and thence up to the top, there occurred implements of flint, the bones of the above-named animals, the bones also of the elephant, rhinoceros, horse, ox, wolf, &c., and *fragments of pottery* (as at Hohlefels).

THE STALAGMITE.

We shall conclude this chapter with a notice of the stalagmitic floors which sometimes occur in the caves, and which have been formed since their first occupation by the men of the Palæolithic Age. The special question of the time at which the mammoth, the rhinoceros, the reindeer, the Irish elk, and the great carnivores became extinct in Europe, we shall consider farther on in the volume, in the chapter entitled "The Mammoth," although in the next chapter immediately following this we shall go so far as to show that some of these animals survived to the Neolithic Age. And the consideration of the changes in physical geography which have been remarked in connection with the localities of the caves, will be deferred until we have treated of the river-gravel. These, and the floors of stalagmite in such caves as Kent's Hole and Brixham, are the special facts relied on to establish the antiquity of the human remains found in the oldest caves.

As to the stalagmitic floors, this is specified by Sir C. Lyell in his "Student's Elements of Geology"[1] as one of the points on which he rests the antiquity of man; in which he is followed by Mr. John Evans,[2] Professor James Geikie,[3] Mr. A. R. Wallace, and others. Mr. Vivian, at the meeting of the British Association in 1871, speaking of Kent's Cavern, argued that the deposit of stalagmite there, if it went on formerly as it does now, involved the lapse of a million of years.

Since attention has been drawn to the subject, it has, however, been ascertained that the deposit of stalagmitic matter frequently proceeds with considerable rapidity. The rate, of course, depends on the conditions.

Travertin is formed precisely as stalagmites are: each a deposit of carbonate of lime held in solution by water. The travertin is deposited by springs or rivers, and various examples of it occur in France and Italy. The stalactites and stalagmites of caves are formed by water charged with carbonic acid percolating through the limestone rock. In its passage it dissolves a portion of the rock, and reaching the chamber of the cave, the excess of carbonic acid is given out, and the calcareous matter deposited.

[1] Ibid., p. 162.
[2] Ancient Stone Implements, p. 464.
[3] Great Ice Age, p. 500.

The rapidity with which travertin is sometimes formed may be observed at San Vignone, in Tuscany, where the deposition of lime from the stream of a thermal spring is so great that half a foot of solid limestone is deposited every year in a conduit pipe inclined at an angle of thirty degrees. Another example occurs at the baths of San Filippo, among the Apennines. Here the water which supplies the baths falls into a pond, where it has been known to deposit a solid mass thirty feet thick in twenty years.

Mantell, in his "Fossils of the British Museum,"[1] mentions that M. Clausen visited a cavern in Brazil, the stalagmitic floor of which was entire. On penetrating the sparry crust, he found the usual ossiferous bed; but pressing engagements compelled him to leave the deposit unexplored. After an interval of some years he had an opportunity to revisit the scene of his labours, when he found that the excavation he had made was completely filled up with stalagmite, the floor being as entire as on his first entrance.

Another example is mentioned in a communication to "Nature," January 1, 1874, by Mr. W. Bruce Clark, who writes to that journal, that he visited ten years ago a cavern near Buxton, known as "Poole's Hole," and observed some stalagmite, probably one-eighth of an inch thick, which had been deposited on the gas-pipes which were used to light the cave, and which had been laid down six months before. This would give a rate of deposit equal to one inch in four years. In the "Archæological Journal" for March 1875 (p. 127),

[1] Page 482.

speaking of this same cavern, it is stated that there occurs here a large piece of stalagmite which has been supposed to be several thousand years old. "The man in charge of the cavern," we are told, "has excavated the floor near the entrance of the cavern, and has found, at the depth of six feet, numerous articles of Roman times; and amongst them Samian ware in fragments, a perfect fibula, and a denarius of Domitian. This discovery strongly tends to reduce the supposed age of the stalagmite."

M. Reclus, in his work entitled "The Earth," makes the statement that in the cave of Melidhoni, the skeletons of three hundred Cretans, smoked to death by the Turks in 1822, are gradually disappearing under the incrustation of stone which has enveloped them with its calcareous layers.

Another very striking example is afforded at one of the Gibraltar caves explored by Captain Brome (designated as Martin's Cave). Excavating through the black earth, he found nine flint knives, and below, other knives and pottery. He then came upon a two-edged iron sword under six feet of earth—partly under stalagmite. The hilt was surmounted by a globe pommel, and the whole of this portion "appeared to be of silver." The succeeding day he found another sword about four yards from the first, also of iron. He then came upon "a copper plate," which lay beneath "eighteen inches of hard stalagmite," close under the south side of the cave, on which was enamelled a dragon. "The plate," continues the narrative, "is said to be of 'Limoges' work, and of the same period as the swords." "The date is probably at the end of the twelfth or the beginning of the thirteenth century."[1]

We have thus objects belonging to the twelfth or thirteenth century covered by a stalagmitic floor eighteen inches thick, and this covered by six feet of earth, and thus indicating that the formation of the stalagmitic matter has long ceased.

Two more examples, yet more decisive, may be added.

In the Ingleborough Cave, in Yorkshire, careful measurements have been made by Mr. James Farrer, Professor Phillips, and Mr. Boyd Dawkins on the rate at which stalagmite is being accumulated, in connection with a large stalagmite, known from its shape as the Jockey Cap. This stalagmite had in 1845 a circumference of 120 inches, and its apex was 95·25 inches from the roof of the cave. In 1873 its apex was 87 inches from the roof, which, says Mr. Dawkins, "would imply an annual deposit of not less than ·2946." The circumference, which in 1845 was 120 inches, in 1873 was 128 inches—the increase being ·2941 inch per annum.

If, says Mr. Dawkins, the Jockey Cap be taken as a measure of the rate of growth of these deposits, "all the stalagmites and stalactites in the cave may not date farther back than the time of Edward III.;" and "it is evident," he continues, "from this instance of rapid accumulation, that the value of a layer of stalagmite in measuring the antiquity of deposits below it is comparatively little. The layers, for instance, in Kent's

[1] Internat. Cong. Pre-hist. Archæol., 1868, pp. 135, 136.

Hole, which are generally believed [we think Mr. A. R. Wallace demanded for them 500,000 years] to have required a considerable lapse of time, may possibly have been formed at the rate of a quarter of an inch per annum, and the human bones which lie buried under the stalagmite in the cave of Bruníquel, are not for that reason to be taken to be of vast antiquity. It may be fairly concluded that the thickness of layers of stalagmite cannot be used as an argument in support of the remote age of the strata below. At the rate of a quarter of an inch per annum, twenty feet of stalagmite might be formed in a thousand years."[1]

Our last illustration is a fact mentioned to us by Professor Alexander Winchell of the Michigan University. He states in a letter which we received from him, that in one of the lead-caves near Dubuque, Iowa, stalactites three feet long have formed in three years.

The probability is that in ancient times the deposit of this calcareous matter in the caves was much more rapid than it is now. The formation of stalagmites in a cave depends on the supply of carbonic acid furnished to the rain-water entering the cave. A cave situated in a dense forest, where there was an abundant accumulation of decayed vegetation on the soil, would have, as Mr. Thomas Karr Callard has remarked, "the natural laboratory where the rain would find the carbonic acid, to act as a solvent upon the calcareous earth; but as, by the axe of man, the forest decreased, in that proportion the chemicals lessened, and as a consequence the deposit diminished."[2]

[1] Cave-Hunting, pp. 39–41. [2] Nature, January 1, 1874.

Nor is this all: our scientific men strangely ignore the fact, that the supply of carbonic acid which enables spring-water to dissolve limestone and deposit stalagmite is often derived in great abundance from deep subterranean sources, and not from decaying vegetation. The quantity of this gas sent up from below in many localities is enormous, and much greater than that supplied by vegetation.

NOTE.—We were not aware, when referring to the discovery of nephrite at Chaleux on p. 79, that articles of nephrite had been found also at Schussenried. This is a station referred by Dr. Peschel to "the glacial period," and is situated near Langenargen, not far from the eastern extremity of the Lake of Constance. The fauna and flora were Arctic in their character, and worked horns of the reindeer, needles of bone, and objects manufactured of nephrite were found "in the glacial clay." [We shall see that the ice lingered in the north of Europe and in the region of the Alps until the close of the Palæolithic Period.] These articles of nephrite were probably brought into Europe at a very early period in connection with the restless movements of the primitive Scythic or Mongol tribes. We express the opinion elsewhere that the Etruscans belong to the Turko-Finnic or Ugric stock, and it is known that the earliest settlements of these people in Europe were to the north of Italy, among the Rhætian Alps. However this be, the presence of the nephrite in Europe implies relations with Asia, and with the primitive lake-people of Switzerland. See Peschel's "Races of Mankind," trans., p. 430.

CHAPTER VII.

SOLUTRÉ.

A palæolithic village—Explorations of MM. De Ferry and Arcelin—Bones of the reindeer, horse, elephant, &c., and flint implements—The horse-deposit—Sepultures—Explorations of the Abbé Ducrost—Beautiful flint implements—Barbed arrow-heads—Fauna of Solutré—Visited by the French Association—Discussion thereon—Vast numbers of horses represented—Domestication of the horse—The funeral hearths—Contemporaneity of the burials, the flints, and the extinct fauna—Freshness of the bones—Box-tombs—Recent explorations.

SOLUTRÉ has been pronounced "a crucial case." It is not a rock-shelter or a cave, but *a palæolithic village.* The fauna is the same as that of the river-gravels, but many of the implements, in all save the absence of rubbing or polishing, are equal to the finer implements of the Neolithic Age. Let us proceed to give the facts.

The *Crot du charnier* is an uncultivated and arid hillock at Solutré, near Macon, in Eastern France, and is formed of a mass of detrital matter at the base of a high cliff. It has never been disturbed by the plough. When we dig into the soil we find, say the first explorers, MM. De Ferry and Arcelin:—

1. In the subsoil, fragments of recent pottery (probably mediæval) at the depth of from ten to fifty centimetres (four to twenty inches), and mingled with these are flints and bones of the reindeer, the horse, and man.

2. *Amas de rebuts de cuisine.* Beneath this bed of scattered débris we encounter deposits much richer in products of human industry, consisting, according to MM. De Ferry and Arcelin, of the *débris de cuisine.* These refuse-heaps are found at variable levels, from forty or fifty centimetres in depth to two and one-third metres—that is, from eighteen or twenty inches to nearly eight feet. The heaps enclose shivered bones, fragments of reindeers' horns, and numerous flint implements. Some of the reindeers' horns are fashioned into hammers, or handles for tools. The flint implements consist of scrapers, arrow and lance heads, knives, punches, &c.,—some of them beautifully worked. The finer flint weapons are in general extremely thin and light, and sometimes of very large dimensions. Besides the remains of the reindeer, there are found in these refuse-heaps the bones of the horse, the mammoth, the cave-lion, the cave-bear, the saiga, cave-hyæna, wolf, lynx, *Cervus Canadensis,* &c.[1]

With the exception of some of the burned bones, all of the animal bones are astonishingly preserved, having retained a considerable proportion of their gelatine, and the horns of the reindeer being very hard, and emitting, when cut, the odour of fresh horn.

Hearths or fireplaces occur in this stratum, forming so many centres around which the bones are scattered. These hearths present quite uniformly coarse slabs of stone, under which occur débris of burned and fractured bones and worked flints. Below these slabs other

[1] This is the actual fauna, as now ascertained: some of the animals mentioned have been identified in the more recent explorations.

slabs sometimes occur at a certain interval, and this superposition is sometimes repeated several times.

3. *Amas de débris de chevaux.* Outside of, and surrounding, the deposits above described, is a bed which consists almost entirely of the bones of the *horse.* These remains begin where the first end, and, as it were, encircle them. At several points they sink below the kitchen remains, and *run under them.* At one point where this is the case there was accordingly found over the "horse-deposit" a large and beautiful hearth, with the remains of the reindeer and the elephant, numerous flint implements, &c., all resting on a bed, two feet thick, of horse-bones, which enclosed within it, a short distance off, another hearth.

Grouped over the space occupied by the kitchen-débris on the one hand, and the horse-remains on the other, are *human sepultures.* These are of two kinds—those with slabs of stone, and those without slabs. Both are found over the spaces occupied by the kitchen-débris and the horse-deposit. But the funeral slab is always found in either case on a hearth or fireplace; and the skeleton is often found stretched upon it. These graves contain worked flints and bones of the extinct animals.

The burials on the fireplaces are so numerous that they sometimes touch each other. Most of the hearths support one or more skeletons, and the relation of the skeleton to the hearth is proved by the fact that the depth of the skeleton from the surface corresponds invariably with the depth of the hearth. If the hearth is found at 0·60 m., the skeleton is at 0·60 m.; if the hearth is at 1·50 m. or 1·80 m., the skeleton is at 1·50 m. or 1·80 m. These skeletons lie extended on the back, and are for the most part complete and intact—the bones all in place and in perfect order, and having, apparently, been subjected to a moderate heat (the fire-places).[1] There are large hearths and small hearths. Adults lie on the former; children—often young infants—on the latter.[2]

Some of the tombs at Solutré consisted of rude cists or boxes formed of slabs of stone, which may be detached from the rock in the vicinity with little difficulty. One of these, examined by M. de Ferry, was found intact. It had the shape of a rectangular box well jointed and closed, but the stones not squared, and it rested on the *magma* or *breccia* of the horse. The skeleton within belonged to a female, and at its side lay bones of the horse and the reindeer, and three flint knives.

We have followed, up to this point, substantially the account given by MM. De Ferry and Arcelin of their explorations of this station.[3]

Since this original exploration, the locality has been examined with great care by M. l'Abbé Ducrost, and

[1] It is probable, almost certain, that over each principal hearth there stood originally a cabin, and that the dweller in this hut was buried, as the Greenlanders now practise, beneath his hearth. The same custom prevails among the Indians of the Amazon, the New Zealanders, the islanders of Torres Straits, and in the great Central African kingdom of Bornou; and formerly prevailed among the Tatar tribes.

[2] There is a great proportion of *aged persons*, showing that the occupants of Solutré did not destroy their aged relatives, as was the fashion in Britain and Ireland in post-Christian times.

[3] "L'Age du Renne en Mâconnais: Mémoire sur le Gisement Archéologique du Clos du Charnier à Solutré," printed in the volume of the International Congress of Archæology for 1868.

re-explored by M. Arcelin, of whose investigations we shall avail ourselves as far as may be necessary in the further presentation of the facts of the case.

The flint weapons found at Solutré have excited the admiration of the archæologists by their beauty of form and their elegant finish. Speaking of the skill with which they were fabricated, we are told that "il faut se rapporter à l'époque des beaux instruments des pays scandinaves pour retrouver le même savoir-faire."[1] We append two examples of these implements, taken from some representations in the volume of "Matériaux" for 1869.

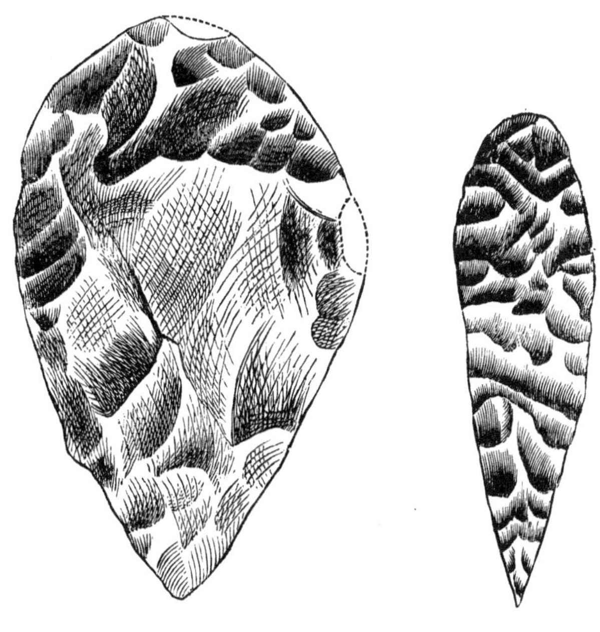

[1] De Mortillet, Matériaux, 1869.

The stemmed and barbed arrow-heads had (as remarked in the previous chapter) been regarded as characteristic of the Polished Stone Age, and M. de Mortillet, at the French Association of 1873, at Lyons, found it difficult to believe that certain stemmed and barbed arrow-heads from Solutré, exhibited by M. l'Abbé Ducrost, were contemporary with the quaternary deposits; but M. l'Abbé Ducrost stated in reply, that he had found at Solutré on the hearths of the age of the reindeer:—1. A type derived from the type of St. Acheul; 2. A type characteristic of Solutré; 3. A transition from this type proceeding towards the type of polished stone; 4. A perfection of edge entirely identical with that of the Polished Stone Age; 5. Instruments common to these two epochs. He cited particularly two whetstones, and two arrow-heads with a distinct stem between the barbs. He had found these objects himself on the hearths.

The significance of this, as we pointed out in the previous chapter, becomes apparent when we remember that the primitive appearance and rudeness of the worked flints of the river-gravels, found with precisely the same fauna as those of Solutré, has been one of the points relied on to separate by a wide interval the Palæolithic from the Neolithic Age.

Solutré has been the subject of many discussions, and came up for formal consideration before the French Association at Lyons in 1873—the members of the Association to the number of two hundred having first made an excursion to Macon, for the purpose of making a personal examination of this capital of the Troglo-

dytes. Several considerable trenches had been opened through the hillock for the inspection of the visitors. We are told in the Report of this excursion given in "Matériaux" (7e, 8e, et 9e livraisons, 1873), that in one of these trenches the excursionists "were so happy as to find a human skeleton reposing on slabs, which themselves rested on a rich fireplace, and in such conditions that *all* the members present admitted the contemporaneity of this sepulture with the animal bones and the quaternary flints."

Having completed their examination, the Association returned to Lyons, and a discussion ensued, embracing all the points involved: 1. The *gisement;* 2. The horses; 3. The flints; 4. The human race.

It was conceded generally that the burials on the fireplaces were contemporary with the worked flints and the remains of the mammoth, reindeer, &c.

M. Cartailhac observed, at the close of the discussion, on the first point: "Cette discussion est de la plus haute gravité et restera célèbre dans l'histoire de la science anthropologique. . . . . Qu'il y ait eu des glissements et des remaniements, peu importe. Mais ce qui est certain, c'est que plus de dix fois un squelette humain s'est trouvé sur un foyer quaternaire et pas un fait ne vient s'opposer à ce qu'on admette la contemporanéité." "M. Broca partage cette opinion et déclare ouverte la discussion sur le deuxième problème; *les chevaux.*"

Under this head it was stated that the number of horses represented in the *amas de chevaux* would amount probably to *forty thousand*—and that it may, indeed, turn out to be double, or even treble this.

The flints are ascertained, contrary to the impressions first received by MM. De Ferry and Arcelin, to occur in large numbers in the horse-deposit, while all of the animals (other than the horse) are represented, though in small numbers, in the same deposit.

A valuable paper was read by M. Toussaint on the question, Was the horse of Solutré *domesticated?* which question he answers affirmatively. MM. Lartet, Christy, and Dupont, he remarks, ascertained that in many of the palæolithic stations we meet with *only certain parts* of the skeletons of the animals whose remains occur, such as the head, with the first cervical vertebræ, the bones of the fore-leg and shoulder, the hind-leg and ham, &c.; the vertebræ and the sides are generally wanting. These authors conclude that the animals were hunted, killed in the forest, and only the parts most readily handled carried back to the station, *which proves that these same animals were never domesticated.*

But at Solutré we find all the parts of the horse in their normal number. The conclusion follows that at this place this animal was slaughtered always *at the station,* and therefore must have been domesticated.

On the other hand, only certain parts (those indicated above) of the reindeer are found at Solutré—a proof that in this case the animal was killed at a distance from the station, and (the meat being stripped from the sides) these parts only brought home for consumption.

The close resemblance of the skeleton of the horse of Solutré to that of the horse of the present day is alone, according to M. Steenstrup, says M. Toussaint, proof that the remains found here belong to the domesticated horse.

[M. Dupont, at the Stockholm meeting of the Anthropological Congress (1874), made an observation which would seem to indicate that he believes the horse of the Palæolithic Age to have been domesticated. In the course of a paper on the domestic animals of pre-historic times he dwelt on the horse, and remarked that it existed in enormous numbers in the quaternary period, "and probably played the same part in domestic life as the ox plays now." [1]]

Dr. Gosse (of Switzerland) remarked that the observations of M. Toussaint had convinced him.

M. de Mortillet, while conceding the contemporaneity of the horses and the hearths, suggested, however, that the horse had been captured with the *lasso.* Captured in this way, the horse, he remarked, falls and *submits.* [2] In reply to this, Dr. Broca asked if there was any trace of the lasso at Solutré?

There is no trace of the kind either at Solutré or at any other Stone Age station; and, moreover, it is difficult to understand, except in rare instances, how the wild horse can be captured with the lasso, unless the pursuer is on horseback.

Another consideration is, that if the lasso was employed in this way in palæolithic times, we ought to

1 Academy, August 29, 1874, p. 239.

2 The American Indians in the West, who live on horseback, and who capture wild horses with the lasso, understand (like Mr. Rarey) how to tame them instantly; but it is not likely that a race of savages who did not ride on horseback would have mastered this secret.

find in the palæolithic caves all the parts of the horse, as at Solutré; but this, as we are informed by M. Lartet, is not the case; we find neither the vertebræ nor the pelvis of either the horse or the bison; and (says Mr. Boyd Dawkins[1]) "from the absence of the vertebræ and pelvic bones of these two animals, M. Lartet concludes that they were cut up where they were killed, and the meat stripped from the backbone and pelvis."[2]

To complete our statement, we add, that "at the surface of the soil (at this station), or at a very slight depth, we find in the surrounding vineyards barbed arrow-heads of stone, fragments of rude pottery, and some polished hatchets. "Here and there we find some Roman and Merovingian remains."[3]

These more recent traces of man at Solutré have caused M. Chabas to question the remote antiquity of the burials which occur at this point. To this M. Arcelin answers: "As for the objection extracted from

[1] Cave-Hunting, p. 340.

[2] When M. Rütimeyer argued that the reindeer, the ox, and the horse were domesticated at Veyrier, M. de Mortillet replied in "Matériaux" (of which he was then editor): "Another consideration which shows that the animal remains which are found heaped up in the stations of the epoch of the reindeer are indeed the remains of wild animals, is that we find in these stations only the head and the limbs among the parts eaten. The sides and vertebræ are wanting. One readily perceives that they are the remains of animals killed far from the habitation, which were slaughtered on the spot, and the choice pieces alone carried away. If these had been domestic animals, they would have been killed, at least in part, near the station, and we should find the remains of the entire skeleton. But this does not happen for the ox, the horse, and the reindeer, any more than for the stag, the ibex, and the chamois."—Bullétin de l'Institut Genevois, Description d'objets trouvés à Veyrier. Par F. Thioly. Lu à la Séance le 7 Mai 1868.

But this is precisely what does happen with the horse at Solutré.

[3] Address of M. l'Abbé Ducrost before the Association at Lyons, Matériaux, Livraisons, 7e, 8e, et 9e, 1873.

the possibility of inhumations posterior to the fireplaces, in the midst of beds of flints and bones, it is long since that we have given the facts in reply to it. There are, at Solutré, burials of every period; each one of these presents certain peculiar characters, and the burials of the age of the reindeer alone are found in the midst of the fireplaces. The trenches opened the 23d of August (1873) by M. l'Abbé Ducrost and myself place this fact in a clear light, and the discussion of the section of anthropology has entirely confirmed our views. I think it useless to insist farther on this point."[1]

The Merovingian and Gallo-Roman traces, as well as the few remains of the Polished Stone Age, at Solutré, all occur near the surface, as do the *box-tombs*, which we have mentioned, formed of rude slabs of stone. These box-tombs occur at a depth of from twelve to sixteen inches.

The Abbé Ducrost, in his investigations, determined, he tells us, to dig deep enough to get entirely clear of these more recent relics; and he informs us that he has been able to discover "at a great depth, and sheltered from all pre-existing profanation," four considerable hearths perfectly intact.

It is proper to remark that, whatever the doubts entertained by some of the French archæologists with regard to the "box-tombs," *there is an entire concurrence* among them in assigning the *fireplaces* and the burials *en foyer* (as Dr. Broca expresses it) to the quaternary period.

M. l'Abbé Ducrost gives a detailed account of one of

[1] Études d'Archéologie Pré-historique, Les Silex de Volgu, p. 80. Par Adrien Arcelin, Paris, 1875.

the hearths which he encountered, and which occurred at the depth of 1 metre ·40 (4 ft. 7 in.). At this point, having first passed through a friable earth, containing *pêle-mêle* bones of o..en, reindeer, and horses, he struck an enormous slab, which rested on a fireplace some twelve inches thick, composed of blackish ashes, and containing implements in flint and bone, and burned bones, the greater number of which belonged to the reindeer.

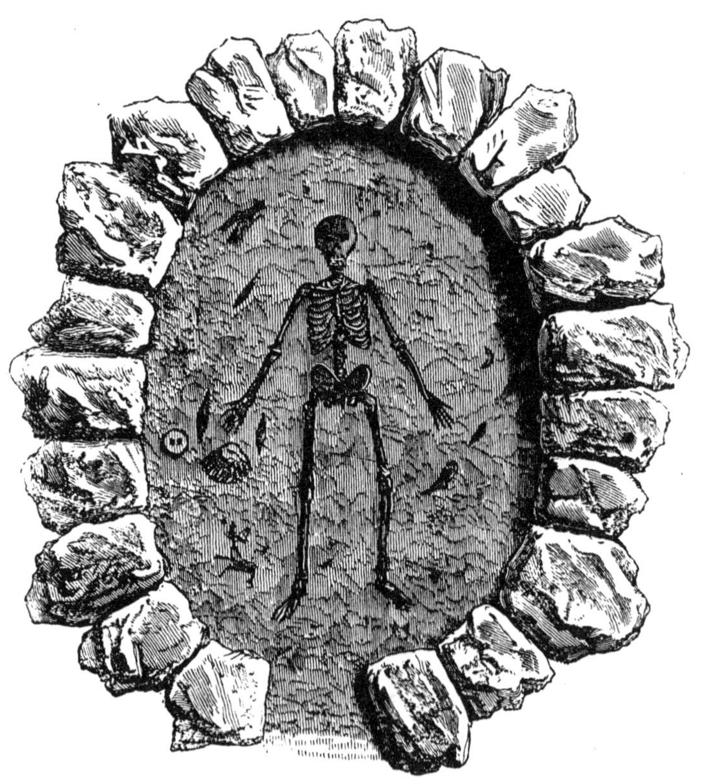

Sepulture at Solutré.

The slab was surrounded by a compact circle of stones, forming a sort of border for it, and on it at full length reposed a skeleton. Under the right hand of this were placed two lance-heads of flint "taillées à grand éclat," perfectly preserved and of large size; a great number of smaller arrow-heads; a valve of *Pecten jacobæus*, pierced with a hole; and a small figure of a reindeer carved in *molasse*.

The funeral couch or the fireplace itself was a confused *mélange* of ashes, burned bones, bones of the reindeer broken for the marrow, and débris of flints in every form.

Outside of the circular wall enclosing the hearth were numerous horns of the reindeer, and bones of the mammoth, cave-bear, wolf, fox, hyæna, marmot, &c.

The arrow-heads and lance-heads were of all forms and sizes, sometimes of the type of the river-gravel, sometimes presenting the rudiments of the barbed type of the Neolithic Age; but in general the form was that lozenge type which we call *Solutréen*.

The other hearths examined by M. l'Abbé Ducrost presented the same features.[1]

With regard to the box-tombs found near the surface, the Abbé Ducrost believes them to be Gallo-

[1] The fauna encountered on or about all the hearths discovered in this exploration embraced the elephant, reindeer, horse, urus, cave-bear, cave-hyæna, lynx, wolf, &c. The implements included "the rude hatchet of the Valley of the Somme," as well as the forms found in the caves, and the leaf-shaped spear-heads peculiar to Laugerie-Haute, Solutré, and one or two other stations. *Etudes sur la Station Pré-historique de Solutré, Par M. l'Abbé Ducrost et M. le docteur L. Lartet, Archives Museum d'Histoire Naturelle de Lyon*, tome i. p. 7, 1872.

Roman, or of some comparatively recent date. But it must not be forgotten that M. de Ferry found one of these "intact," as he expresses it, and containing three flint knives and bones of the horse and the reindeer by the side of the skeleton.

Again: even in the surface deposits at Solutré, the fauna seems to be the same as that below; there is no "modern" fauna, while great numbers of flint implements of the palæolithic type occur. This inclines us to the opinion that nearly *all* of the remains at Solutré are of quaternary date, those extending to a depth of sixteen inches below the surface, as well as those at from one to three metres of depth.

In his *résumé* of the results of his explorations, the Abbé Ducrost remarks:—

"If one desires an approximative date [for the palæolithic remains at Solutré], I think that we may accept the method employed to measure the advance of the delta of the Rhone, and applied to Solutré by MM. Ferry and Arcelin. Taking for a point of departure the blue clays of the Saône, which are nearly contemporary with the station of Solutré, for they still contain bones of the *Elephas primigenius*, which are met with more abundantly in the beds immediately above, and for a unit of time the mean distance which separates us from the Roman epoch, of which one perceives frequently the incontestable traces in the banks of the river; taking into account also certain disturbances which may have introduced into the upper beds the human relics, or some exceptional inundations, we reach, for the deposition of the lehm comprised between the Roman débris and the clays, which one may observe whenever the river is low, an approximative epoch of 7000 to 8000 years." (See Addenda.)

The remains of the horse abound in all of the palæolithic stations; on the contrary, they are almost unknown among the animal bones of the Neolithic Age; the horse-deposit at Solutré cannot, therefore, be of neolithic date; nor do we find any such accumulations of horse remains in the Gallo-Roman or Merovingian period. This deposit is, therefore, of the Palæolithic Age—evidenced, farther, as we have remarked, by the fact that the bed at some points *runs under* the *amas de rebuts de cuisine*, and is found at a depth of *thirteen feet;* and by the presence in it (both among the loose, uncemented bones, and in the solidified magma) of the palæolithic flints and the bones of the mammoth and other extinct animals.

The large proportion of skeletons belonging to *aged persons* at this station implies a degree of filial regard which is not common among savages, while there is something equally touching in the graves of the little children.

These burials, the finely-cut weapons, the fresh condition of the animal bones (emitting the odour of fresh bones), are difficult to be reconciled with the antiquity claimed for the contemporaries of the mammoth, among whom the artisans of Solutré seem to have been a numerous and thoroughly organised tribe.

And if, moreover, the horse at Solutré was domesticated, the discussion about the antiquity of man is at an end. When Abraham was in Egypt, we hear only of *asses;* the horse does not appear to have been known in that country at that time.

If the remains of this animal had been found under the same circumstances in connection with a recognised later date (as, for example, during the Bronze Age), no doubt would be entertained that the fact noticed by M. Toussaint (the presence of all the parts) was conclusive that it had been domesticated. It is so difficult to realise this in the Palæolithic Age, that we hesitate to yield to the evidence; for our own part, after much reflection, we do not see how this can be avoided.

With regard to the skulls from Solutré, we will merely quote the language of Dr. Pruner Bey: "Cet homme quaternaire" (he is pronouncing his verdict on Solutré) "est constitué homme dans toute la force du terme. Rien dans son physique n'indique un rapprochement avec les Simiens . . . rien de la brute dans ses us et coutumes, dans ses croyances," and much more to the same effect.

The life of the Palæolithic Age is presented at Solutré under conditions that do not exist anywhere else. It was not the abode of a family or a small company like Moustier or the Kesslerloch, but *a tribal village*, and the phenomena are upon a scale that leaves no room for misconception.

Note.—Since the above was written, MM. Ducrost and Arcelin have carried their examination of Solutré yet farther (during 1875 and 1876). They have dug deeper than in all the previous explorations, and represent that there is a uniform stratification at this station of the relic-beds, as follows:—1. At the bottom, a bed containing bones of the mammoth, reindeer, *Cervus Canadensis*, horse, cave-bear, cave-hyæna, cave-lion, &c., and flint implements of the types of St. Acheul and Moustier, together with tools and ornaments of bone. 2. The bed represented by the magma of the horse, which contains occasionally also the reindeer and the elephant, and flint flakes which may have served as knives. 3. A zone of considerable thickness, which is nearly barren of relics, but contains some thinly-scattered débris of bones and flints of the type of the lowest bed; at certain points there is a second bed of *magma de cheval*. 4. Another bed, which they call the Reindeer bed. This contains bones of the mammoth, reindeer, *Cervus Canadensis*, horse, &c., but not the cave-bear, cave-lion, nor hyæna. There appear here the beautiful weapons of the type *Solutréen*, numerous tools in bone, and some attempts at sculpture. 5. The surface bed, in which we find polished hatchets, objects in iron and bronze, and graves, Neolithic, Gallo-Roman, and Burgundian.

We would remark on this:—1. It is thus clearly established that the horse-deposit is of Palæolithic date. 2. The bed No. 4 contains not only the reindeer but the mammoth: the absence of the great carnivores merely shows that the climate had become colder, as we know was the case towards the close of the Palæolithic Age. 3. It may be noticed that *bone* as well as flint implements are found in bed No. 1. 4. From the character of the implements, and the presence of the hyæna and bear, we may infer that the sepulture delineated on p. 106, and previously brought to light by the Abbé Ducrost, belongs to the date represented by bed No. 1. We have thus the burials from the oldest period. (See Matériaux, 1876, p. 496.)

The most extraordinary fact at Solutré is the immense accumulation of the horse remains in a distinct layer; it is astonishing; and we can conjecture no explanation of it, except that it was connected with funeral rites. It is not a refuse-pile: the flints are of one form, and, according to one authority, have not been used; the bones are burned—whether universally or not is left in some doubt.

But what can be the explanation of the vast number of individuals represented? At the meeting of the French Association at Lyons in 1873, Dr. Gosse, of Switzerland (who remarked that

M. Toussaint had convinced him of the domestication of the horse at Solutré), added that among the Kirghis Cossacks of the present day it is the custom, on the death of any member of the tribe, to burn hetacombs of animals, proportioned to the rank of the deceased. M. de Meyendorff, he said, who was fourteen years Governor in the Caucasus, states that he several times assisted at funeral repasts where from two hundred to three hundred horses and from three thousand to four thousand sheep were slaughtered (Matériaux, livraisons 7e, 8e, et 9e, 1873).

It may be merely added that, from an examination of some of the human skulls from this station, Dr. Pruner Bey referred them to a Mongoloid race.

Was this the metropolis of a Tartar tribe—those tribes which have often mustered (as in the battles of Tscenghis Khan) two or three hundred thousand cavalry?

CHAPTER VIII.

FARTHER REMARKS ON THE CAVES.

Survival of the reindeer, cave-bear, &c., to neolithic times.

THE older Swiss lake-dwellings and the lower beds of the French and Danish peat belong, as has been mentioned, to the Age of Polished Stone. Their date is probably some 1000 or 1200 B.C. The fauna of the lake-dwellings and the peat is different from that of the palæolithic caves. It is called, in contradistinction to the other, a modern fauna. We no longer (it is alleged) meet with the mammoth, the cave-hyæna, the cave-bear, &c. We encounter, on the other hand, along with wild animals now existing, the remains of the domestic animals.

Anthropologists tell us that a fauna had died out, and a new one been introduced; and that this implies a vast lapse of time.

The station of Solutré brought us in full view of the Palæolithic Age, with its huge pachyderms and its powerful carnivores; the picture it revealed left upon the mind an impression—if not a conviction—that those palæolithic hunters were but little removed from the life of our day. We propose now to advance a step farther; we propose to show that the distinguishing animals of the Palæolithic Age (or some of them) *lived down to the Neolithic Age*[1] (which seems to have been almost reached by the dwellers at Solutré).

If the reindeer and the cave-bear have left their remains in the caverns of the Neolithic Age, and if, moreover, they were the contemporaries in Europe of the mammoth and rhinoceros, *then* a presumption arises, of course, that the mammoth and rhinoceros, though they may have become extinct prior to the Neolithic Age, are not far removed from it. If this be so, the fauna of the older caves and the river-gravel does not necessarily, or even presumptively, possess a great antiquity.

We mention first, then, the cave of Veyrier, near Geneva, at the foot of Mount Salève, in Switzerland. This cave yielded an immense number of flint implements, knives, saws, &c., evidently manufactured on the spot; and the black soil in which they are found is literally paved, we are told, with the bones of horses, bulls, pigs, reindeer, stags, chamois, marmots, Alpine bears, wolves, and storks; half of which are reindeer bones.

Professor Rütimeyer identified the horse as the *Equus caballus*, " le cheval d'aujourd'hui et aucune des modifications connues à l'état fossile." The remains of the ox he referred to the *Bos taurus*, or the present domesticated species.

We have spoken of the cave near Thäyngen, where the tame ox, the domestic pig, the present domesticated

[1] In a future chapter we shall proceed yet further, and show that most of them lived down to historic times.

horse, and the dog,[1] (?) occurred in association with the mammoth, rhinoceros, and reindeer.

Veyrier and the Kesslerloch belong to the Palæolithic Age, and we mention them on account of the presence of the domestic animals. Whether these animals were actually *domesticated* is a question which has been raised; but if our present domestic animals were already in Europe (though not actually tamed) in the Palæolithic Age, it is not probable, as M. Dupont has observed, that there was any *hiatus* between the Palæolithic and Neolithic Ages. (See Addenda.)

The remains of the reindeer were found by M. Perrault in a rock-shelter at the Camp of Chassey (Saône-et-Loire), along with polished stone implements. It is alleged, however, that there has been a "remaniement," and we do not, therefore, rely upon the case. But no such suggestion has been made with regard to the cave of Lombrive (Ariège), where M. Garrigou found mingled together the bones of the reindeer, urus, bear, dog, and small domestic ox, nor to the case mentioned by M. Reboux, near Paris, where he found the remains of the reindeer with polished flint implements superimposed on the bones of the elephant.[2]

Another illustration occurs at the Cave of Espalungues, Hautes-Pyrénées, examined by MM. Garrigou and Martin. In the upper layer of this cave the fauna was fox, horse, wild boar, stag, chamois, wild goat, reindeer, ox, sheep, &c. The lower bed contained the same

[1] The remains of the domestic dog occur also in the Swabian caves, and were found at the cavern of Nero in Southern France. The domestic fowl was found at Gourdan, Lherm, and elsewhere.

[2] Congrès d'Anthrop. et Archéol. Pré-hist., 1867, p. 106.

fauna, but is regarded by MM. Garrigou and Martin, from "the coarseness of its wrought objects, its worked flints, and its sculpture; from the reddish-brown colour of the bones, and from the absence of gelatine and their adhering to the tongue, to pertain to an age more ancient than the preceding."

On the upper bed they remark: "We conclude from the presence of the aurochs, the existence of domestic animals, the discovery of bones gnawed by dogs, the almost complete preservation of the gelatine in the bones, and their deeper colour, and by the discovery of a bone finely sculptured, that the upper beds belong to a period more recent than the lower beds."[1]

These beds are both of the same age, and in both we find the remains of the domestic animals; and the period belongs, in fact, not to the Neolithic, but to the transition age, as is proved by the sculptured bones, the remains of the horse, reindeer, aurochs, and chamois, and the absence of pottery. On the other hand, the presence of the dog, sheep, goat, and ox imply that "the Reindeer Epoch" in Southern France comes down to the Polished Stone Age.

It will be seen elsewhere that the remains of the reindeer occur in the Danish peat, and also in the English and Scotch peat, which beds are admitted on all hands to be of the Neolithic Age.

If, then, the reindeer (so prominent a feature of the Palæolithic fauna) was living in these regions in the Polished Stone Age, that is to say, a few thousand years

[1] Quoted in American Journal of Science, 1864, p. 277.

ago, it is not difficult to imagine that the mammoth was living in the same regions a few centuries earlier.

Another of the characteristic fauna of the river-gravels and the caves is the great Irish elk; and the remains of this animal also have been found in the Irish peat, and in the peat of the valley of the Somme near St Valéry.[1]

We now propose to show that the remains of the cave-bear also (considered to be the oldest of the palæolithic animals) have been found in neolithic beds.

Sir John Lubbock (Pre-historic Times, p. 283) informs us, that the bones of this animal have been found in Italy, "apparently in conjunction with a polished stone implement and even pottery;" but he is incredulous as to its being contemporaneous with the pottery and the stone-axe found near it. In Northern Europe, he proceeds to say, no such case has been met with.

But the evidence seems to be that the remains of the cave-bear have been found with relics of the Neolithic Age in Northern Europe, Middle Europe, and Southern Europe.

M. Regnoli explored some seventy caverns in the mountains of Northern Italy.

In the Grotta all' Onda, at the foot of Mount Matanna, he found instruments in bone, barbed arrow-heads of stone, polished stone implements, two axes,—one of diorite, and one of jade,—a polisher of serpentine, and bones and teeth of the cave-bear, bearing traces of human work, and unworked bones of the cave-bear

[1] See chap. on "The Mammoth;" and Palafittes of the Lake of Neufchâtel, by M. Desor, in Smiths. Report for 1865, p. 400.

belonging to at least four individuals. The other animal remains were stag, hare, wild boar, badger, ox, sheep or goat, &c.

In the Grotta del Tamaccio, on Mount Cigoli, he found human bones, bones of the ox, stag, sheep, hog, &c., and the teeth of a bear which appeared to be *Ursus spelœus.*

The Grotto of the Goths, in the mountain called Colle Maggiore, yielded arrow-heads of stone, pottery, charcoal; bones of the cave-bear, and of another species of bear; the worked tooth of a bear; a bodkin made of the cubitus of a bear; and bones of the stag, marmot, and ox. The objects manufactured into implements belong, we are told, to "the Neolithic Age."[1]

A similar association is mentioned by M. Lioz at the caverns of Velo, province of Verona, where he found a complete skull of the cave-bear; and among the numerous bones belonging to the same animal he dug up a very fine [polished] axe of porphyry, and another of serpentine.[2]

Again, at the Grotto of Minerva (Aude), in France, we are told that the cave "contained only bones of the great bear, mingled with those of the horse, goat, sheep, &c."[3]

Mr. Boyd Dawkins informs us that "the presence of the sheep or goat, short-horned ox, and dog, was unknown in Europe before the Neolithic Age."[4]

[1] Matériaux pour l'Hist. de l'Homme, 1re série, tome iii. p. 496; ibid., 3e livraison, 1873, p. 142; ibid., p. 144.

[2] Matériaux, 1re série, tome i. p. 303.

[3] Ibid., 1re série, tome ii. p. 117.

[4] Macmillan's Magazine, December 1870.

Objects of the Neolithic Age have also been found in Austria associated with the remains of extinct animals. In the caverns of Byciskâla and of Shap, in Moravia, Dr. Wankel has discovered a great number of polished stone hatchets, worked bones, and pottery, in the same beds with the bones of the cave-bear and cave-lion. And, so far as the existence of pottery in the Palæolithic Age is concerned, we are told that Count de Wurmbrandt found in the caverns of Peggau the same primeval carnivores, and in the same earth numerous fragments of vases.[1]

Another instance of the point under discussion is reported in the volume of the International Congress of Pre-historic Archæology for 1868, in a paper entitled, "Researches into the Caverns of Moncluses," in Valencia, by Don Juan Vilanova y Piera. These caverns are stated to belong to "the Palæolithic Age." In one of them, the cave of Las Maravillas, the author found, at the depth of several metres, instruments belonging to "the First Age," and among them some very fine arrowheads, "perfectly identical with those of the Swiss palafittes," mingled with the bones of the extinct mammifers. In the upper tiers of this deposit were more recent bones, mingled with fragments of Roman pottery.

With regard to Sir John Lubbock's statement, that "in Northern Europe no such case has been met with," we have the express declarations of Professor Nilsson to the contrary. "Along the coast of the Baltic," he says, "from Ystad to Trälleborg and Falsterbo, there

[1] Matériaux, Janvier 1872, p. 40.

lies a ridge—consisting of gravel and stones—called the Jära-Wall." He then proceeds to state that under this ridge there are in several places peat-bogs, which lie beneath the surface of the sea, which peat was formed in fresh water. The stone implements, he says, are found in this peat, and with them have also been found bones of the cave-bear. He farther states that in other peat-bogs (as that of Kullaberg) the bones of both the cave-bear and the reindeer have been found, and that flint flakes occur in this peat in great numbers.[1]

Mr. C. Carter Blake mentions an instance of the occurrence of the bones of the cave-lion in the peat of England, at Holderness, near Hull. The bones are in the museum of the Hull Royal Institution.[2]

As we shall see elsewhere, the remains of the mammoth have also been found in the peat-bogs; in America this is frequently the case, while the remains of the American mastodon are nearly always found in the peat formations, or in some formation contemporary therewith—often, indeed, on the surface of the ground.

These facts at once break the back of the argument for the antiquity of the Palæolithic Age, based on the presence of the remains of the extinct animals.

In a subsequent chapter we shall have much more to say on this point, and shall show that the aurochs, the urus, the reindeer, the megaceros, the cave-lion, lived in Europe down to the Historic Period, and that the mammoth, the rhinoceros, and the hippopotamus, disappeared from the same theatre no great while before.

[1] Nilsson on the Stone Age, trans., pp. 252–254.
[2] Nature, May 11, 1871.

CHAPTER IX.

THE RIVER-GRAVEL.

IF we observe the valleys of the Thames, the Seine, the Somme, the Tiber, and other rivers in various parts of the world, we find at variable levels—sometimes more than 100 feet above the present water-courses—*gravel-deposits,* indicating that the streams formerly ran at these higher levels. The gravel-deposits of the Somme river, first explored by M. Boucher de Perthes, are the most famous, and may be selected as a typical example. Between Amiens and Abbeville these gravels, sometimes on one side of the river, sometimes on the other, occur at heights varying from ten to one hundred feet above the present river-level. This deposit rests immediately on the chalk, and near the bed of the river, has superimposed upon it a deposit of peat or silt. This peat or silt is sometimes thirty feet thick—contains implements of iron, bronze, and polished stone—and was formed, of course, after the gravel was laid down. The gravel contains palæolithic implements (at the higher as well as the lower levels) and bones of the mammoth, rhinoceros, reindeer, and other extinct animals. It is admitted that these gravel beds are post-glacial, but Sir Charles Lyell, Sir John Lubbock, Mr. Evans, and the archæologists generally, assign to them a vast antiquity, and maintain that they afford conclusive evidence that man inhabited this region tens of thousands of years ago. The peat alone, according to M. Boucher de Perthes, implies the lapse of some thirty thousand years since it first began to

Flint Hatchet from the River-gravel.

cover the gravel, and Sir Charles Lyell and Sir John Lubbock, without explicitly accepting, substantially acquiesce in this conclusion.

The gravels (in some places twenty or thirty feet

thick) were, as remarked, laid down before this Neolithic Period set in. It is represented that they occur at two distinct levels, and they are described as the high-level gravels and the low-level gravels; the former

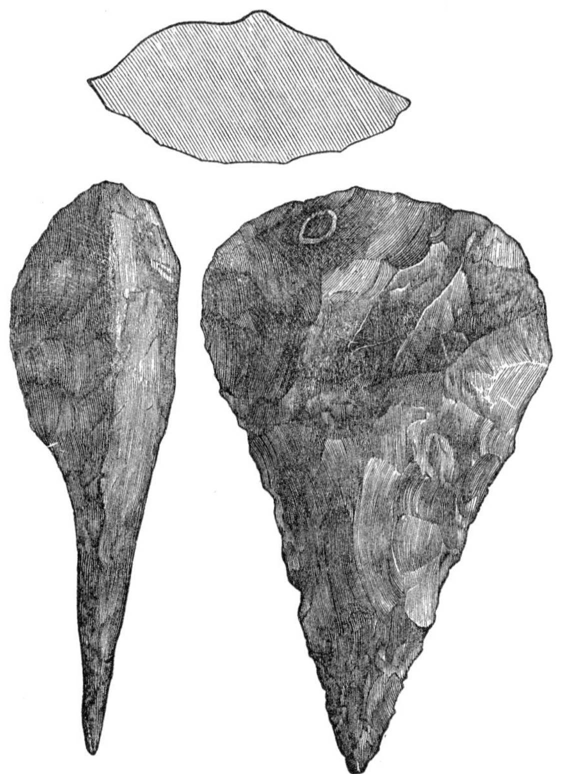

Spear-head from the River-gravel.

being laid down first, and the river, through the lapse of tens or hundreds of thousands of years, gradually *excavating* the valley, and then depositing the low-level gravels. The antiquity of the human relics found is to be measured, therefore, not only by the time which must have elapsed since the mammoth roamed in this region, but by the additional time required for the Somme river (some fifty feet wide) to excavate a valley one or two hundred feet deep and a mile or a mile and a half wide.

And these are not all of the evidences of the great lapse of time which has taken place. There have been marked changes in the physical geography of Europe; the relative positions of the sea and land on the coasts have been changed, and it is observed that in the interior, alterations have occurred in the superficial and subterranean lines of drainage. Since the reindeer and the musk-sheep and the great snowy owl were to be met with in France, the climate too, we are told, has moderated some twenty degrees.

These river-gravels, as we have stated, are [generally] admitted to be post-glacial, it having been observed that in several localities they rest upon the boulder-drift. They were deposited at the close of the Glacial Period, and their age is to be measured by the date of this period. This Sir Charles Lyell, in the last edition of his "Principles," fixed at about 800,000 years ago, but in the fourth edition of his "Antiquity of Man," he modifies this estimate considerably, and accepts the figures of Sir John Lubbock, which fix the Glacial Epoch at about 200,000 years ago.

It may assist the reader to lay before him the following diagram from Sir C. Lyell's "Student's Elements of Geology." It represents an ideal section of a valley containing these implement-bearing gravels, and applies to other valleys than that of the Somme.

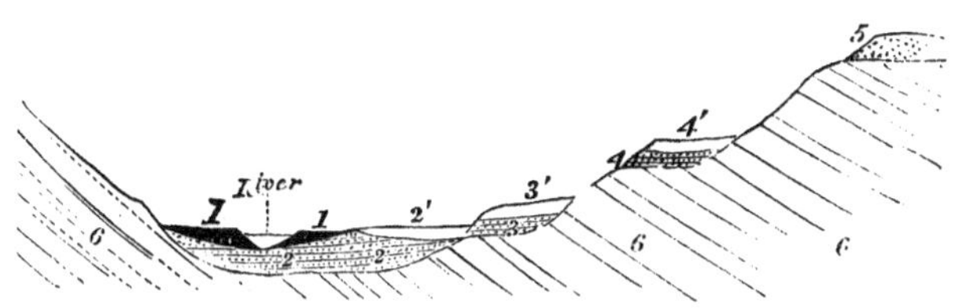

"The peat No. 1," he says, "has been formed in a low part of the modern alluvial plain, in parts of which gravel No. 2 of the recent period is seen. Over this gravel the loam or fine sediment 2′, has in many places been deposited by the river during floods which covered nearly the whole alluvial plain.

"No. 3 represents an older alluvium, composed of sand and gravel, formed before the valley had been excavated to its present depth. It contains the remains of fluviatile shells of living species associated with the bones of mammalia, in part recent, and in part of extinct species. Among the latter, the mammoth (*E. primigenius*), and the Siberian rhinoceros (*R. tichorinus*), are the most common in Europe. No. 3′ is a remnant of the loam or brick-earth,[1] by which No. 3 was overspread. No. 4 is a still older and more elevated terrace, similar in its composition and organic remains to No. 3, and covered in like manner with its inundation-mud, 4′."

[1] This loam or loess covers the gravel, and is found high up on the slopes of the valleys, and in fact on the tops of the hills, several hundred feet above the river.

Having thus presented the views of the anthropologists on this subject, we shall proceed now to present our own, which are as follows:—

1. *The post-glacial river did not excavate the valley at all.* The Somme River, from its source (twelve miles N. E. of St. Quentin) to its mouth at St. Valéry, is 124 miles in length, and above Abbeville (which is twelve miles from its mouth) is about fifty feet wide. The fall of the river from its source to its mouth is 220 feet, or 1·77 feet per mile. This is *the present fall* of this little stream. Before the valley was excavated (supposing this to have occurred), it had a fall of little more than one-third of this: for the plateau at St. Valéry was 140 feet above the sea, and the fall from above St. Quentin was only eighty feet for the 124 miles. The little sluggish stream, spread over this plateau, must have had a depth of about half an inch.

With this stream Mr. Evans, Sir John Lubbock, and Sir C. Lyell excavate this broad and deep valley, removing the vast volume of the chalk which filled it, and rolling its angular flints into sand and gravel, and depositing them in strata sometimes thirty feet thick at its edges.

There are, moreover, in the gravel rolled pebbles larger than a man's head, and sandstone boulders, some of which weigh a ton. Sir John Lubbock speaks of one which he observed eight feet six inches in length, by two feet eight inches wide, and three feet four inches thick.

We may add to this that, as Mr. James Parker, F.G.S., has shown, *there are no water-bearing strata on the hills, or the valley-slopes along, or at the source of the Somme;* there are not now, and never could have been, any *springs* to supply the Somme with water; this river is sustained and fed by the turbaries or peat-bogs along its course, which hold the rain-water in suspension, and supply it to the river as from a sponge. The bogs are sometimes a mile wide, and extend several miles in length without interruption, while here and there may be observed large pools and even lakes of water (fifteen or twenty feet deep) from which the peat has been dug.[1]

But this peat has been formed since the valley was excavated, and, therefore, the river is posterior to the valley.

2. But how then shall we explain the occurrence of the implement-bearing gravels, eighty feet or more above the present level of the river? Our opinion is, that when those gravels were deposited, the valley was filled by water from bluff to bluff—a body of water one or two miles at least in breadth, and 100 or 150 feet deep. It was *the Palæolithic Flood,* an event now well recognised by geologists. It is a secondary question whether this flood was occasioned by an inflow of the sea, or by the Pluvial Period of Mr. Tylor. That there was such a flood, covering no inconsiderable area in Belgium, in France, in England, in the valley of the

[1] On the Relation between the Somme River and the Somme Valley. By James Parker, Esq., F.G.S., &c.

M. Omalins d'Halloy remarked at the Congress of Brussels (1872), that the excavation of the valley of the Lesse had taken place before the Quaternary Period, and M. Capellini expressed his concurrence in this opinion. See Matériaux, 1872, pp. 421, 422.

Tiber, in the valley of the Mississippi, and elsewhere, there is no doubt—what Dr. Andrews designates as *The Flood of the Loess.*

With regard to the *fact* of this flood there is no question; the only question is as to the *extent* of it. There are some indications that it was even more serious than has been supposed.[1]

M. Boucher de Perthes referred the deposition of the gravel to a great "cataclysm;" M. D'Orbigny, rejecting the theory of marine action, connected the phenomena with "immense inundations of *fresh* water;" Mr. Alfred Tylor propounded the theory of a Pluvial Period following the Glacial Period; Professor Andrews, of Chicago, as remarked, recognises, from his observations in the United States and in Europe, "a palæolithic flood."

Even Mr. Evans, who is a firm believer in the excavation theory, allows that there was at this epoch[2] "a considerably greater annual rainfall," and speaking of Mr. Tylor's Pluvial Period, remarks: "To some extent this opinion is probably correct." And Mr. Prestwich is much more explicit; before the Royal Institute, in 1864, he expressed himself in the following remarkable language:—

[1] For the opinion of scientific men on this point we may refer to Mr. S. J. Mackie, F.G.S., editor of the "Geologist," 1864, p. 118; to M. Le Hon, quoted in the "Anthropological Review," 1869, p. 167; to the Report of M. Dupont on the Belgian caves; to an article entitled, "Man as the Contemporary of the Mammoth and the Reindeer," in the Smithsonian Reports, translated from "Aus der Natur," 1867; to Professor Dawson's "The Story of the Earth and Man," p. 290; to the views of M. Belgrand, quoted by Professor Busk in the Journal of the Anthropological Institute, January 1873, p. 433; to M. Figuier's "Primitive Man," trans., pp. 57, 125; and to many other writers.

[2] Ancient Stone Implements, pp. 569, 613.

"For these and various other reasons I am confirmed in the opinion I expressed in 1859, that the evidence, as it stood, seemed to me as much to necessitate the bringing forward of the great extinct animals towards our own time, as the carrying back of man in geological time. . . . If, on the contrary, they [the modern valley alluvia and the later quaternary beds] followed in immediate succession—and I think we have evidence that such was the case, for there seems reason to believe that some of the larger pachyderms still existed at the commencement of the Alluvial Period, whilst we know that many of the ruminants lived on uninterruptedly from one period to the other—I do not, for my part, see any geological reason why the extinct mammalia should not have lived down to comparatively recent times, *possibly not further back than eight thousand or ten thousand years.*" "But (he continues) this only brings us to the threshold of that dim and mysterious antiquity in which first appear those rudely-wrought flints." . . . . (He then proceeds to speak of the time required for the excavation of the valleys by the streams.) "But," he then continues, "if the views here proposed be correct, it would follow that with rivers so large in proportion to those now occupying the same valleys, with floods of a force now unknown in the same districts, with cold so severe as to shatter rocks and to hasten the removal of their débris, we should have, I contend, agencies in operation so far exceeding in power any now acting, that it is impossible to apply the same rule to the two periods. The change described must have progressed with a rapidity of which we at the present day can in these latitudes hardly form an adequate conception."[1]

It will be observed that the only difficulty in Mr. Prestwich's mind is about the *excavation of the valley;* apart from this, he is prepared to bring down the period of the extinct mammalia to "six or eight thousand years ago." But as the excavation theory is now pretty well exploded, and as Mr. Prestwich recognises the mighty floods of the Post-Glacial Period, we may regard this eminent geologist as practically discountenancing the views put forth by Sir Charles Lyell and Sir John Lubbock.

Different opinions, as we have intimated, have been entertained as to the character of the flood which closed the Quaternary Period—as to whether it was an inundation of the sea, or a rise in the rivers occasioned by an extraordinary rainfall and the melting of the post-glacial snows and ice. The absence of marine shells, and the presence of fresh-water and land shells, point, on the one hand, to fluviatile action, as does the fact that "the constituents of these river-drift gravels are, in all cases, derived from beds now *in situ* along the valley," and never from the beds of other valleys. But, on the other hand, the loess deposit caps the hills, and seems to spread over the district—beyond the range of the gravels; while the absence of a marine fauna does not necessarily exclude the idea of an inundation of the sea; for unless the submergence had continued for a long period, there could have been no marine flora, and without a marine flora there could have been no marine

[1] Proceedings of the Royal Institute, 1864, p. 221.

fauna. There are extensive marine deposits which yield no marine organisms; and if the marine fossils are wanting in the river-gravel, those of the land and the fresh-water are usually equally wanting.

Our own impression is that the flood was at once the result of extraordinary rains, melting snows, and an invasion of the sea. It was the closing storm of the Quaternary Period: there were oscillations of the land, and the river-valleys were filled by their swollen streams. At Menchecourt, in the suburbs of Abbeville, in what are designated as the "low-level" gravels, marine shells have been found at a height of about forty feet above the river-level; and in the valley of the Ouse, again, marine shells are found in the gravel on the old Nene, twelve miles from the sea. In fact, in the Fen country of the East of England, remains of the seal, the walrus, and the whale have been found at a distance of nearly fifty miles from the sea—as at Waterbeach, near Cambridge, &c.

That the land at the mouth of the Somme has greatly altered its position in relation to the sea, is seen by the fact that at St. Valéry the gravels fringe the coast at an elevation of a hundred feet above the present sea-level. When the gravel was deposited, the sea must have been a hundred feet higher than it is at present (unless we make some abatement for the erosion of the coast by the waves). (See Addenda.)

Mr. Alfred Tylor, F.G.S., who has published several papers on this subject, has established the fact that the distinction between the high-level and the low-level gravels is an error—the gravel deposit being a continuous one over the slopes of the valley; and Mr. Tylor contends, as we do, that it is all of one period. The existence of river-floods he regards as proved by the gradual slope and continuity of the gravels upon the sloping sides of the valley, and by the loess or warp of similar mineral composition and colour, extending continuously over the whole series of gravels, and finishing with a well-defined bank near the present stream. The palæolithic deposits, following upon the Glacial Period, and clearly posterior (as Mr. Tylor believes) to the formation of the valleys in which they lie, are of such great dimensions and elevation that they must have been formed under physical conditions very different from our own. They indicate, he believes, a *Pluvial Period*, "which must have immediately preceded the true Historical Period." The existence of a Glacial Period, Mr. Tylor thinks, almost necessitates that of a Pluvial Period, commencing prior to the Glacial, and continuing after it, occupying a region south of that occupied by the ice and snow.

The extraordinary rainfall which characterised this period is referred to as follows by Professor Dawson in his "Story of the Earth and Man":—"The rainfall," he says, "must have been excessive, the volume of water in the streams very great. . . . It was the springtime of the Glacial Era, a spring eminent for its melting snows, its rains, and its river-floods."

And so M. Belgrand (who, according to Professor Busk, has enjoyed unusual opportunities for studying this subject), in his work on "Le Bassin Parisien aux Ages Anté-historiques," remarks that the floods in Palæolithic times were extremely violent, and that the amount of rainfall was so great that it rolled on the surface of even the most permeable soils. "Dans l'âge de la pierre," he says, "les pluies étaient tellement abondantes que leurs eaux ruisselaient à la surface des terrains les plus perméables. Il résultait de là que la première partie de la crue de Paris, celle qui est due aux terrains imperméables, était considerablement augmentée, et que la deuxième partie, due aux eaux de sources, était aussi beaucoup plus grande, puisque les eaux ruisselant à la surface du sol, les sources étaient alimenties autant qu'elles pouvaient l'être, l'absorption des eaux pluviales dans les terrains perméables étant alors au maximum." Citing this, in his address as president of the Anthropological Institution of Great Britain in 1872, Mr. Busk proceeds to remark, that "when once, therefore, the latter (the permeable areas) were rendered impermeable, as M. Belgrand supposes to have been the case in Palæolithic times, whether by saturation or any other cause, the total impermeable area, that which mainly supplies flood water, . . . would be four times as large as at present."[1]

M. Belgrand (who is a firm believer in *Tertiary* Man) makes another point in this discussion which has an important bearing upon the date of the Palæolithic Age. The peat, it will be remembered, is directly superimposed on the gravels, and the lowest stratum of this peat is of the Neolithic Age. M. Belgrand thinks that this peat (which occurs in the valley of the Seine

[1] Journal of Anthropological Institute, January 1873, p. 433.

as in the valley of the Somme) is an evidence that the change from the large rivers of the Palæolithic Age to the small rivers of the Neolithic Age must have taken place *suddenly*. This he conceives to be proved by the fact that peat never grows in turbid, muddy water, and if the change in question had been a gradual one, the valleys would have been filled not with peat, but with gravel, sand, and alluvium. In the valley of the Marne there is no peat, because, owing to the impermeable nature of a part of its course, it is subject to violent floods of muddy water. So the Seine valley down to Montereau contains much peat, but below this point, where it is joined by the Yonne, no peat occurs, because the Yonne, like the Marne, receives its waters from an impermeable district, and is subject to similar floods of muddy water. In Palæolithic times the floods were so violent that the water became muddy in all cases.

This shows that the transition from the Palæolithic Age to the Neolithic Age was *abrupt*, and the immediate superimposition of the peat shows that there was no *gap* between these periods, as has been generally assumed.[1]

It appears from the foregoing discussion that the river-gravels in themselves carry no evidence of a great antiquity: they may be very old, or they may be quite recent. They were the result of violent floods; they were deposited in valleys already excavated; and they were deposited rapidly.

[1] The opinion of M. Belgrand with regard to the excessive rainfall of the Palæolithic Period is shared by M. Dupont. See Matériaux, 1872, p. 396.

The relics of man found in these beds create a presumption that they are not (geologically) very old; the argument for their antiquity rests—1. On the presence of the remains of the extinct animals; and 2. On the physical changes which may be recognised to have occurred since their epoch on the coast-lines of Europe, or in the interior lines of drainage. These will be considered in the proper place.

There are two data for fixing the date of these gravels—1. They were laid down just upon the close of the Glacial Age; 2. The peat began to form just after the subsidence of the Palæolithic Flood. When was the Glacial Age? When did the Danish peat and the French peat begin to form?

It is proper to mention that a human jaw was found in the "high-level" gravel at Moulin-Quignon (Abbeville) in 1863. This bone, when sawn asunder, *emitted distinctly the odour peculiar to bone;* and the authenticity of the relic was accordingly questioned. The British and French *savants* had several conferences at Abbeville and Paris on the subject, and the matter was very minutely investigated. It was finally unanimously agreed that no fraud had been practised; but Dr. Falconer and Mr. Busk doubted *the age* of the fossil on the ground of its *freshness.* This, however, cannot be a valid ground of objection in view of the freshness of the animal bones at Solutré, on which we have remarked.[1]

[1] M. de Quatrefages remarks on this: "It is known that some doubts were raised at different times touching the authenticity of this relic; but they must have been removed by the discovery, in the same locality, of a second jawbone presenting the same characters, and the quaternary origin of which no one disputes."—Matériaux, 1875, p. 61.

CHAPTER X.

THE PEAT OF THE SOMME VALLEY.

Estimated by M. Boucher de Perthes to be 30,000 years old—This calculation apparently approved by Lyell—Observations of Professor Andrews—Infers that the peat must have formed very rapidly from the erect stumps of trees in it—Farther evidences of the recent date of the peat from the relics found in it at great depths—Lubbock on this peat or silt—Traces of a pile-village—Objects of iron and bronze, and Roman relics, found many feet below surface—A Roman causeway—Table of the different strata—The Bronze Age in Gaul fixed by M. de Perthes about 200 B.C.—Boat laden with Roman bricks at bottom of peat—Observations of Mr. Parker.

WE shall have occasion to say something about the peat-bogs of Europe in general elsewhere, but it is necessary to take up here the peat of the Somme valley, as it forms a member of the deposits which we have been discussing.

Sir Charles Lyell and Sir John Lubbock urge that this bed alone represents a vast lapse of time, while it takes us back only to the beginning of the Neolithic Age. M. Boucher de Perthes made a calculation which would require about 30,000 years for this peat to form. Sir Charles Lyell, while he is cautious about committing himself on the point, offers this calculation as the best that can be furnished on the subject.

The lower part of the valley of the Somme, at Abbeville, where M. Boucher de Perthes pursued his investigations, is filled with peat or silt—the peat constituting ordinarily only one in a series of five or six deposits; the pure beds of peat are the exception, but it sometimes occurs in this way, and attains a thickness of over thirty feet.

The observations of Professor Andrews, of Chicago,[1] on the estimates of M. Boucher de Perthes, are more judicious than those of Sir C. Lyell.

"M. Boucher de Perthes," says Dr. Andrews, "has with praiseworthy care sought to determine the age of this bed; but as he was probably unacquainted with the phenomena of forest peats in process of actual formation, he has very excusably overlooked some of the most important data. The growth of the peat at present," Dr. Andrews remarks, "is doubtless imperceptible (as M. de Perthes states) to the modern inhabitants—and very easily explained. The peat-beds of the Somme valley belong to the class of forest peats, and not to that of moss growths. Forest peats, as may be seen in thousands of localities in the United States, are formed as follows: The annual crop of fruit, twigs, leaves, and windfallen trunks, furnished by the trees and shrubbery of a dense swamp, amounts to an immense mass of vegetable matter. These, added to a thick undergrowth of grass, herbs, and moss, are all pressed against the ground by the winter snows. In the spring they are flooded and protected from decay. In the summer they are partly protected from oxygenation by the extreme wetness of the soil into which they have been pressed. Hence they are only slightly rotted

[1] American Journal of Science and Art, October 1868.

when they are finally covered up by the fall of the next autumn's crop. To one who studies the actual quantity of this material, a growth of two or three feet in a century is by no means improbable. The increase of the peat *depends on the presence of the forests.* But the forests of the Somme valley have disappeared centuries ago—and with their disappearance the peat ceased to grow."

"Boucher de Perthes," proceeds Dr. Andrews, "states that he has found, deep in the peats of the Somme, numerous trunks of trees standing erect where they grew, generally birches or alders. These trunks were sometimes a metre in height, but generally less. Now, as stumps of trees do not stand long uncovered in the damp air of a swamp without decay, it follows that all which are found standing erect in the peat must have been covered to their present summits before they had time to rot away. Applying M. Boucher de Perthes' estimate of one and a half or two inches in a century for the growth of the peat, the above-mentioned stumps must have stood uncovered without decay from 1950 to 2600 years! But one hundred years is a long lifetime for an oak-stump under such circumstances, and every trace of almost every other tree would disappear in fifty years. Birch-stumps are especially perishable. There were prostrate trunks of oak in the peat four feet in diameter, and so sound that they were manufactured into furniture. They must have been covered by the peat in a hundred years. The rest of the calculation is easily made."

Dr. Andrews adds that most of the erect trunks were

shorter than three feet, and seem to have disappeared altogether. Thus, while it is evident that the accretion in some places has been equal to three feet in a century, the average rate must have been lower.

So much for the pure beds of peat. But the diggings described by M. Boucher de Perthes in his "Antiquités Celtiques et Anté-diluviennes" were not in these beds, but in those mixed alluvial beds in which the peat is only one of five or six layers. He tells us that he excavated at a number of points in the valley on both sides of the river, and that he found everywhere the same succession of beds, which he represents to be as follows:—

I. Terrain alluvien.
II. Terre végétale.
III. Tuf calcaire poreux.
IV. Sable limoneux, bleu.
V. Tombes renfermant des sépultures celtiques.
VI. Autre couche de sable limoneux.
VII. Terrain diluvien détritique.
VIII. Terrain secondaire, craie blanche.

He gives us the following diagram (see next page) illustrating this succession of beds.

Now we are told by Sir John Lubbock, that M. Boucher de Perthes found in these strata a rich harvest of interesting relics belonging to the various periods, and that he has "carefully noted the depth at which these objects are found."

"Taking," Sir John quotes from M. de Perthes (and which we translate), "for the mean limit of the soil of the valley, a height of two metres above the level of the Somme, it is at thirty to forty centimetres from the surface that we meet most abundantly the traces of the

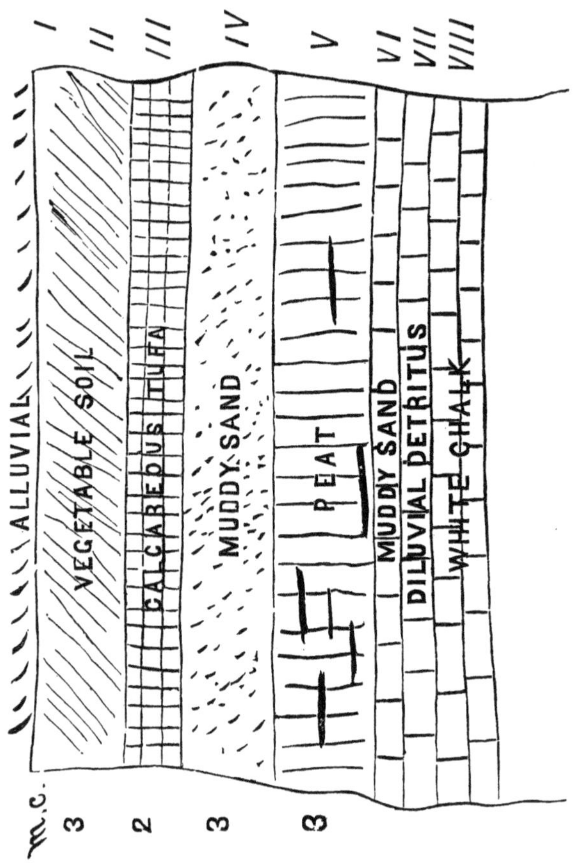

Middle Ages. Fifty centimetres lower, we commence to find remains of the Roman, then of the Gallo-Roman, period. We continue to follow these last for a metre, that is, down to the level of the Somme. After these come the pure Gaulish vestiges, which descend without interruption to nearly two metres below this level, a proof of the long habitation of this valley by this people. It is at one metre lower, or at about four metres below this same level, that we arrive at the centre of the soil which we have named Celtic, that which was trod by the primitive Gauls or the peoples who preceded them." These measurements are, of course, only given "comme terme approximatif."

We are taught to believe that Roman relics occur ordinarily at about the depth of from three to five feet, and remains of the Gallo-Roman period at a depth of from five to six feet—the remains of the Neolithic Age occurring at about the average depth of from fifteen to eighteen feet. The result, of course, is that if the age of the Roman relics is fixed at about 1600 years, 6000 or 7000 years must have elapsed since the Neolithic Period.

We have taken the trouble to examine the work of M. Boucher de Perthes, and do not find these statements confirmed.

For example, at p. 54, vol. i., of the "Antiquités Celtiques et Anté-diluviennes," we are told by the author that in the Marais de Boufflers, between Abbeville and Hesdin, at the depth of several metres, a *paved subterranean causeway* was encountered.

At p. 147, vol. i., he informs us that near the gate of Bois (Abbeville), at the depth of five or six metres in the peat, he found a copper poniard some twelve inches in length.

At p. 155, vol. i., he mentions finding a lump of iron between Abbeville and Epagne, at seven or eight metres deep, in digging a well in the marl. It was *under* the marl, and its antiquity, says M. Boucher de Perthes, "is certainly very great." He suggests that it may have been a scraper or a ploughshare.

A kind of iron spade, he says, was found in 1842, at Condé-Folie (Somme), at the depth of six metres (twenty feet).

In 1844 another object of iron, which resembled a *hache à sapeur* was found at the gate of Hocquet, beneath a stratum of gravel, at the depth of three metres below the level of the Somme, that is, five or six metres from the surface.

At p. 186, vol. i., at La Portelette, at Abbeville, at the depth of from twelve to fifteen metres, he found the traces of a pile-village. This was thirty metres distant from the river, implying a larger body of water.

The layers of dressed wood or rafters belonging to the pile-settlement occurred between the "sable limoneux" and the "terrain diluvien détritique," *i.e.*, between VI. and VII. of the diagram.

At IV. of the diagram some beautifully polished hatchets of flint and jade were found, seven metres from the surface. Near this level, but a little higher, and six metres distant from the hatchets, they found a statuette in ivory, representing a man holding a palm and a sort of gridiron: "*c'était probablement Saint-Laurent.*"

Continuing his excavations at this point (p. 201, vol. i.), the author found a fragment of iron at the depth of thirty-six feet, which he says was perhaps introduced "accidentally." Near it lay a hatchet of green porphyry.

Subsequently other excavations were made at La Portelette, and the charcoal, flints, vases, &c., characteristic of the "Celtic Period" were found at "the usual depth"—that is, as we understand it, at twelve or thirteen metres from the surface. But at one metre above these remains, as we are told, M. de Perthes encountered "*des pièces romaines de cuivres frustres*," or Roman relics, thirty-six feet or more from the surface.

At p. 213, vol. i., we are told that in May 1844 the ground between the Pont Rouge and the Marcadi Gate was excavated for a gasometer. At the depth of six metres M. de Perthes found fragments of a large Roman amphora, and on the same level "some medals of the Lower Empire." These were immediately under the layer of peat. Some very delicately worked knives of black and blue flint, and some flint axes, were found at the same time and at the same depth.

A few centimetres lower down they found an iron chisel.

In 1853 M. Boucher de Perthes excavated again between the river and the gate Marcadi, at a point one hundred metres distant from the excavation for the site of the gasometer. He reached the same Celtic soil (VI. of the diagram), encountering vases and worked flints, also a fine axe of sandstone seventeen centimetres long, and another of highly polished jade. Digging one metre below this bed, he reached what he calls "a second Celtic bed," where he found a vase "almost entire," having a place in the side for a light of rosin or wax.

Near by were the head of a urus, and some worked flints. This vase, M. de Perthes tells us, "is not of high antiquity"—having been "hardened in the fire *and turned on the wheel.*"

M. de Perthes expresses the opinion that it *sank* to the position where he found it; but the vase was about six inches in diameter by seven inches in height, and not, we should think, well adapted to sinking through beds of sand and peat many feet thick. Moreover, as the fact of its having been turned on the wheel implies a Roman origin, it must, on M. de Perthes's hypothesis, have had a considerable distance to travel, if the Roman or Gallo-Roman stratum occurs five or six feet from the surface.

The stratum in which this vase was found was immediately preceded by a bed of peat, which bed, we are told, presently raises itself to the surface, and is no longer dominated by the humus. This same bed, we are told, has been signalled at seven metres below the soil of the city. It was in this peat, where it shows itself at the surface, that M. de Perthes found certain Roman dishes at the depth of one metre, on which circumstance he made his well-known calculation as to the rate of the formation of the peat. But, supposing no other error to exist, M. de Perthes seems to have forgotten that the time which has elapsed since the dishes were placed where they were found includes not only the period represented by the accumulation of the peat, but the farther period represented by the twenty-three feet of silt deposited above it. Since that peat ceased to form, twenty-three feet of sand and gravel and mud have gathered over it; and it is strange that neither M. Boucher de Perthes nor Sir C. Lyell recognised the propriety of taking this into account in connection with this calculation.

At p. 447 of vol. i., M. de Perthes sums up the results of his explorations in the peat or silt, and to use his own language, casts a retrospective glance at the several strata which he had penetrated at many different points, commencing "par le sol que nous foulons, et en indiquant, lit par lit, les débris que nous avons rencontrés." The following is a description of these beds in their order; and is worthy of *the special attention* of the reader.

First Bed, or Modern Soil.—Arts of civilisation, scoriæ, glazed pottery of different colours, porcelain, &c.

Second Bed.—Transition from modern times to the Middle Ages; iron; some copper; French, Flemish, Spanish coins; Venetian glass, &c.

Third Bed.—Middle Ages. Coins of the first races and of the Lower Empire, in bronze, zinc, and gold, but little silver; less of iron than copper, &c.

Fourth Bed.—Gallo-Roman Epoch. Marbles, statues, fragments of columns, stone tombs, coins of the Consular Age; iron more rare; copper keys; bronze figures, &c.

Fifth Bed.—Gaulish Period. Iron more and more rare; swords and lances are of copper; Gaulish coins of gold, but not of silver; some Greek pieces, &c.

Sixth Bed.—First Celtic Period. We no longer find coffins or entire skeletons; there are broken bones, ashes, cinders, rude vases; no iron; a few relics of copper; polished stone hatchets with their sheaths, &c.

Seventh Bed.—Second Celtic Period,—an undefined period,—other vases found under the first (hand-made); ashes, charcoal, broken and calcined bones. Flints roughly hewn into hatchets, knives, &c. Trees found squared and hewn without iron tools. Urns more and more rude. This is at four metres below the level of the Somme, and at eight to ten metres below the soil inhabited to-day. We have traversed three or four beds of gravel or of peat intermingled with layers of sand, ashes, bones, charcoal, &c.

Eighth Bed.—The diluvium or drift; broken and rolled flints; ferruginous sand.

From this analysis of the relic-beds at Abbeville, we learn—1. That in the Third Bed, characterised by coins of the Lower Empire, we find "less of iron than copper" [bronze?]; *i.e.*, the Bronze Age continued some time after the Christian era; we learn, 2. That in the Fourth Bed (in the Gallo-Roman Period) iron is yet more rare; 3. That in the Gaulish Period (Fifth Bed), along with Gaulish coins, *the swords and lances are of copper* (bronze). This was about B.C. 150 or 200. The Gauls had no coinage prior to B.C. 300. 4. In the Sixth Bed, just below this, we come to the relics of the Neolithic Age.

These dates, it will be observed, are widely different from those given in the works of Sir C. Lyell, Sir J. Lubbock, and other writers on pre-historic archæology.

The coinage of the Gauls follows at once upon the Stone Age.

Nor is this all: the peat takes us back to the river-gravel on which it rests; it began to form as the floods of the Palæolithic Age passed away. We obtain thus a clue to the date of the Palæolithic Age.

The peat is not all of precisely the same age; it formed at particular spots according to the conditions presented. It ceased to form in some places, while its formation continued in others. Some of it we know to be post-Roman. This will appear by the following extract from Sir C. Lyell's "Principles of Geology:"—

"We are informed," says Sir Charles Lyell, "by Deguer, that remains of ships, nautical instruments, and oars have been found in many of the Dutch mosses; and Gérard, in his history of the valley of the Somme, mentions that in the lowest tier of that moss was found *a boat loaded with bricks, proving that these mosses were at one period navigable lakes and arms of the sea,* as were also many mosses on the coast of Picardy, Zealand, and Friesland, from which soda and salt are procured. The canoes, stone hatchets, and stone arrow-heads found in peat in different parts of Great Britain, lead to similar conclusions." [1]

There were, of course, no bricks in Gaul before the Roman Period.

Canoes have been found in the peat of the Somme valley in other instances, as at the place called Saint-Jean-des-Près, on the left bank of the canal; at Abbeville, at the depth of twelve feet; at Estrebœuf, near Saint-Valéry; and at Picquigny, between Abbeville and Amiens. In this last case there were several skele-

[1] Principles of Geology, twelfth edition, vol. ii. p. 512.

tons in the boat, and a bronze sword, and coins of the Roman Emperor Maxentius (A.D. 306–312).

We not only learn from these discoveries that the peat is a recent formation, but we learn also that even as late as the Roman Period the sea extended far up the Somme valley. The presence of a considerable body of water at Abbeville at a yet earlier period is indicated by the traces of a pile-village observed by M. Boucher de Perthes at La Portelette, thirty metres distant from the river. When that pile-village existed, the water at this point must have been at least six or eight feet deep, and the Somme, now only some fifteen or twenty yards wide, must have constituted an estuary one hundred or one hundred and fifty yards wide.

The conclusions to be drawn with regard to the growth of the peat from the foregoing facts are corroborated by the statements of Mr. James Parker, F.G.S., and M. D'Archiac. In his paper on the Somme valley, Mr. Parker states that he inquired of a couple of men who were working at a peat-pit in this valley as to whether the peat was still growing, its rate of growth, &c., and they informed him that it does grow at present, and, according to their idea, about a metre in a century is the rate. Mr. Parker thinks this an average estimate, as, in 1861, when they were altering the moat surrounding Abbeville, he observed two or three feet of peat in it, which they were clearing out, and "he thought that they would at least have cleared their moat once in a century."

M. D'Archiac's estimate, as may be seen in a future chapter on the Peat, considerably exceeds this.

CHAPTER XI.

THE GREAT EXTINCT ANIMALS.

The association of the relics of man with the bones of these animals suggestive of a high antiquity—Erroneous impression with regard to the disappearance of wild animals—The buffalo, wapiti, moose, &c.—Disappearance of the elephant, rhinoceros, and lion in certain districts in India—Survival of the so-called extinct animals to recent times—The urus and aurochs—The reindeer—The great Irish elk—The mammoth and mastodon—The megatherium—Identity of the cave-lion with the Asiatic lion—Of the cave-hyæna with the spotted hyæna—Of the cave-bear with brown bear—Of the palæolithic horse with present horse—Palæontologists deceived by the greater size of ancient animals.

THE facts of the last chapter dispose effectually of the peat of the Somme valley; but the question still remains, what is the age of the river-gravels? We have already suggested that they immediately preceded the beginning of the Peat Period. But, as in the case of the bone-caverns, we have yet two principal difficulties to meet—1. The presence of the remains of the extinct animals; and 2. The physical changes which have since occurred in the crust of the earth. To the first of these two questions we propose to address ourselves in the present chapter.

When one fully comprehends that in Western and Central Europe, man and the mammoth have lived together; that within the same human period the hippopotamus and the rhinoceros roamed in the Thames valley, and that with these the reindeer ranged as far south as the Pyrenees; it is difficult to have any other impression than that man must have been on the earth longer than has been generally supposed. That lions, and hyænas, and elephants, and hippopotami, constituted the distinguishing fauna of the region afterwards known as Gaul some 4000 or 5000 years ago, must be carefully explained to us before it can be accepted.

We find man and these animals together; we have believed that man is recent, and that the animals are very ancient; we must, therefore, carry the age of man back, or bring the age of the mammoth forward. We shall proceed to show that all of these extinct animals have lived down to a comparatively recent period—some of them down to historic, and even post-Roman times. If this shall be made clearly to appear, the main argument for the Antiquity of Man is set aside.

There are very great misconceptions about the disappearance of a fauna. Wild animals are constantly vanishing from regions where they abounded, and, indeed, from the face of the earth; and we may judge from what we observe to-day, in some measure at least, of what probably occurred after the advent of man in Europe.

The bison, for example, now driven to the western part of the United States, and destined soon to become entirely extinct, abounded, within the present century, in the valley of the Kanawha, in West Virginia, and grazed in herds, as did the moose, two centuries ago, in the valley of the Connecticut.

The Salt Lick in Kanawha county, West Virginia, then called the "Great Buffalo Lick," was such a resort of the buffalo [bison] and elk (*Cervus Canadensis*) at the close of the last century, that Daniel Boone, the famous Kentucky hunter, about 1789, returned eastward into this region, and settled just on the opposite side of the river from the lick, in order to enjoy his favourite pastime.

The moa (which stood ten feet high) has become extinct in New Zealand within a very recent period, and the gigantic and grotesque dodo was found by navigators in the island of Mauritius in the sixteenth century.

The stag and the fallow-deer—formerly slaughtered by hundreds in England at a hunting-match—are now only preserved with the greatest care; and the bustard, formerly seen in Britain in large flocks on the heaths and downs, is now confined to the county of Norfolk.

The brown bear lingered in Belgium until the Middle Ages, and in Scotland until the eleventh century. The wolf was found in Scotland in 1306, and in Ireland in 1710.

The hippopotamus in ancient times was found near the mouth of the Nile; now it is rarely seen even in Lower Nubia; and it is fast disappearing from South Africa, only two being left in Cape Colony in 1838.

One of the most suggestive facts on this subject is the disappearance of the elephant, and rhinoceros, and the lion, from Northern India. Three centuries ago, the Mogul Emperor, Baber (the great-grandson of Tamerlane), in his public memoirs, mentions the occurrence of the rhinoceros, wild buffalo, and lion in the neighbourhood of Benares, and that of the elephant near Chunar. "In the jungles around Chunar," he remarks, "there are many elephants," and he elsewhere states that they are found in the district of Kalpe, and "as you advance east they increase." The translator of this work, in a note on this passage, written some sixty years ago, observes: "The improvement in Hindustan must be prodigious. The wild elephant is now confined to the forests of Himâla and to the ghâts of Malabar. A wild elephant near Karrah, Manikapore, or Kalpe, at the present day, is totally unknown."[1]

At this time the rhinoceros has long been extirpated, with not (says Figuier) *so much as a tradition* of it remaining in all the parts where Baber mentions its former existence. The lion was numerous within the district north-west of Delhi within the memory of living men; but already *hardly a tradition survives there of this formidable animal.*[2]

In a few centuries this wonderful change has taken place in the fauna of this country; India has been almost cleared of the elephant, the lion, and the rhinoceros, while the tiger is driven to the jungles along the great rivers; but it is more surprising that the memory of these animals has perished in regions which they so recently inhabited. May it not be, then, that it is not so very long ago since the disappearance of the American mastodon and the Siberian mammoth, and may not man, in a few thousand years, readily have lost the remembrance and the tradition of their presence?

[1] Figuier's Mammalia, pp. 148, 150.

[2] Ibid., p. 143.

Indeed, the lion has not only disappeared from nearly all of the provinces of India; in ancient times he was common in Asia from the shores of Syria to the banks of the Ganges and the Oxus. We know that they were numerous in Palestine—being the subject of frequent allusion in the Old Testament, and the fact being indicated by the names Lebaoth (Josh. xv. 32), Beth-lebaoth (Josh. xix. 6), Arieh (2 Kings xv. 25), and Laish (Judges xviii. 7; 1 Sam. xxv. 44); nor is this all; as we shall have occasion to mention presently, they were found *in Europe* at the beginning of the Christian Era.

We shall now notice in order the following animals which constituted specially the fauna characteristic of the Quaternary Period: the urus, the aurochs, the reindeer, the great Irish elk (megaceros), the mammoth, the woolly rhinoceros, the cave-lion, the cave-bear, &c.

The Urus.—This animal is mentioned by Cæsar as existing in the Hercynian Forest; we find it mentioned again as late as the twelfth century of our era in the poem of the Niebelungen Lied, and, according to Herberstein, it survived in Germany to the sixteenth century. (See Addenda.)

The Aurochs, or European bison, is mentioned by both Pliny and Seneca as existing in their time; it is also named in the Niebelungen Lied; existed in Prussia until 1775; and is still found wild in the Caucasus. Twelve herds, also, are carefully preserved in the forests of Lithuania by the Czar of Russia.

The Reindeer.—It is of more importance to our present inquiry to ascertain when the reindeer disappeared from Western and Central Europe.

And, first, we have it, on the authority of Cæsar, that it existed in his day in the Hercynian Forest (De Bel. Gal. vi. 26). It has been questioned by some whether Cæsar really refers to the reindeer in this passage; but it seems to have been forgotten that the same writer mentions the reindeer elsewhere in his account of the Germans, who, as we are told, "et pellibus aut parvis rhenonum tegumentis utuntur" (De Bel. Gal. vi. 21); and this testimony is corroborated by that of Sallust: "Germani infectum rhenonibus corpus tegunt" (Fragm. incertæ sedis. 18. Dietsch). Mr. Boyd Dawkins (p. 79) admits the existence of the reindeer at this time in Germany, as does Mr. Conrad Merk in his account of "The Excavations at the Kesslerloch, near Thäyngen" (p. 11 trans.).[1]

If, however, the reindeer existed in Central Europe at the beginning of the Christian Era, the argument from "the extinct animals" at once loses all significance.

But, again, the reindeer is proved to have been living in the North of Scotland in the twelfth century by a passage in the Orkneyinga Saga, in which we are told that the Norwegian jarls of that age used to cross the seas to Scotland (from the Orkney Islands) to hunt him.

About A.D. 600 we find a passage in Isidore (Orig. xix.

[1] Brandt and Schaaffhausen admit the same fact. See Archiv für Anthrop., Januar 1876, s. 264.

"It is important also," adds Professor Schaaffhausen, "that upon a Roman mosaic floor in the Louvre in Paris a reindeer is represented grazing under a fir tree."

c. 23) implying that the reindeer was hunted at that time at no remote distance from the Rhine.[1] This statement is borne out by another from a work written in the fourteenth century by Gaston de Foix (third count of that name and Lord of Béarn), entitled "Le Miroir de Phébus des déduits de la Chasse." This nobleman at an early age joined a crusade in behalf of the distressed Teutonic knights against the Paynims of Lithuania; and this matter disposed of, being passionately fond of hunting, he crossed over into Norway and Sweden to hunt reindeer. In the work mentioned, referring to this journey, he writes of the reindeer: "J' en ay veu en Norvegne et Xuedene et en ha oultre mer, mes en Romain pays en ay je peu veu."[2]

The bones of the reindeer abound in the cemetery at Björkö, near Stockholm, which dates about the ninth or tenth century. They also occur in the ruined towers of the North of Scotland, called "burghs" or "brochs," some of which are of the twelfth century—along with the bones of the red-deer, short-horned ox, horse, goat, &c.

Professor Filhol found in the cavern of Mas-d'Azil (Haute-Garonne) great numbers of the worked horns of the reindeer, mingled with chipped flints and remains of the ox, sheep, dog, wild goat, and aurochs.[3] His

[1] Renones sunt velamina humerorum et pectoris usque ad umbilicum atque intortis villis adeo hispida ut imbres respuant. Dicti autem renones a Rheno Germaniæ flumine ubi iis frequenter utuntur. Isid. Orig., xix. c. 23.

[2] By "the Roman country" we understand Prussia, which, at that time, was the possession of the Teutonic order, but which, as well as Denmark, owned allegiance to the Holy Roman Empire.

[3] Matériaux, 1875, p. 93.

remains occurred again, with polished stone, at the camp of Chassey, Saône-et-Loire.

The bones of the reindeer were found, with bronze objects, and bones of the ox, stag, and wild boar, in the valley of the Tardoire, France.[1] They were found again, with bronze spear-heads, arrow-heads, knives, &c., in the shell-marl of the Walthamstow marshes (near London), accompanied by the bones of man, the wolf, the fox, the beaver, the wild deer, &c. They have been found again in the layer of peat underneath the alluvium of the Thames at Crossness; in the peat of Yorkshire; and, in several places, in the peat of Scotland and Ireland.[2] They have been found in the Danish peat, and in the more recent layers of that peat—that is to say, in the layer assigned by archæologists to the Bronze Age. This fact is stated by Professor Worsaae in his "Primeval Antiquities of Denmark."[3]

Professor Steenstrup is of opinion, adds Professor Worsaae, that the animal "existed to a much later period in these forests, and that it was only exterminated by the slings, the weapons, and the traps of the inhabitants."

All these facts are abundantly sufficient to justify Professor Dawkins in the declaration that "the reindeer was probably living in the Bronze and Iron Ages."

For the purposes of our argument it is only necessary to show that it survived to the Neolithic Age.

[1] Matériaux, 1874, p. 14.

[2] British Quarterly Review, April 1874, p. 346.

[3] English translation, p. 10. See also an article by Steenstrup in Matériaux for 1872, p. 301, who states that the reindeer and the elk are "often" found in the Danish peat-bogs.

One of the principal evidences for the remote date of the Palæolithic Age, on which a great deal of stress is laid, is the long time required for the change which took place between the Palæolithic and Neolithic Ages, *in the climate* of Europe. The Arctic fauna, characteristic of the river-gravels and the caves—the reindeer, the musk-sheep, the Alpine hare, &c.—we are told, had given way to the animals appropriate to milder and less rigorous climatic conditions. "These and similar facts," says Sir John Lubbock, "though they afford us no means of measurement, impress us with a vague and overpowering sense of antiquity." But if we find the reindeer in England, France, and Denmark in the Bronze Age—then the change in question must have taken place since then. Now Professor Worsaae fixes the Bronze Age in Denmark at from B.C. 600 to A.D. 200; and the whole argument from the change of climate thus falls to the ground. (See Addenda.)

It has, in fact, been assumed, without sufficient warrant, that the reindeer requires an almost Arctic climate; but it thrives in the mountains north and east of Mandchuria, a comparatively temperate region, and existed until quite recently in the Southern Urals. It lived in Scotland, as we have seen, in the twelfth century; and the present climate of Scotland does not differ very materially from that of those regions of Norway where it now exists. The reindeer moss grows abundantly not only in Scotland, but even in England.

As Mr. H. H. Howorth suggests, the explanation of the fact that experiments to introduce the reindeer in Scotland have failed is found in a passage contained in

Mr. Laing's admirable narrative of a residence in Norway. The hair of the reindeer does not, Mr. Laing says, throw off wet well, and even parts from the skin after any continuance of moisture. With our damp climate and wet ground (he proceeds) the animal would be drenched through the hair to the skin for weeks together, and would die of cold or rot, as our sheep often do in wet seasons. In Norway the heavy rains occur in spring or autumn, at which seasons what is rain below is dry snow higher up in the Fjeldes. Our highest hills do not afford in summer this kind of refuge from rain and damp to an animal whose coat keeps out any degree of cold, but will not stand continued moisture. (Laing's "Residence in Norway," p. 264.)

Mr. Howorth remarks on this: "It is the damp of our latitudes now-a-days that the reindeer cannot endure. It is strange that no use has been made of this fact hitherto in our zoological reasoning; for it is a very potent reason why so many foreign animals die here. In our menageries the beasts do not suffer so much from cold and other assigned causes as damp. Diseases of the lungs are the scourges of such establishments, and these induced not by cold but damp. The camel, the tiger, &c., can endure the exceedingly bitter cold of the Thibetan plateau with impunity, because the cold is a dry parching cold. . . . That our climate has grown damper is probable from the contemporaneous extinction of the spruce fir with the reindeer, the former of which, as well as the other linear-leaved trees, according to Ermann, especially likes a dry air. Such climatic changes would probably first be felt by the vegetation. . . . With the disappearance of the forest, the forest animals disappear too—notably the elk, the sable, &c."[1]

The Great Irish Elk (*Megaceros*).—It has been represented that this great deer is more ancient than even the mammoth. It survived, however, to historic times. We proceed to establish this by the following facts.

At the meeting of the Geological Society of Dublin, in December 1861, Dr. Petrie stated that he had in his possession an iron sword which had been found in association with the bones of the megaceros in the county of Meath.

The leg of a megaceros, with a portion of the tendons, skin, and hair on it, was found about 1864 in the county of Wexford, on the estate of H. Grogan Morgan, Esq., a specimen of which was sent to the Royal Dublin Society, and exhibited by Mr. Peale, Professor of Veterinary Surgery, to his class.[2] In this same paper it is stated that Archdeacon Mansell mentions the discovery of a megaceros at Rathcannon, Limerick county, and with it a number of jet rings, and the bones of a dog or bear.

In an article published forty years ago in the "Penny Magazine," on the great Irish elk, it is stated that the head of one of these animals, some stone hatchets (the palæolithic hatchets were not recognised at that time),

[1] Journal of Anthropological Institute, 1873, pp. 221–224.

[2] Dublin Quarterly Journal of Science, January 1865. Paper by R. H. Scott, Esq.

and several bones of the urus were found together in the same drain.[1]

Colonel Hamilton Smith mentions the discovery, near Xanthen, on the Rhine, beneath an altar of stone, of the head of an Irish elk, and a quantity of ashes.[2]

The crannoges of Ireland all belong to a recent date. In one of these in Lough Crea, as we learn from a paper read in November 1863 before the Royal Irish Academy, the head of a megaceros, together with the bones of the ox, sheep, goat, pig, dog, wolf, &c., were dug up at the depth of thirteen feet. With these animal remains were found iron implements, a crozier of brass, a battle-axe, a cast for a coin, bone and stone implements, &c.[3]

Professor Jamieson and Dr. Mantell note the discovery in the county of Cork, Ireland, of a human body found in a peat-bog, at the depth of eleven feet. The soft parts were converted into adipocere, and the body, thus preserved, was enveloped in a deer-skin of such large dimensions as to lead them to the opinion that it belonged to the extinct elk. Professor Daniel Wilson, who is our authority for this case, mentions another which leaves less margin for doubt. At a meeting of the Archæological Institute, June 3, 1864, the Earl of Dunraven exhibited an imperfect Irish lyre, found in the moat of Desmond Castle, Adare, the material of which was pronounced by Professor Owen to be bone of the Irish elk.[4]

[1] Penny Magazine, p. 300.
[2] Natural History of the Human Species, p. 154.
[3] Dublin Quarterly Journal of Science, 1864, p. 125.
[4] Pre-historic Man, 2d edition, p. 37.

In the first edition of "Prehistoric Man" (we are not sure that it is in the later editions), Dr. Wilson affirms that "skeletons of the Irish elk have been found at Curragh, Ireland, in marshes, some of the bones of which were in such fresh condition that the marrow is described as having the appearance of fresh suet, and burning with a clear flame."[1]

The statements with reference to the freshness of the bones are corroborated by the "Dublin Quarterly Journal of Science."[2] According to this authority, a centesimal analysis of a skeleton by Professor W. Stokes yielded 43·45 of phosphates, with fluates, and 42·87 of animal matter; and Professor Apjohn states that "the cartilage and gelatine had not been even perceptibly altered by time."

There are allusions in the "Book of Lismore" to the chase of a great black deer, which is supposed to have been the Irish elk.

At the meeting of the Boston Society of Natural History, in 1868, Professor Agassiz remarked that Brandt had proved, from an examination of ancient documents in the Sclavonic tongue, that the *Bos primigenius* was living in the forests of Lithuania and Poland up to the eleventh and thirteenth centuries, and added, that "the presence of *Cervus megaceros* in the marshes of Europe up to the fourteenth century is also made probable." (See Addenda.)

To the same effect we read in "Matériaux pour l'Histoire de l'Homme:" "Le *Bos cervi figurâ* de César n'était ni un Élan, comme le suppose Lenz, ni un

[1] Vol. i. p. 98. [2] January 1866, p. 22.

Cervus euryceros [megaceros], comme le croit Eichwold, mais bien un Renne, et M. Brandt croit l'avoir prouvé. Suivant lui, le *Machlis* ou l'Achlis que Pline distingue positivement de l'Élan, et le *Schelch* du poëme des *Niebelungen*, ne sont autre que le *Cervus euryceros.* En effet, cette grande espèce vivait en Allemagne au xième siècle; et n'y devint complètement inconnue qu' à partie du xiième siècle, époque à laquelle on la trouvait encore en Irlande."[1]

Such is the conclusive evidence for the recent existence of this great member of the palæolithic fauna.

The Mammoth and the Woolly Rhinoceros.—(In this discussion we shall speak also of the American mastodon, the companion of the *Elephas Americanus.*) The bones of the mastodon were found in miry clay, above a stratum of rock-salt, on the island of Petit Anse, Louisiana, in association with pottery, stone hatches, cane baskets, &c. These remains were found at the depth of twelve feet. Whether they are all contemporary we are not prepared to say. If they are, it is very certain that this gigantic animal lived at a recent date.[2]

A similar association of the bones of the mastodon with fragments of pottery was found by Professor Holmes on the banks of the Ashley River, near Charleston, S.C.[3]

Whatever value is to be attached to these discoveries,

[1] Décembre 1872, p. 534. It is added in a note: "D'après Hibbert, selon Ranking (Wars and Sports, London, 1826), il aurait été détruit par les Romains."

[2] Proc. Acad. Nat. Sci. of Phil., 1866, p. 109.

[3] Ibid., July 1859, pp. 178–186, and 1847, p. 125.

the circumstances under which the bones of both the mastodon and the mammoth occur in America warrant the declaration of Professor Shaler in the "American Naturalist," that "there can now be no doubt that a few thousand years ago these companion giants roamed through the forests and along the streams of the Mississippi valley." They fed, says Professor Shaler, upon a vegetation "not materially different from that now existing in that region." "The fragments of wood which one finds beneath their bones seem to be of the common species of existing trees; and the reeds and other swamp plants which are embedded with their remains, are apparently the same as those which now spring in the soil." "Almost any swampy bit of ground," says this writer, "in Ohio or Kentucky contains traces of the mammoth and mastodon;" and at Big Bone Lick "the remains are so well preserved, as to seem not much more ancient than the buffalo bones which are found above them."[1]

The remains of these animals (in America) occur in the most superficial deposits—those of the mastodon ordinarily in peat-bogs, swamps, and the shell-marl of small lakes and ponds. The bones of the mammoth occur also in the peat-bogs, but most generally in the river-gravel deposits. Professor Winchell remarks that he has himself "seen the bones of the mastodon and elephant embedded in peat, at depths so shallow that he could readily believe the animals to have occupied the country during its possession by the Indians." Sir C. Lyell states that "in 1845 no less than six skeletons

[1] American Naturalist, vol. v. pp. 606, 607.

of the mastodon were found in Warren County, New Jersey, six feet below the surface, by a farmer who was digging out the rich mud from a small pond which he had drained."[1]

Dr. Kage, quoted by Professor Hall ("Natural History of New York," vol. iv.), says: "Cuvier states that the mastodons discovered near the Great Osage River were almost all found in a vertical position, as if the animals had merely sunk in the mud. Since that time many others have been found in swamps, a short distance beneath the surface (frequently some of the bones appearing above the soil), in an erect position, conveying the perfect impression that the animal (probably in search of food) had wandered into a swamp, and, unable to extricate himself, had died on the spot. . . . We think it probable that the mastodon was alive in this country at a period when its surface was not materially different from its actual state, and that he may have existed contemporaneously with man."

"Of the very recent existence of this animal," Professor Hall continues, "there seems to be no doubt; the marl-beds and muck swamps where these remains occur are the most recent of all superficial accumulations (indeed, they are now forming)." This report on the geology of New York was made in 1843.

"That they [the mastodon and mammoth] were exterminated by the arrows of the Indian hunters is the first idea presented to the mind of almost every naturalist."[2]

[1] Student's Elements, p. 160.
[2] A Second Visit to United States, by Lyell, vol. i. p. 349.

It is well known that in parts of the United States, Wisconsin especially, there are found artificial mounds representing animals, such as the bear, the deer, the fox, birds, reptiles, &c. In Grant County, in that State,

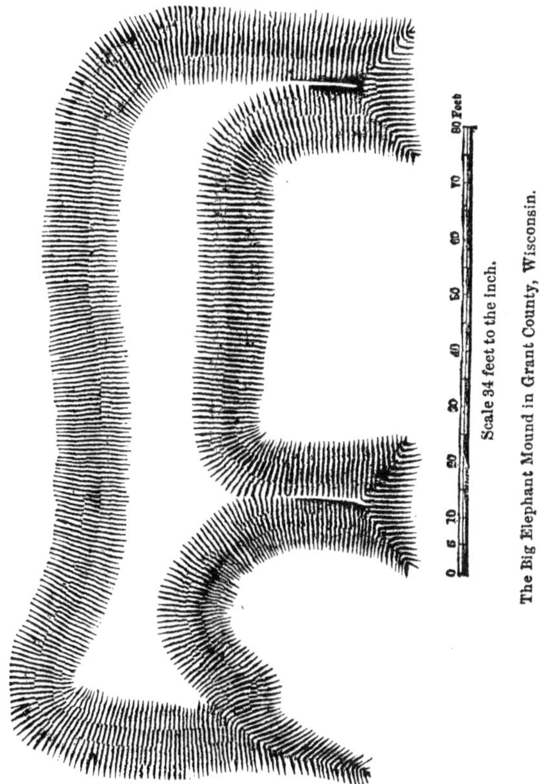

The Big Elephant Mound in Grant County, Wisconsin.

there exists a mound called " The Big Elephant Mound " (see the annexed cut), which there is good reason to believe was intended to represent the mastodon or mammoth. Such, at least, is the opinion of Dr. Hoy of Racine, Wisconsin, well known in scientific circles. The mound is described as "accurately representing a great elephant."

The cut which we give is taken from the Smithsonian Report for 1872.

There is nothing improbable in the supposition that the mastodon was known to the Mound-Builders.[1] It is of some significance that a tradition of this animal (or the mammoth) existed among the Indians. Mr. Jefferson, in his "Notes on Virginia," mentions it as existing among the Delawares, and a French officer, by the name of Fabri, mentions it, in 1748, in a letter to Buffon, as prevailing among the Canada tribes.

We find it again among the Indians of Ohio. In vol. v. of the "Natural History of New York," Professor Mather states that Mr. Stickney, for many years the

[1] It has been suggested that the trunk of the elephant is delineated on the monuments represented in Stephens' work on Central America; but we are unable to see any good grounds for the opinion. There are, however, some cuts (one of which we reproduce) in M. de Waldeck's work on Mexico and Yucatan which unquestionably represent the head of the elephant, and which were taken from the ruins at Palenque.

"It is Clavigero, I believe," says Bradford in his 'American Antiquities,' "who says that a tomb in the city of Mexico, upon being opened, was found to contain the bones of an entire mammoth, the sepulchre appearing to have been formed expressly for their reception. Mr. Latrobe relates that during the prosecution of some excavations near the city of Tezcuco, one of the ancient roads or causeways was discovered, and on one side, only three feet below the surface, in what may have been the ditch of the road, there lay the entire skeleton of a mastodon. It bore every appearance of having been coeval with the period when the road was used" (see Latrobe's Rambles in Mexico, vol. i. p. 145). "American Antiquities," by Bradford, p. 226.

Indian agent of the United States for the tribes north-west of the Ohio, informed him that "particular persons in every nation were selected as the repositories of their history and traditions; that these persons had others who were younger, selected for this purpose continually, and repeatedly instructed in those things which were handed down from generation to generation; and that there was a tradition among the Indians of the existence of the mastodon; that they were often seen; that they fed on the boughs of a species of lime-tree; and that they did not lie down, but leaned against a tree to sleep."[1]

In a paper read before the Troy meeting of the American Association for the Advancement of Science, Professor Winchell, speaking of the Post-Tertiary phenomena of Michigan, remarked: "These beds are the sites of ancient lakelets slowly filled up by the accumulation of sediment. They enclose numerous remains of the mastodon and mammoth. These are sometimes found so near the surface, that one could believe they have been buried within 500 or 1000 years. What is, perhaps, most interesting of all, is the discovery of flint implements in a similar situation. The arrow-head was found seven feet beneath the surface, in a ditch excavated in the southern part of ~~Washetow~~ County. The mastodon remains found near Tecumseh, but a few miles distant, lay but two and a half feet beneath the surface. The Adrian mastodon was buried about three feet."[2]

Professor Barton, of the University of Pennsylvania,

[1] Nat. Hist. of New York, Part iv., Geology, by W. W. Mather, p. 44.
[2] Annual Scientific Discovery, 1871, p. 239.

discovered the bones of a mastodon at the depth of six feet in the soil; and in the middle of the bones, and in a sac which was probably the stomach of the animal, he found a mass of vegetable matter, partly bruised, and composed of leaves and branches, among which was a rush belonging to a species now common in Virginia. Professor Mitchell, in his Appendix to "Cuvier's Theory" (p. 376), referring to another skeleton found in Goshen County, New York, states that "beneath the bones, and immediately around them, was a stratum of coarse vegetable stems and films, resembling chopped straw, or rather drift stuff of the sea."

In a monograph by Dr. J. C. Warren, of Boston, on the Newburgh mastodon, after mentioning that it was found just beneath the soil, in a small pool of water, the writer gives an analysis of the bones as follows:—

"A portion of the epiphysis of a vertebral bone yielded, when dried at 300° F.—

Animal matter (bone cartilage)	27·73
Bone earth (phosphate and carbonate of lime) and phosphate of iron	72·27
	100·00

"A portion of the bone, with cancelli, yielded, by drying, a little above 210° F.—

Water	6
Bone earth (phosphate and carbonate of lime) and phosphate of iron	64
Bone cartilage[1]	30
	100

[1] "Nothing," says Sir C. Lyell, "is more remarkable than the large proportion of animal matter in the tusks, teeth, and bones of many of these extinct mammalia, amounting in some instances to 27 per

In South America the bones of the megatherium are found under circumstances similar to those which characterise the occurrence of the mastodon and mammoth bones in North America. Colonel Hamilton Smith, in his "Natural History of the Human Species," states that they are met with in Brazil on or near the surface. "How could they," he asks, "have resisted disintegration four or five thousand years, subjected to a tropical sun and periodical rains? Yet they often occur on the surface, and the bones of the pelvis have been used for temporary fireplaces by the aborigines wandering on the pampas beyond the memory of man."

Few traces of the mammoth have been found in the peat deposits of Europe; but in a few instances such remains have been found in this formation, and must, therefore, be regarded as indicating the survival of this animal to the Neolithic Period.

Two perfect heads of the mammoth were brought to light by excavations made for a railway in 1847 at Holyhead. They were found in a bed of peat three feet thick, which passes into the sea, and is exposed at low-water. Sir Charles Lyell remarks on this discovery that "it is not improbable that this mammoth survived most of the lost species which were its contemporaries in what has been called the Cavern Period." He thinks

cent.; so that when all the earthy ingredients are removed by acids, the form of the bone remains as perfect, and the mass of animal matter is almost as firm, as in a recent bone subjected to similar treatment."—Second Visit to United States, vol. ii. p. 364. And Dr. Foster observes to the same purport: "Mastodon bones, however, of a much older date, recovered from peat swamps, have so much of the gelatinous matter yet remaining in them, that a nourishing soup might be extracted."—Prehistoric Races of the United States, p. 370.

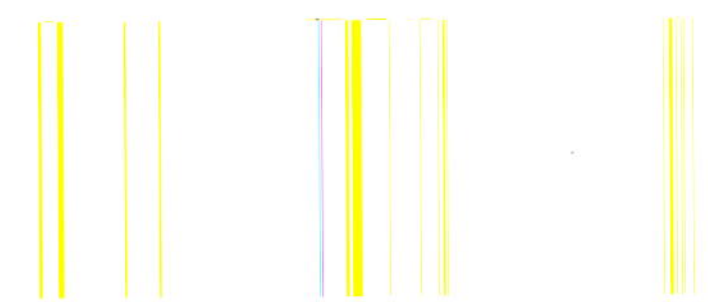

that it probably belonged to "a date intervening between the era of the lake-dwellings and that of the oldest epoch to which man has yet been traced back."[1] But this admission is fatal to Sir Charles's theory: the survival of one mammoth to the period of the lake-dwellings, or to a date nearly approaching that period, destroys the presumption of a remote antiquity for the Palæolithic Age.

The molar tooth of another mammoth (as we also learn from Lyell) was taken a few years before 1851 from a submerged forest, containing much peaty matter, at Torquay. It was stained with the black colour of the peat, and retained much of its animal matter. In this forest-bed, which is partly on the shore, and partly under the sea, bones of the red deer, wild hog, horse, and *Bos longifrons* (a neolithic fauna) occur in the peat. There was among the bones an antler of the red deer, fashioned into a tool for piercing.[2]

The Rev. D. Fisher found the remains of a mammoth, which had been overwhelmed in a bog, near Colchester, the small bones of the feet being in their natural position; and in an address before the Geological Society (reported in "The Geologist" for 1864, p. 64), Mr. G. S. Poole stated that the remains of the mammoth and the tichorine rhinoceros had been found in a peat-moss above thóse of man and fragments of pottery.

Another instance of the discovery of the bones of the mammoth in the European peat occurred at Sprottau,

[1] Principles, vol. i. p. 545.
[2] Ibid., p. 544.

in Silesia, the remains being associated with *Pinus sylvestris*.[1]

It is proper to recall in this connection the fresh condition of the reindeer bones from the palæolithic station of Solutré.

Having considered the circumstances under which the remains of the mammoth occur in America and Europe, we shall now refer to the extraordinary preservation of the tusks, bones, and flesh of this animal and of the rhinoceros in Siberia.

Throughout all the lowland of this country, from the borders of Europe to the extreme point nearest America, and from latitude 56° to the Arctic Ocean, the bones of the mammoth are found in countless numbers, and great quantities of fossil ivory have been collected from the banks of the Irtish, the Obi, the Yenisei, and the Lena, in so fresh a state as to constitute an important article of commerce. Similarly, in Northern Russia, as we are told by Tilesius, thousands of tusks have been collected and used in turning. In the east of Siberia, where the cold is intense, and the ground frozen to the depth of 500 feet, *entire carcasses* of the mammoth and rhinoceros are found in an almost perfect state of preservation. In 1772, Pallas obtained, in latitude 64°, from the banks of the Wiljui, a tributary of the Lena, the carcass of a rhinoceros (*tichorinus*) taken from the sand in which it had been frozen. This carcass emitted an odour like putrid flesh, part of the skin being covered with a short crisp wool and with

[1] Meyer, Palæol. 540, cited in Quarterly Review, vol. cxiv. p. 378.

black and gray hairs. Professor Brandt, in 1844, extracted from the cavities in the molar teeth of this skeleton a small quantity of half-chewed pine leaves and coniferous wood. And the blood vessels in the interior of the head appeared filled, even to the capillary vessels, with coagulated blood, which in many places still retained its original red colour.

Thirty years later, that is, in 1803, Mr. Adams obtained the entire carcass of a mammoth much farther to the north, on the banks of the Lena, in latitude 70°, "and so perfectly had the carcass been preserved, that the flesh, as it lay, was devoured by wolves and dogs."

In 1846, during a flood of the Indigirka, a young Russian engineer witnessed the *disentombment* of a mammoth.

Another carcass was found on the Tas, between the Obi and Yenisei, with some parts of the flesh in so perfect a state that the ball of the eye is now preserved in the Museum of Moscow. (See Addenda.)

The remains of the mammoth are also found in great abundance in Alaska, and it was stated not long since that parties from San Francisco were entering on the business of collecting from this region fossil ivory on a large scale.

All of these facts render it not only probable, but almost certain, that the mammoth, the mastodon, the megatherium, and the tichorine rhinoceros were living at a very recent date. The same evidences present themselves alike in North America, South America, Europe, and Siberia. The remains are found on the surface, and in a more or less well-preserved condition. Is it credible that the mastodon remains obtained in all parts of the United States, a few feet in the peat, possess a high antiquity? Is it credible that the carcasses of the mammoth found in Siberia are 100,000 or 200,000 years old? *Credat Judæus Apella.*

The Cave-Lion.—This member of the so-called extinct fauna M. Gervais, Mr. Boyd Dawkins, and Mr. Sandford regard as only a variety of the existing lion—identical in species—in which opinion Sir John Lubbock seems to concur.

The lion, as we have mentioned, survived in Europe to the time of Aristotle, who states that it was found in his day in the country between the Acheloüs and the Nestus. It is mentioned by Herodotus that they attacked the elephants in the army of Xerxes, near the mountains of Thessaly. This does not appear extraordinary when we remember that they seem in ancient times to have been common in Palestine, and that they are occasionally seen even now in the valley of the Euphrates. History does not inform us of the presence of the lion in South-Western Europe, but both the lion and the hyæna abound even to-day in Morocco, and the presumption is natural that they were formerly familiar to the ancient Iberians. (See Addenda.)

"There is not one solitary character," says Mr. Boyd Dawkins, "by which the animal [the cave-lion] can be distinguished from the living lion."[1]

The Cave-Hyæna.—Of this animal Sir John Lubbock observes, that "it is now regarded as scarcely distin-

[1] Popular Science Review for 1869, p. 153.

guishable from the *Hyæna crocuta* or spotted hyæna of South Africa."[1] (See Addenda.)

The striped hyæna, as we have just stated, is still common in Morocco and in Abyssinia; as we are told by the traveller Bruce, "they were a plague, both in the city and in the field, and, I think, surpassed the sheep in number."

The Cave-Bear.—We have mentioned that the great bear of the caves has been found in Italy with relics of the Neolithic Age, and that its bones have been found in the peat-bogs of Denmark. It is only necessary to add that M. Gervais identifies it with the common brown bear of Europe.

The Cave-Horse, described by Professor Owen as belonging to a different race from the present horse, there is every reason to believe, only differed as the wild horse differs from the domesticated horse. At the meeting of the Philadelphia Academy of Sciences in 1865, Dr. Leidy exhibited the bones and teeth of the so-called "Fossil Horse" of America from California, and observed that "most of the remains, among them including an entire skull, are unchanged in appearance, and are undistinguishable from the corresponding parts of the mustang or recent Indian horse of the West, though taken from auriferous gravel a considerable depth from the surface." To the same effect the author of the paper in "Aus der Natur" (1867), entitled "Man as the Contemporary of the Mammoth and Reindeer," remarks that the palæolithic horse "has been improperly regarded as differing from that of the present day."

[1] Prehistoric Times, p. 285.

Wild horses inhabited different countries in Europe down to a recent date. Ekkehard mentions them as existing in Switzerland in the eleventh century; Lucas David alludes to them as existing in Russia in 1240; and Herberstein, at the beginning of the seventeenth century, speaks of the bisons, the uri, the elks, and the wild horses of Lithuania.

Professor Owen has described the horse found in the palæolithic caves as the *Equus spelæus*, misled, no doubt, by its small size, to distinguish it from the present species; but there exists in Virginia, on Chincoteague Island, off the coast of the county of Accomac, a diminutive pony, which seems to have acquired its proportions by a sojourn of a few centuries on that island; and taken from the island, as we are told, the breed rapidly assimilates to the ordinary horse. These ponies were certainly not on Chincoteague Island at the beginning of the seventeenth century. The Indian tradition was that a ship was wrecked on this coast, and the crew rescued and taken to the mainland, while some horses on board were left on the island. Thus a race of ponies has been created in less than three centuries.

It is well known that on the Shetland Isles the oxen, sheep, and swine, as well as the horses, are diminutive.

We have thus fulfilled our promise, and proved the recent existence of the so-called palæolithic fauna. The cave-horse, the cave-bear, the cave-lion, the cave-hyæna are still living; the cave-lion is mentioned historically in Europe a few centuries before our era; wild horses scoured the plains of Russia a few centuries ago; the urus survived to the sixteenth century; the aurochs still survives; the reindeer is traced down to the beginning of our era—and even to the twelfth century; the great elk survived equally as late; the mastodon, and the mammoth, and the woolly rhinoceros are found under circumstances that imply their existence a few thousand years ago.

One circumstance which deceived the palæontologists in this matter was the great size of the carnivores whose remains were found in the caves. But it is well ascertained now that, even in the Neolithic Age, the denizens of the forest attained larger proportions than those of their degenerate successors of the present day. The deer were larger, as well as the bears and the lions. In Scotland there are traditions of deer, in the days of Fionn, far larger than any now existing. Ossian, according to this tradition, spoke of "deer as big as horses."

The fact is explained by the Rev. W. Greenwell, in his article on Grime's Graves in the "Journal of the Ethnological Society of London" for 1870. The bones of the red deer, he says, found in these Neolithic Flint Mines, are much larger than the present Scotch red deer. "This might," he remarks, "have been expected, because the red deer of Scotland is now confined to a small area in Britain, and that of a high elevation and almost entirely devoid of vegetation, except ling and very coarse grasses, whereas in pre-historic times, and much later, it occupied a country abounding in wood, and possessing a much more varied and nutritious flora than is now possessed by the Highlands of Scotland."[1]

Where the conditions have not greatly changed, as in Russia and Siberia, the brown bear is found to have equalled in size the cave-bear, as is proved by specimens of that animal (of recent date) preserved in the Zoological and Zootomical Museums of St. Petersburg.[2]

The fact mentioned a page or two back with regard to the Chincoteague ponies and the animals of the Shetland Islands, illustrates the powerful influence exerted on the development of an animal by its *habitat* and environment.

[1] Journal of the Ethnological Society, London, vol. ii. p. 428. M. Brandt speaks to the same purport. According to him, in the degree that different countries experience gradual changes in the constitution of their soil and in their vegetation, the animal species offer corresponding modifications adapting them to the new conditions. He cites in proof the *Cervus elephas* (red deer), contrasting the giant stags of Mandchouria and Southern Siberia with those met with in the forests of Europe. See Matériaux, December 1872, p. 536.

At the meeting of the *Société d'Anthropologie*, May 15, 1873, M. Roujou exhibited a fragment of the horn of a stag found at Choisy-le-Roi, of Neolithic Age, which measured twenty-two centimetres in circumference above the first antler. He also showed a tusk of a wild boar of the same epoch, nine centimetres in circumference. Matériaux, 7e, 8e, et 9e liv., 1873, p. 389.

[2] Matériaux, December 1872, p. 530.

CHAPTER XII.

THE EXTINCT ANIMALS—CONTINUED.

The elephant, rhinoceros, lion, cameleopard, &c., found on north-western coast of Africa at the beginning of the Christian Era—Remains of African animals in Spain—Evidence from Egyptian and Assyrian monuments of the existence of elephants in Assyria down to twelfth century before Christ—The black obelisk in the British Museum—Elephants in Northern China about 1200 A.D.—Represented in ancient bronze relic from Siberia—The hippopotamus—Recent presence of, in Lower Egypt and Algeria, and in India—Represented in Trojan stratum at Hissarlik—The Behemoth of the Book of Job—The crocodile in Palestine.

WE have not yet quite done with this head. On it hinges the whole controversy. We desire to add a few words to what we have said about the extinction of the elephant and the rhinoceros.

Anthropologists seem to have forgotten, or to have overlooked the fact, that the elephant and the rhinoceros, eighteen centuries ago (like the lion and hyæna at the present day), inhabited the north-west regions of Africa, ranging in the vicinity of the Straits of Gibraltar. This important fact is attested by Herodotus, Pliny, and Strabo, and in the fragment entitled the "Voyage of Hanno." From these authorities it is evident that these animals, as well as the cameleopard, the lion, the bear, and the crocodile, during the period 500 B.C. to 100 A.D., were common in the African territory contiguous to the south-western parts of Europe. The testimony in regard to the rhinoceros is given only by Strabo, but all of the other writers mention the elephant.

The "Voyage of Hanno" is an official report of an exploration of discovery made to the Carthagenian Government about 500 B.C., by the commander of a large fleet fitted out for the examination and colonisation of the western coast of Africa. "When we had passed the Pillars on our voyage," says this account, "we came to Cape Soleis [Cantin], a promontory of Libya. . . . Here elephants and a great number of other wild animals were feeding."[1]

Herodotus, writing a little later, and giving an account of the Western Libyans, says, the country "is mountainous, and full of wood, and abounding with wild beasts; here are found serpents of an enormous size, lions, elephants, bears, asps, and asses with horns."[2]

Pliny, in his "Natural History," says: "Africa produces elephants beyond the deserts of Syrtes, and in Mauretania," and, he adds, in "Ethiopia."[3]

The statement of Strabo is, that in Mauretania the country produces large serpents, elephants, antelopes, buffaloes, lions, &c.; and again, that it is said "the rivers of Mauretania contain crocodiles: above Mauretania, on the exterior sea, in the country of the Western Ethiopians, as they are called, Iphicrates says that cameleopards are bred here, and elephants, and the animals called *rhizeis*, which are in shape like bulls, but in manner of living, size, and strength in fighting,

[1] Quoted in Lenormant's History of the East, trans., vol. ii. p. 263.
[2] Book iv. § 191.
[3] Book viii. chap. 11.

resemble elephants." He states once more that the Mauretanians wear the skins of lions, panthers, &c., and that the foot-soldiers present as shields the skins of elephants.[1]

Elsewhere we have called attention to the discovery of the bones of the African elephant in Spain and Sicily. If the animal was on the African side of the Gibraltar Straits at the beginning of our era, and his bones occur in recent deposits in Spain, is it strange if a hardier species lived a few thousand years ago in Central and Western Europe?

The complete skeleton of a rhinoceros was found in one of the Gibraltar caves or fissures by Captain Brome. Is this remarkable if the rhinoceros lived in Mauretania eighteen hundred or two thousand years ago? In these same (Neolithic) Gibraltar caves occurred bones of the African lion, the leopard, lynx, serval, spotted hyæna, and ibex.

The monkey, as we know, is still found on the rock of Gibraltar [in Europe].

But we have further to remark on the presence of the *cameleopard* and the *crocodile* in the region now known as Barbary, at the beginning of our era.

Such facts all go to show that we have very inadequate ideas on the subject of the extermination of

[1] Strabo, Book xvii., chap. 3, § 4, 5, 7, 8.

This is the source from which the Carthagenians obtained the elephants which figure so conspicuously in their wars, and it was from the same quarter that the Romans obtained the elephants and the hippopotami for the amphitheatre.

At a very early period the elephant, doubtless, was found in Egypt, which is to be inferred from the name of the island of Elephantine, below the first cataract, in hieroglyphics A B = "Elephant-land."

wild animals. Why should Europe be exempt from the wild animals that characterise the other continents? and why should their bones in association with human bones remand the human race to a remote antiquity?

In ancient times the elephant was to be found in another quarter, where his presence has been little suspected—we refer to the valley of the Tigris.

Sir Gardiner Wilkinson long ago, in his "Manners and Customs of the Ancient Egyptians," reproduced an Egyptian tomb at Qournah, of the time of Thothmes III., on which the Asiatic elephant is represented as part of the tribute brought to that prince by a people from the region of the Upper Euphrates, called the *Rutennu* (about 1500 B.C.). That the elephant should have existed in Northern Syria seemed so inadmissible, that Egyptologists explained that "the Rutens extended their rule to the very confines of India"[1]—about 1500 miles distant! (See Addenda.)

The elephant and the rhinoceros are delineated on another monument—the famous black obelisk (in the British Museum) of Shalmaneser II. (B.C. 858–823). In this instance a people called the *Muzri*, from the region of the head waters of the Tigris (Kurdistan), are represented bringing tribute to the Assyrian monarch — among other offerings, the rhinoceros, the elephant, and the camel. They also bear on their shoulders elephants' tusks.

It was deemed impossible in this case also that the elephant and the rhinoceros should have existed in Western Asia, and accordingly it was again suggested

[1] Birch's Egypt, p. 99.

that they must have come from India, whence they had been procured by the Muzri "through traffic."[1]

In a previous work,[2] we remarked that this was incredible, and expressed the opinion that the animals in question appertained to the country of the Muzri, as was farther evidenced by the "elephants' tusks" which constituted part of the tribute.

The point seems to be now settled by the stele of Amenemheb, a military officer of the time of Thothmes III., and Amenophis II., which has been translated by M. Chabas. This inscription, says M. Lenormant, "establishes the fact that in the time of Thothmes III. the elephant was hunted in the neighbourhood of Nineveh," of which there can be little doubt, as the statement is explicit that King Thothmes "captured one hundred and twenty elephants for the sake of their tusks in the country of Nineveh."[3]

At a yet later period the elephant was still hunted on the Tigris. For this we have the testimony of an Assyrian inscription. On the prism of Tiglathpileser I. (about 1120 B.C.), also preserved in London, this monarch recites one of his hunting exploits: "I killed ten full-grown elephants in the country of Harran, and on the banks of the Khabour [an affluent of the Tigris] I captured four elephants alive. I brought their skins and their tusks, with the living elephants, to my city of Alassar [Asshur]."[4] The worthy successor of Nimrod

[1] Smith's Ancient History of the East, p. 290.

[2] The Recent Origin of Man.

[3] Comptes Rendus de l'Academie des Inscriptions et Belles-Lettres, 1873, pp. 157, 165, 178.

[4] Ibid., p. 182.

goes on to state that he had destroyed 920 lions—120 of which were laid dead at his feet, and 800 captured with his chariots of war.

There is another inscription to the same effect on the broken obelisk of Tiglathpileser I., also in London, and which dates from an epoch later than his reign.[1]

Later than the twelfth century B.C., we do not read on the Assyrian tablets of the chase of the elephant in Assyria, although ivory is constantly referred to in enumerating the royal treasures. The animal had by this time been driven farther north and east, and in the ninth century B.C., the Muzri bring their tribute of ivory and the living elephant and rhinoceros, then become unfamiliar to the eyes of the Assyrian monarchs.[2]

Is it by any means improbable that the elephant was living at this time—or a thousand years before this —in Siberia?

If we pass from 1200 B.C. to about 1200 A.D., we find Marco Polo stating that Kublai-Kaan, the Grand Khan of Tatary, had 5000 elephants.[3] (See Addenda.)

[1] "With his bow he overcame elephants, he captured elephants alive, which he transported to his capital of Asshur."

[2] Many specimens of ivory have been obtained from the excavations at Nimrud. Part of an ivory staff and several entire elephants' tusks were discovered by Mr. Layard (Nim. and Bab. p. 195).

Mr. Birch informs us that in the time of Thothmes III., "ivory was imported in considerable quantities into Egypt, either in boats laden with ivory and ebony from Ethiopia, or else in tusks and cups from the Rutennu" [Assyria]. Transactions of Royal Society of Literature, iii., second series.

The walls of the palace of Menelaus, described by Homer, are panelled with ivory; the Chaldee paraphrase on Genesis xlix. 33 represents Jacob's bedstead as made of ivory; and, as we shall see, the elephant is delineated on one of the objects obtained by Dr. Schliemann from Mycenæ.

[3] Marco Polo's Travels, Bohn's edition, p. 202.

Was the wild elephant in Northern China in the twelfth century of our era? It is probable, and yet it is barely *possible* that the Tatar king had brought these 5000 elephants from his province of Yunnan on the frontiers of Birmah.

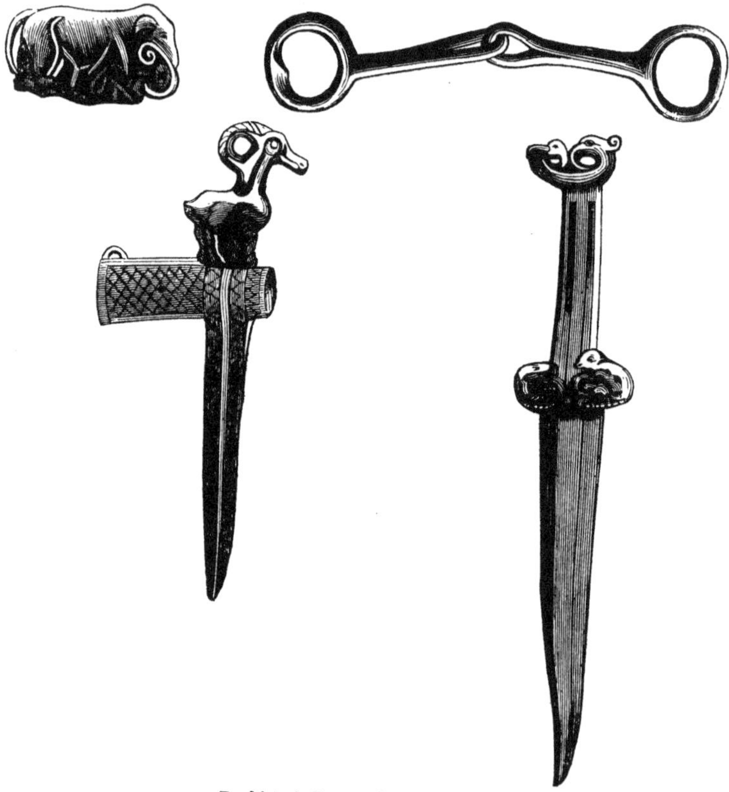

Pre-historic Bronzes from Siberia.

A number of pre-historic bronzes were obtained about 1872 near Krasnojarsk, in Southern Siberia, by M. Lapatine, a Russian engineer, an account of which was published in "Matériaux pour l'Histoire de l'Homme" for 1873. These bronzes, we are told, differ entirely from the utensils or weapons in use among the Tatars, and have nothing in common with the classic forms, or with those of the pre-historic epochs of Europe; nor are they Chinese, or Hindoo.

Similar objects are found in the Kurgans, or Strangers' Graves, which occur in great numbers on the banks of the Yenisei. Certain animals are represented on some of these bronzes from Krasnojarsk, and among them we find one which appears to be an elephant.

The *Hippopotamus* is now confined to Central and Southern Africa, but in ancient times it abounded in Lower Egypt, and as late as the year 1600 the traveller Zerenghi killed two of them near Damietta. Its bones (*H. amphibius*) have also been found in the river Chelif, in Algeria.

It was found in India in the time of Alexander the Great, as is attested by the letter of Alexander to Aristotle, and by Onesicritus and other ancient authors.[1]

Dr. Falconer tells us, in his "Palæontological Memoirs,"[2] that he was informed by Raja Radhakanta Derva, the eminent Indian scholar, that the hippopotamus of India is referred to under names of great antiquity, significant of "*Jala-Hasti*," "Water-Elephant," or "Living in the Water." This inference, he says, is confirmed by the opinion of Henry Colebrooke and H. H. Wilson.

It is equally interesting to find that the hippopo-

[1] See Buffon's Natural History, vol. vii. p. 453. London, 1812.

[2] Vol. ii. pp. 573–80.

tamus lived on the shores of the Hellespont in the twelfth century B.C. This has been proved by a vessel of pottery, bearing the form of this animal, discovered in the bed above the Trojan bed, at Hissarlik, by Dr. Schliemann. There is no trace of Egyptian influence in these relic beds, and the pottery appears to have been manufactured on the spot. But if the hippopotamus lived at this time in the Troad, it must have existed also in Thrace. (See Addenda.)

This discovery throws unexpected light on the passage in the Book of Job describing Behemoth, which is now generally supposed to signify the hippopotamus. But why should a writer, addressing the inhabitants of Syria or Palestine, select for the purposes of illustration an animal with which they were not acquainted, dwelling minutely on its habits and peculiarities? The author, it is suggested, had visited Egypt; but his readers had not, and his allusions would have been lost on them unless Behemoth was an object with which they were familiar.

The same is true of his description of the *leviathan* or the *crocodile*, which doubtless lived at that day in the Asiatic rivers running into the Mediterranean, for several of the older writers state that the crocodile yet inhabits the Nhar Zurka, a river of Samaria, flowing westward through the valley of Sharon; and the Rev. J. G. Wood, in his "Bible Animals," informs us that a crocodile eight feet long has been recently captured in this stream.[1]

[1] Page 519. It is not improbable that the Asiatic crocodile is referred to in Psalm civ. 26, and Isaiah xxvii. 1.

Pliny speaks of the crocodile "at the mouth of the Nile." Nat. Hist., viii. 25. It is not seen now below Minzeh.

With regard to the hippopotamus,[1] the language of Job seems to be sufficiently explicit as to his *habitat:* "Behold, he drinketh up a river, and hasteth not; he trusteth that he can draw up *Jordan* into his mouth." Heretofore the critics, who assumed that the hippopotamus of the Nile must have been in the writer's mind, have explained away the word *Jordan.*

It appears to us that the considerations presented in this and the preceding chapter completely destroy the argument for the antiquity of man drawn from the extinct animals.

NOTE.—The presence of the rhinoceros in Syria at a recent date seems to be established by the discovery of the bones of this animal by Dr. Fraas, in association with the bones of the ox, the bison, the bear, the goat, and the sheep, in the grottoes of the Libanus. This interesting fact was announced by Dr. Fraas at the Congress of German Anthropologists held in August 1876 at Jena.

---

[1] We have not thought it worth while to discuss the question whether the behemoth of Job is really the hippopotamus; we may remark, however, that despite the opinion now most generally prevailing on the subject, our own opinion leans rather to the elephant. How can the expressions, "He curveth his tail like a cedar," "his Maker hath furnished him with his weapon," and "his nose pierceth through snares," apply to the hippopotamus? They may apply to the trunk and the tusks of the elephant.

CHAPTER XIII.

RECENT CHANGES IN PHYSICAL GEOGRAPHY.

The argument for the antiquity of the Palæolithic Age from the physical changes on the surface of the earth since that epoch—They imply a movement of several hundred feet in the crust of the earth—But this does not necessarily involve a great lapse of time—Such movements common to the Glacial Age, and to be expected in a modified form in the Post-Glacial Period—The Palæolithic Flood—Elevations and subsidences of the land have continued since the Palæolithic Age—In analogy with the history of the Tertiary Age—Earthquakes—Volcanic convulsions in the region of the Rocky Mountains and in India—Secular movements of the land—In Sweden, in Scotland, South of England, Hanover, &c.; Puzzuoli, Crete, Cagliari; Texas, New Jersey, Nova Scotia, &c.; Chili, Peru; Australia, China, Siberia, Nova Zembla—Elevation of 200 feet at Uddevalla since Glacial Period—Remarkable instance at Södertalje—The Island of Möen—Coast of Norway.

THE next point to be considered is the alleged changes which have taken place in the crust of the earth since the date of the palæolithic river-gravels. It is alleged that caves inhabited by man during the Palæolithic Period, and which were then swept by rivers, now stand unconnected with the existing lines of drainage, and elevated far above the streams of the adjacent valleys; as, for example, Brixham Cave, on the coast of Devonshire, and King Arthur's Cave, in the peninsula of Gower, Glamorganshire. On the south coasts of England the gravel in which the worked flints occur is 100 feet above the level of the sea; and, as has been previously noticed, the gravel deposit is found at the same elevation on the opposite coasts of France. Sir Charles Lyell was particularly impressed with the presentation which characterises the gravel on the Hampshire coast; he remarks that it constitutes a plateau, or table-land, along the coast, intersected by the river-valleys of the small streams of the Southampton, the Avon, the Stone, &c., all of which have been excavated laterally through the gravel plateau since the Palæolithic Age.

We are farther told, that when man first appeared in England that region was united to the Continent—the land standing higher—that the bed of the North Sea between England and Holland was a great undulating plain, traversed from south to north by a mighty river, which united the waters of the Thames and the Rhine into a common trunk, and discharged itself into the Northern Ocean. The rivers of the south coast of England united with the Seine and the Somme, and ran westward into the Atlantic. The continuity of the Mediterranean was interrupted by at least one bridge of land between Europe and Africa.

Sunken forests, running out into the sea, are observed on the east coasts of Scotland and England, as well as along the coasts of Brittany, Normandy, and the Channel Islands. Incredible numbers of the teeth and bones of the mammoth, rhinoceros, reindeer, horse, and other animals, are dredged up by the fishermen in the German Ocean, and have been likewise obtained from the English Channel—pointing to the occupancy of this submerged region by these animals during the Quaternary Period. Such are the facts—admitted by us to be, in substance, correctly stated.[1]

Taking the most extreme view of the case, conceding that the British Islands, as represented, were, at the date of the Palæolithic Age, joined by a broad tract of country to France and Holland, we would remark that the British Channel and this part of the North Sea are quite shallow. "An elevation of from twenty to thirty fathoms would," says Professor Geikie, "drain nearly all of the German Ocean between England and the Continent, and twenty fathoms more would lay dry the same sea between Scotland and Denmark."

A subsidence of 150 feet would, therefore, have let the waves of the sea roll in between the British Islands and Holland. The probability, however, is that the subsidence was greater than this, and that there was then a partial re-elevation.

We do not think that a movement to this extent in the crust of the earth, especially in North Europe, need be held to involve a great lapse of time.

It is recognised among geologists that the Glacial Age was especially a period of unrest, characterised by repeated and alternating elevations and subsidences of the land. There are evidences that England, Scotland, and Ireland were submerged at this period to the height of 1200 feet; and at Moel Tryfan, in Wales,

[1] We do not accept Sir C. Lyell's view of the gravel "plateau" of the Hampshire coast; and we have seen no proof that England and the Continent were united during the human period: this last may be true; it is by no means improbable; we only say that we think it has been rather assumed than established. The mammoth ranged over the now submerged plain of the North Sea; but man may not at that time have reached Northern Europe.

fifty-seven species of marine shells in stratified sand and gravel, overlying the boulder drift, were obtained by Sir C. Lyell and the Rev. W. S. Symonds, at the height of 1390 feet. Some of the Scandinavian geologists—and Mr. James Geikie is inclined to agree with them—believe that that region was submerged to the height of 2000 feet; and the region of the Alps sank, according to M. Morlot, 1000 feet; according to Charpentier, 3000 feet. Oscillations in the level of the land, moreover, in all probability took place, the land, after having been covered by the sea, rising again to be again submerged, and again re-elevated, how often it is impossible to say.[1]

The close of the Glacial Age was followed by a period of comparative repose, and this marks the advent of man in Western Europe. It was then that the palæolithic hunters settled in the valleys of the Thames and the Somme, and dwelt in the caves of Périgord and the basin of the Meuse. The land had been re-elevated; England, as we have intimated, being probably united to the Continent.

But stability had not been entirely restored to the crust of the earth; the land in the North of Europe sank again, and the Palæolithic Flood—due partly to the waves of the sea, and partly, no doubt, to the copious rainfall which Mr. Tylor denominates the Pluvial Period—overwhelmed the habitations of the contemporaries of the mammoth.

[1] During the Pleistocene Period (to use the present English term for the Quaternary Period of the French geologists) the basin of the Mediterranean sank 3000 feet, and the region of the Sahara (the former basin of an inland African Sea) was elevated 3000 feet.

The land rose again, but not to its former elevation. The extent of this movement cannot be accurately defined; we may suppose, however, that the downward and upward movements amounted together to some hundreds of feet, possibly 500. As the land in Scotland and Sweden is still rising, the process of re-elevation may have proceeded continuously down to the present time.

The fact that there was a *Flood*—a flood which, in the opinion of M. Dupont, overtook the dwellers in the valley of the Lesse, implies that the inundated regions were overflowed *suddenly*. The great volume of the loess in the valley of the Rhine, and the great mass of gravel in the basin of the Somme, the Thames, and such rivers, leads to the same conclusion. To the same effect we have pointed out that M. Belgrand argues the rapid transition from the great rivers of the Palæolithic to the smaller rivers of the present age, from the formation of the peat in the Seine valley.[1]

The subsidence of the waters was doubtless consummated as rapidly as M. Belgrand suggests, in consequence of a diminution of the rainfall, and a rapid re-elevation of the land. It does not follow that the entire movement of re-elevation was consummated at once; as we have remarked, a slow secular movement of elevation, in addition, may have continued to the present time, interrupted, no doubt, by new movements of depression, but on the whole the upward movement prevailing.

[1] The sudden disappearance of the palæolithic fauna is another link in the chain of evidence.

There is nothing at all strange in a rapid subsidence and re-elevation of the land in Northern Europe at the close of the Glacial Age. On the contrary, the geological history of the Glacial Age leads us to *expect* that the unstable conditions which characterised that period would, before they ceased entirely, re-manifest themselves in a modified degree in the Palæolithic Period. It was the last murmur of the angry elements before the wintry sun of the Quaternary Period should greet with the face of April the inauguration of Man.

Nor were these great movements of the crust of the earth peculiar to the Quaternary Period. M. Elie de Beaumont refers the elevation of the Western Alps, including Mont Blanc, to the close of the Miocene Epoch, and that of the Eastern Alps, along the Bernese Oberland, to the close of the Pliocene.

There was a general rise of the continental area of Asia after the Secondary Age. The occurrence of nummulitic limestones in the Himalaya Mountains at the height of 16,000 feet above the sea, shows that this great range has been lifted up 16,000 feet since the Eocene seas covered the elevated plateau of Thibet and Central Asia. The same marine shells are found from Burmah to Eastern Bengal—from Scinde along Baluchistan to the Himalaya—and again, in Persia, along the Caspian Sea, in Syria, in Asia Minor, and in Egypt—showing that all this vast area was under the sea in the Tertiary Age. The Suliman range of mountains in Eastern Afghanistan has been elevated since the elevation of the districts mentioned. Indeed, nearly the whole continent of Asia was under water in the Tertiary Age—the northern portion thereof having been elevated in the Miocene and Quaternary Periods.

The fauna of the Miocene strata of Greece show that during that period there were vast grassy plains in the place of the present broken and mountainous surface, and these plains were probably united with Asia Minor, spreading over the present area where the deep Ægean Sea with its numerous islands now rolls.

The Carpathians in Hungary and Transylvania, as well as the Apennines, were elevated about the same time.

The loftiest peaks of the mountains of the north-west in the United States, according to Hayden, were beneath the waters of the ocean at "a very recent period;" and Professor Alexander Agassiz, in his recent trip to Peru, observed extensive saline basins at the height of 7000 feet, and noticed in Lake Titicaca a salt-water genus of amphipod crustaceans at the elevation of nearly 13,000 feet.

We propose to show that these movements of the crust of the earth have continued since the Tertiary and Quaternary Periods, and in some instances exhibit a very marked character.

Humboldt tells us that on the 14th of September 1759, the mountain of Jorullo in Mexico was seen to rise from a level plain to a height of 1681 feet—which proves that *Force* as well as *Time* is an element in geological action.

The earthquake at Lisbon was felt on the North

American lakes and the coasts of Sweden—over an area four times the extent of Europe.

According to Chinese and Japanese accounts, several volcanic mountains have risen from the bed of the sea on the coasts of Japan and Corea in historical times. In the year 1007 a roar of thunder announced the appearance of the volcano of Toinmoura on the south of Corea, and after seven days a mountain four leagues in circumference towered up to the height of 1000 feet.

For the effects of earthquakes in modifying the physical geography of different regions, we may refer also to the convulsion in the Mississippi Valley in 1812; to the earthquake of Cutch in India in 1819; and to that in New Zealand in 1823.

This action, of course, is paroxysmal, but paroxysmal action has given form to the vast region east and west of the Rocky Mountains in the United States. The geologist who should follow in the track of Professor Hayden's "Exploration of the Territories," would probably relinquish his belief in Uniformitarianism, and demand more energetic forces than Sir Charles Lyell's two-and-a-half feet per century for the elevation of a coast. The surface-phenomena of this region are, says Professor Hayden, "only the dim departing evidences of a series of events which once were performed here on a scale that almost baffles human conception." The evidences of volcanic action, commencing in the later Miocene or earlier Pliocene Epoch, and continuing down "to the commencement of the present period"—the existing geysers and hot springs "being the faint departing remnants of these once terrific forces"—point to something which must be described by a broader word than *earthquake*: it was a fiery convulsion which extended east and west of the Rocky Mountains, and over the whole Pacific slope, and altered the whole face of the country from the headwaters of the Yellowstone to the valley of the Rio Grande and the Gulf of California. The most recent effect of this volcanic activity was the basaltic outflow, which, by way of illustration, may be seen in the Great Snake River basin (100 miles wide by 175 miles long), or in the valley of the Rio Grande for 130 miles southwards from the Conejos River, covering the country like a blanket. The upheavals, the depressions, the inundations, the erosion, the ice-action, the subterranean throes, of which Idaho, Montana, Oregon, Washington, Wyoming, Utah, Nevada, Colorado, New Mexico, Arizona, and California were the theatre, seem to have been without a parallel elsewhere, if we may judge by the marks which the storm has left. As to the date of these events, Professor Hayden observes: "The lake-deposits are certainly of very moderate date, at least as late as, and perhaps later than the Pliocene. Upon this rests a huge bed of drift, which was deposited still later, and then comes the outflow of basalt."

"As I have frequently said," he again remarks, "the effusion of the basalt is a modern event, probably occurring, for the most part, near the commencement of our present period, after the entire surface reached nearly or quite the present elevation." "The hot-springs, which are now slowly dying out, are, of course, the last of this series of events."[1]

In California, says a writer in the "Encyclopædia Britannica," the volcanic outflow is of Pliocene date. The coast range of mountains, he observes, have been much disturbed, and in part elevated, during the most recent Geological Epoch, as large masses of Pliocene are found in various localities to have been turned up on edge; but in the Sierra, he adds, the volcanic activity seems to have been more general, and to have continued to a later date than in the Coast Range.

While the western part of the continent of North America was passing through these convulsions, evidently connected with them, beginning in the Miocene Period, and continued or renewed in the Post-Pliocene Epoch, India was the theatre of very similar disturbances. The outflow of trap, commencing on the southern line of the Vindhya and Aravulli ranges, covers in Central India an area of 200,000 square miles, and has in some places a thickness of 4000 feet.

These volcanic disturbances, as we have intimated, are hardly spent yet in North America—as the Yellowstone Geysers, and innumerable others, as well as the frequent earthquake shocks in California, testify—and as the mountain of Jorullo testifies. In South America the Volcanic Epoch has embraced within its devasta-

[1] United States Geological Survey of Montana, Idaho, &c., 1871, pp. 30, 42, 48; and the volume for 1872, pp. 35, 36, 43, 44, 51. See also "Explorations and Surveys West of the One Hundredth Meridian," in charge of Lieutenant George M. Wheeler, United States, America. Vol. iii., Geology, 1875, p. 525.

tions the crowded thoroughfares of civilised man, and the earthquake is as familiar to the Peruvian as the avalanche is to the peasant of the Alps.

Let us pass to those elevations or subsidences of the land which appear to be unconnected with volcanic action, and which have occurred since the Palæolithic Age. The examples might be indefinitely multiplied, but we shall select only a few of the most striking. The crust of the earth is never at rest; movements of upheaval or subsidence are in progress in all parts of the world at present, as they have been in the past.

Sweden.—At the northern extremity of the Gulf of Bothnia, the continent is emerging at the rate of five feet three inches per century, while the terminal point of Scania, on the south, is gradually being buried under the waters of the Baltic, as is proved by the submerged forests. Several streets of the towns of Trelleborg, Ystad, and Malmö have disappeared, the last having sunk five feet two inches since the observations made by Linnæus. The Baltic Mediterranean communicated at a recent period with the North Sea by a wide channel, the deepest depressions of which are now occupied by the lakes Mälar, Hjelmar, and Wenern. Considerable heaps of oyster-shells, says M. Reclus, are found in several places on the heights which command these great lakes, and the celebrated kjökken-möddings of the Danish islands are in great part composed of oyster-shells. The oyster will not live in water containing less than sixteen or seventeen parts in one-thousand of salt; but the Baltic Sea, into which its tributaries bring a large quantity of fresh water, does not contain more than five parts in one-thousand of salt; and yet the heaps of oyster-shells on its shores prove that the Baltic and the inland lakes were once as salt as the North Sea. This former saltness of these lakes and the Baltic Sea was communicated by means of a former strait occupying the depressions in which the Swedish engineers dug out the Trolhätta Canal, and which at that time connected the North Sea with the Baltic. When the sluices of this work were being constructed, there were also found, at the height of forty feet above the Cattegat, various marine remains mingled with the relics of human industry, such as boats, and anchors, and piles.

These facts are a vindication of the name Scandinavia—the Island of Scand—and explain why the ancient writers describe this peninsula as an island.

This geological change has occurred since the beginning of the Neolithic Age—since the formation of the shell-mounds on the Danish coasts. In one of these, and one containing stone implements of the very rudest type, it will be remembered objects of bronze were found. The change has, in fact, occurred *since the Bronze Age.*

Sir Charles Lyell suggests that the upward movement of the Swedish coast was a uniform one, and equalled about two and a half feet per century. But the movement is not "uniform," and M. Bravais has, moreover, shown that at Altenfjord the lines of erosion are not parallel, but that while the upper bank of Altenfjord has risen at its eastern end 219 feet, at the entrance of the bay it has risen only ninety-one feet.

The movement is irregular in a particular locality, and is sometimes accelerated and sometimes retarded.[1]

Scotland.—In the neighbourhood of Edinburgh the beach has been elevated twenty-five feet since the Roman Period. Fragments of Roman pottery, along with bones apparently of deer, and littoral shells, have been found at this height on the shore at Leith. There is a similar presentation at Inveresk, a few miles below Edinburgh; and again at Cramond, at the mouth of the Almond, above Edinburgh, the old Roman quays of Alaterva have been lifted up some twenty feet or more, and thrown back far from the shore.

The foundations of old Roman docks are observed, again, several miles up a small stream near Falkirk. Twenty miles above Falkirk, and seven above Stirling, in Blair-Drummond Moss, not many years since, the remains of a whale, and a rude harpoon of horn with a wooden handle, an oaken quern, a wooden wheel, and flint arrow-heads, were found. In the neighbourhood of Falkirk, in 1821, an ancient canoe was found at the depth of thirty feet below the surface of the carse or alluvium. In the carse, below Stirling, an iron anchor was found. This carse is about twenty-five feet above high-water mark.

On the western coast, more than twenty canoes have been dug out of the flat lands along the banks of the Clyde. Five of them lay buried under the streets of Glasgow, one of which contained marine shells. Twelve

[1] In the present century, near Morup, on the coast of Sweden, a stone observed by Bexell in 1816 had, in the summer of 1871, receded 120 feet from the shore.—Academy, March 1, 1872.

others were found about 100 or 125 yards back from the river, at the average depth of about nineteen feet, or seven feet above high-water mark; but a few of them were buried only four or five feet, and, consequently, more than twenty feet above the sea-level. Some of these canoes were rudely hewn out of a single trunk, but others "were cut beautifully smooth, evidently with metallic tools." Two of them were built of planks, and elaborately constructed—the planks having been fastened to the ribs partly with oaken pins, "and partly with what must have been square nails of some kind of metal." In one of the canoes a beautiful celt of greenstone was found; "in the bottom of another was found," says Sir C. Lyell, whose account we are following, "a plug of cork, which could only have come from the latitudes of Spain, Southern France, or Italy.[1] And, remarkable to tell, although the fact is not mentioned by Sir Charles, the canoe in which the cork plug was found was "a large rude one hollowed out of the trunk of an oak."[2]

The upheaval of the beach of the Firth of Forth, since the time of the Romans, has been 26½ feet, or 0·195 inches a year; but since 1810 this rate has increased to 0·546 inches in a year.

England and the Baltic Region.—The coasts of the South of England, of Cornwall, of Yorkshire, as well as those of Brittany and Normandy, and those of Hanover, present submerged forests and submarine peat-mosses. On the coast of Schleswig, at the bottom of the port of

[1] Antiquity of Man. p. 52.
[2] Professor W. King in the "Christian Observer" for May 1863.

Husum, there was discovered, in the midst of a forest of birches, *a tomb of the Age of Stone.* According to John Paton, Denmark and Schleswig-Holstein have lost, since the year 1240, one-eighteenth of their territory.

Submerged forests fringe the coasts of Pomerania and Eastern Prussia. On the point of Samland the church of St. Adalbert, built at the close of the fifteenth century, some four and a half miles from the sea, is now only one hundred paces from the beach.

Italy.—The movements of elevation and subsidence at Puzzuoli, on the Bay of Baiæ, is familiar to geological students. Sir C. Lyell reaches the conclusion, that "since the beginning of the Christian era the relative level of land and sea has changed twice," and that "each movement, both of elevation and subsidence, has exceeded twenty feet." At one point on the coast the elevation has exceeded thirty feet.

The town of Conca, once situated near the mouth of the Crustummio, has been entirely under the sea for some centuries. And at Trieste, pavements may be seen under the sea.

Near Cagliari, in the south of Sardinia, ancient pottery, mixed with modern sea-shells, was found at the height of nearly 300 feet.

Crete.—On the island of Crete, at the western extremity, there are ancient ports now twenty-five feet above the sea, while at its eastern extremity buried cities may be seen beneath the waves.

North America.—On the western side of the Atlantic,

the shores of the Bay of Matagorda, on the coast of Texas, have risen from eleven to twenty-two inches from 1845 to 1863. Along the coast of New Jersey the sea has encroached, within sixty years, upon the sites of former habitations, and entire forests have been prostrated by the inundation. The north side of Nova Scotia is sinking, while the south is rising. The city of Louisburg, on the island of Cape Breton, was in the eighteenth century the stronghold of France in America; but the rock on which the brave General Wolfe landed has now disappeared, and the sea flows within the walls of the city.

South America.—On the coasts of Chili the evidences of upheaval are very manifest. Here the coast was not raised by any uniform movement; there seem to have been intervals of comparative repose.

On the Isle of Chiloe Darwin found heaps of modern shells at a height of 347 feet. On the north of Conception, several lines of level, cut out by the waves during the present period, are found at an elevation of 600 to 1000 feet; while near Valparaiso these levels are no less than 1295 feet above the sea. Darwin ascertained that at Valparaiso, during the seventeen years between 1817 and 1834, the ground had risen ten feet seven inches, or about seven and a half inches a year.

In front of Arica, on the coast of Peru, the sea has receded 165 yards in forty years. In front of Callao, on the island of San Lorenzo, at a height of eighty-five feet above the sea, Darwin discovered, in a bed of modern shells, roots of sea-weed, bones of birds, ears of maize, plaited reeds, and some cotton thread, almost entirely decomposed,—the relics of human industry almost exactly resembling those observed in the *huacas* or burial-places of the ancient Peruvians.

Australia.—If we pass to Australia, we learn from the "Transactions of the Philosophical Institute of Victoria," that in twelve months the bottom of Hobson's Bay rose four inches; that the beach at Williamstown, which five years before was covered by the tide, was at the date of the statement covered with a green vegetation, and was occupied by tents and houses. Flinder's soundings are no longer reliable, for where he found ten fathoms of water, there were then but seven. The railway between Adelaide City and the port rose four inches in the year after it was opened. The conclusion drawn from these facts is, that for some time a rise of four inches per annum has been going on.[1]

Asia.—China presents extraordinary alterations in its physical geography. We may mention, though it does not come strictly under the subject we are discussing, the wanderings of the Yellow River. Instead of emptying into the Yellow Sea, as it did twenty-five years ago, it now empties into the Gulf of Pecheli—more than 380 miles in a straight line from its former mouth. Cities that were built on its delta plain are now far removed from the sea. Putai, which is said to have been, in the year 220 B.C., one li (one-third of a mile) from the sea-shore, in A.D. 1740 was 140 li inland (nearly fifty miles).

[1] Chambers's Journal, 1860, article on "Progress of Science."

In the description of China compiled by Du Halde from the diaries of the Jesuit missionaries, who, between 1708 and 1717, mapped out the Chinese Empire, we learn that "the mountain Ki-she-shan, which formerly was united to the territory of Yungping-fu, is now 500 li (160 miles) distant in the sea from the city." Du Halde argues, and adduces facts to prove, that Corea and the ancient Chantsien were formerly contiguous, that the whole Gulf of Pecheli was dry land, and indeed that there was, when the Chinese abridgment of Chorography entitled Kwang-in-ki was prepared, a continuous plain from Peking to Corea. If the land in this region were raised 240 feet, this would now be the case; the Gulf of Pecheli would disappear.

The land around the Gulf of Pecheli has risen some fourteen feet in the last 250 years. If, instead of rising fourteen feet, it had subsided fourteen feet, "probably one-third of the low thickly-populated parts of China would then be beneath the sea." [1]

That Northern and Western Siberia has very recently been elevated from beneath the sea is well known. A thin coating of sand and fine clay, containing marine shells identical with those of the adjacent seas, extends over the *tundras* or mossy deserts which stretch between the Obi and the Yenisei, from latitude 60° to the sea, and between the Yenisei and Lena, from the Arctic circle to the sea. This sand and clay contains the bones of the mammoth. But at a later period probably,

[1] American Journal of Science, vol. xlv. (second series), pp. 213, 221, *et seq.*

as we gather from Chinese documents of great antiquity, the land towards the north is reported to have terminated at no great distance beyond the mountain chain of Northern Tartary. This fact is stated by Colonel Hamilton Smith, who adds in a note that the shadow of a gnomon set up in A.D. 1260, by order of Kobli-kay, Emperor of China, proves that the northern coast of North-Eastern Asia then ranged between 53° and 54° north latitude, it being now above 70°. The skeletons of whales, we are further told, have been found 800 miles up the Lena.[1]

A remarkable example of the elevation of the land is reported in "Notice," No. 89, published in the year 1874 by the Hydrographic Office, Washington, giving an account of the explorations in the northern seas, about Nova Zembla, during 1872. One of the results of these explorations was the discovery of the Gulf Stream Islands, in the exact place where the examinations of the Dutch expeditions of 1594–97 located a sandbank with eighteen fathoms of water over it, the depth of the water between it and the coast being fifty to sixty fathoms. This would indicate that the sea-bottom in that region has risen more than 110 feet in three hundred years.

UDDEVALLA AND SÖDERTELJE.

We desire now to call special attention to the following observations in Sweden, Norway, and Denmark.

[1] Natural History of the Human Species, p. 119; and Memoir read at Geographical Society, 8th February 1841; also Biblioth. Orientale d'Herbelot, t. iv. p. 171.

We learn from Sir C. Lyell[1] that in 1862 Mr. J. Gwyn Jeffreys visited Uddevalla, on the west coast of Sweden, and collected eighty-three species of shells characteristic of the Glacial Period from certain beds elevated 200 feet above the sea. "He also," continues Sir C. Lyell, "obtained evidence that a littoral and shallow-water deposit underlay the shells proper to deeper water—a fact clearly implying a depression of the bed of the sea previous to that upheaval, which has since carried up the land where the marine shells are found to the height of more than 200 feet. As to the date of this last upheaval, M. Torell has shown *that it by no means reaches back to the Glacial Period*, to which the shells above alluded to belong. Those shells, so characteristic of a cold climate, are specifically identical with those now living in the seas of Spitzbergen, ten degrees of latitude north of Uddevalla. M. Torell detected, however, at the same height of 200 feet above the sea, the remains of a marine testacea *agreeing with species now proper to the fauna of the adjacent and more temperate seas.* It appears, therefore, that the series of movements in the district under consideration consisted, first, of a depression converting the shallow water into deep sea, at a time when the cold was very severe, and then of an elevation of more than 200 feet, when the waters of the sea had acquired their present milder temperature."

We would remark on this, first, that the "depression" referred to seems to have been *rapid;* we pass at once

[1] Principles, vol. ii. p. 192.

from the shells of the shallow water to those of the deep water.

Secondly, the upheaval "by no means reaches back to the Glacial Period." The climate had become what it is now. Since this date (which, as we shall have occasion to show hereafter, is *very recent*) the land at Uddevalla has risen 200 feet.

But, again, Sir Charles Lyell gives an account of another elevation and depression of the land in Sweden, as striking as the above; we quote his own words:—

"Some phenomena in the neighbourhood of Stockholm appear to me only explicable on the supposition of the alternate rising and sinking of the ground since the country was inhabited by man. In digging a canal, in 1819, at Södertelje, about sixteen miles to the south of Stockholm, to unite Lake Mälar with the Baltic, marine strata, containing fossil shells of Baltic species, were passed through. At a depth of about sixty feet they came down upon what seems to have been a buried fishing-hut, constructed of wood, in a state of decomposition, which soon crumbled away on exposure to the air. The lowest part, however, which had stood on a level with the sea, was in a more perfect state of preservation. On the floor of this hut was a rude fireplace, consisting of a ring of stones, and within these were cinders and charred wood; on the outside lay boughs of fir, cut as with an axe, with the leaves or needles still attached. It seems impossible to explain the position of this buried hut without imagining first a subsidence to the depth of more than sixty feet, then a re-elevation. During the period of submergence, the hut must have been covered over with gravel and shelly marl, under which not only the hut but several vessels also were found, of a very antique form, and having their timbers fastened together by wooden pegs instead of nails."[1]

The actual depth at which this hut was found was sixty-four feet, and near it, as we learn from another source, lay an *iron anchor* and some *iron nails*.[2]

There has, accordingly, been a movement of 128 feet since the iron anchor was left on the bed of this sea. The shells of Baltic species point to a similarly recent date—these dwarfish shells (mussel, cockle, and other marine species) occurring, by the way, we may remark, on a raised beach near Upsala, a hundred feet above the sea, and also at Linde, 130 miles west of Stockholm, at a height of 230 feet above the sea: in other words, the land 130 miles west of Stockholm has risen 230 feet since the date of the Danish Shell-mounds, in one of the oldest of which (judging by the rudeness of the stone implements) objects of bronze were found.

THE ISLAND OF MÖEN AND NORWAY.

The other examples to which we desired particularly

[1] Principles of Geology, vol. ii. chap. xxxi. p. 187.
[2] Archiv für Anthropologie, August, 1875, s. 17.

to refer are the phenomena on the Island of Möen (Denmark), and on the coasts of Norway.

Our information again is derived from Sir C. Lyell.

The most wonderful dislocations and foldings of the cretaceous and drift strata, which Lyell states to be subsequent to the origin of the drift, occur in the north-eastern coast of this island. These contortions

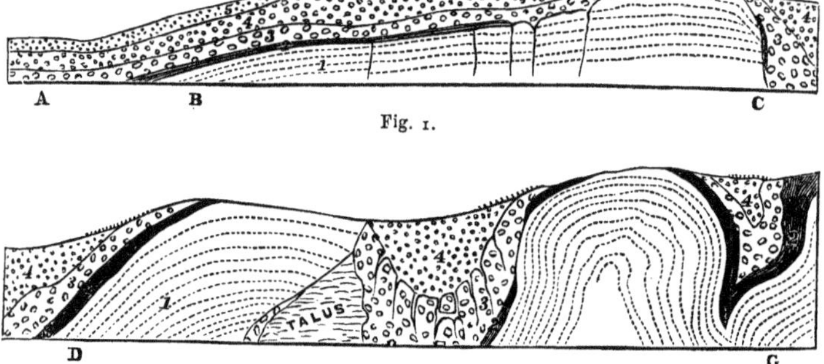

Fig. 1.

Fig. 2.

and dislocations in the strata referred to illustrate the violent energies at work in the Glacial and Post-glacial Periods, and go far to disprove the Uniformitarian theory. (See the cuts.[1])

But we desired to call attention particularly to the

[1] These cuts (from the "Antiquity of Man") represent the cliffs on the north-east coast of Möen. In the low part of the island, at A, fig. 1, the drift is horizontal; at B it changes; at C, where the cliff is 180 feet high, there is a sharp flexure. Passing to fig. 2, between D and G we observe a great fracture in the rocks, with synclinal and anticlinal folds exhibited in cliffs nearly 300 feet high.

But the most wonderful shiftings and faultings of the beds occur in the Dronningestol, part of the same cliff, where the drift becomes thoroughly entangled and mixed up with the dislocated chalks.

elevation of the land at this point since the Post-glacial Epoch. During the Glacial Period, the land (according to M. Puggaard and Sir Charles Lyell) subsided to the depth of 400 feet. After the close of this period, we are told, it was again elevated 400 feet. The Post-glacial Epoch in Denmark, as we shall see hereafter, corresponds in point of time with the Neolithic Age; and, therefore, the land on the Island of Möen has risen 400 feet since the Polished Stone Age.

The rise of land in Norway since the Glacial Epoch is yet more remarkable: Marine shells, identical with those now living a few degrees farther north in the same seas, have been observed by Professor Keilhan, of Christiana, on the south coasts of Norway, at a height of 600 feet above the sea, showing that an elevation of the coast has occurred to this extent since the close of the Glacial Age in the North of Europe. This elevation is not confined to the south coasts, but is traceable along the west coast from Cape Lindesnæs to North Cape.[1]

This has all occurred (as will appear from a future chapter) since man entered Scandinavia with implements of polished stone.

But if this be true, if such changes as these have occurred within the past few thousand years, must a change in the relative level of sea and land, no greater

[1] Lyell, Principles of Geology, eleventh edition, vol. i. chap. vii.; vol. ii. chap. xxxi.; Antiquity of Man, 4th edit., pp. 63, 64.

in extent, require us to associate a remote antiquity with the Palæolithic Age?

The Palæolithic, that is to say, the Post-glacial Age, we have already remarked, fairly inherited the commotions and perturbations of the Glacial Age; it would be strange if the disturbances of this last-named period had terminated abruptly.

CHAPTER XIV.

THE THREE AGES, AND THE RECENT USE OF STONE IMPLEMENTS.

The use of stone implements in all parts of the world down to a recent period—Co-existence of the Three Ages—Stone used along with iron, as well as bronze—Lingered in interior after metal had reached the coasts—Used by common people when the chiefs had metal—Ancient Irish—The Fennians and Æstii of Tacitus—Testimony of Cæsar—St. Jerome—Chaldæa and Assyria—Stone implements in oldest Chaldæan tombs along with metal—Egypt—Stone implements found in tombs down to Greek Period—Delineated on monuments—Found in the valley of the Nile on the surface—Troy—Stone and bronze found here together in all the relic-beds—Greece—Marathon, Mycenæ, Athens—The Etruscans—The Massagetæ ignorant of iron—Palestine—Recent use of stone in India, and in China and Japan—The Ichthyophagi—The Altai region and Africa—Mexico and Peru—The Pacific Islanders—North American Indians and the Mound-Builders—The Indians used polished and unpolished implements, the latter, in some instances, of palæolithic type—Stone implements used in North-Eastern Siberia a hundred years ago, and in Norway—No gap between the Palæolithic and Neolithic Ages—Brixham Cave—The Belgian caves—Gourdan—Grotto of Duruthy—Coast of Cheshire.

We propose to show in this and the succeeding chapter—

1. That stone and bronze have often been in use together; that bronze and iron have often been in use together; that stone and iron have often been in use together; and that all three have been in use together.

2. That stone, bronze, and iron are found together in

the Chaldæan tombs; that bronze and iron weapons (and occasionally flint) are found in the Assyrian ruins; that stone continued in use in Egypt down to the eighteenth dynasty; and that it continued to be used, together with bronze, in the Troad, down to the seventh century B.C.

3. That in India stone implements were in use in the seventh century of our era; in Japan long after the beginning of the Christian era; in China in the ninth and tenth centuries of our era; in Palestine, at a date not fixed, but apparently recent; in Ethiopia, in the fifth century before Christ; in Greece, along with iron and bronze; and that it is used at the present time in various parts of Africa along with metal; that there has been no Stone Age in Africa, or in the region of the Altai; and that iron was unknown to at least one great Scythian tribe at the beginning of our era.

4. That in America stone and bronze implements, as in the Troad, flourished together, and constituted what may be called a Stone-and-Bronze Age.

5. That the metals do not make their appearance in Western and Northern Europe until some four or five centuries before the Christian era, and that stone implements continued in use in the same regions after the Christian era.

6. That in Gaul and Britain, in Southern Germany, in Holland, in Poland, in portions of Russia, there was, properly speaking, no Bronze Period.

7. That there is no gap, as the archæologists affirm, between the Palæolithic and Neolithic Ages.

Archæologists have been compelled to admit that

stone and metal implements are found together, and they attempt to explain it by saying that the ages "lapped," or that in such cases there has been what the French call a "*remaniement*," or disturbance of the beds.

We shall show that metal and stone occur together in *innumerable* instances; we shall cite many instances where there can have been no "*remaniement*" of the beds; we shall show that iron implements occur often with stone implements, in which case the suggestion that the ages have "lapped" would imply that the Stone Age had lapped the Iron Age *across* the Bronze Age; and we shall show, finally, that stone implements continued in use down to the Merovingian epoch in France, and as late, and later, in other parts of Europe.

If stone continued in use as late as this, or as late as the Christian era, it is no answer to say that "we admit that stone may have been used long after the Stone Age," because the point is *the antiquity* of the Stone Age, and if stone was used after the Christian era, the Stone Age, pure and simple, cannot be *very far* behind.

There *was* a Stone Age in Western Europe—a period when the metals had not reached that region; we only deny the remote antiquity of that period, and negative that antiquity by showing that stone had not ceased to be used, and, in some quarters, exclusively used, after the conquest of those regions by the Romans.

The archæologists assign to the Second Stone Age in Europe an antiquity of some 6000 or 8000 years, without undertaking to say when it began. This, in their scheme, is followed by some 1500 or 2000 years of the Bronze Age.

But in the Troad it is evident that stone and bronze flourished side by side some 2500 or 3000 years ago; iron was not common among the Etruscans; and in Britain, while iron was precious two or three centuries after the Christian era (being used for ornaments), stone implements were still in use. The bronze, we are expressly told by Cæsar, was imported.

There was a difference, which is to be noted, along the coasts, and in the interior of the western and northern parts of Europe; the tribes on the coasts obtained metal from Etruscan, Phœnician, Greek, or Roman vessels, when the inland tribes relied exclusively on stone and bone.

Again, the chiefs and the rich could afford to procure metal by barter, when the poor had to content themselves with stone.

Some of the tribes were, of course, more advanced than others. Thus Tacitus informs us that the Fennians (Finns) "depend for their support on their arrows, to which, for the want of iron, they prefix a pointed bone."[1]

In the second book of his Annals the same author gives us a speech of Germanicus to his army, on the banks of the Weser, in the modern province of Hanover, in which Germanicus tells his soldiers, speaking of their enemies, that "their shields are nothing but osier twigs intertwined, or slight boards daubed over with glaring colours, while *in their foremost ranks* a few only are pro-

[1] Manners of the Germans, § 46.

vided with pikes and javelins, the rest of the army having nothing but *stakes hardened in the fire*, or weapons too short for execution." This is a description of the Chaucians, whom Tacitus represents as "beyond all question the most respectable of the Germans."

The Æstians, on the right of the Suevian (Baltic) Ocean, he tells us, were unacquainted with iron, "their usual weapon being a club."

Herodian, who wrote about 200 A.D., speaks of iron as even at that time very precious in Britain, the inhabitants, he says, "wearing iron about their bellies and necks, which they esteem as fine and rich an ornament as others do gold."

Cæsar speaks of the Cantii, or people of Kent, as following agriculture, but the tribes of the interior he represents as living on milk and flesh, and clothing themselves with skins (De Bel. Gal., v. 14). Speaking of the Germans, he tells us they wore skins, or pieces cut from the skin of the reindeer; and of the Suevi, whom he describes as the most numerous and powerful of the Germans, he states that their clothing was nothing but the skins of wild beasts, and that even this covering was so scant that a large portion of the body was exposed; and this was the case even in the coldest regions.[1]

St. Jerome, in the fourth century, describes the Attacotti, a Scottish tribe, who seem to have lived on the banks of the Clyde, as cannibals; and he informs us particularly of the parts of either sex which they esteemed the most delicate—"partorum nates et fœmi-

[1] De Bello Gallico, iv. 1; vi. 21.

narum, et papillas solere abscindere, et has solas ciborum, delicias arbitrari."

It seems to be a well-established fact that the ancient Irish were cannibals, and it is said to have been a matter "of religious observance with them to eat their parents."

As late as the twelfth century we get a glimpse of them from Giraldus Cambrensis, who states that some sailors, driven on the coast of Connaught, met two men who were naked, except that they were girded with loose belts of untanned hides of animals.

Fynes Moryson gives us a description four centuries later—in the sixteenth century.

The wild or "mere" Irish, he says, do not, as a general thing, eat bread at all. Horses dying were considered a delicate morsel. They willingly ate the shamrock. They had no tables, but ate on the grass. They slept in the open air, or in a poor house of clay. The men and women in many parts went naked all the winter, except a rag about the loins, and a loose mantle on the body. At night they lay naked in a circle about a fire, with their feet towards it.

As for the civilised Irish, he met at Cork "young maidens, stark naked, grinding corn with stones to make cakes of."[2]

What must have been the condition of Ireland two thousand or twenty-five hundred years ago? Is it not plain that, in the absence of outside influences, these people would have been still in their Stone Age in the

[1] American Journal of Science, 1872, p. 160.
[2] Itinerary, part iii. p. 156. Archæologia, vol. xii. p. 460.

sixteenth century? Is it likely that iron utensils were common in this region at the beginning of our era?

Northern Europe was only revolutionised by conquest; the Roman arms rapidly achieved what colonies, like Massilia, and a languid commerce—Phœnician, Etruscan, or Roman—had not effected. But that primitive customs and primitive implements continued in use in many districts even after the rude hand of civilisation had been laid upon them, may well be inferred when we see carts with stone wheels to-day in Palestine, while the Portuguese continue to use a farm-cart furnished with solid wooden wheels, the axles of which revolve with the wheels; and that the inhabitants of Syria, Turkey, Greece, Spain, Portugal, Southern Italy, and Algiers, have not ceased to plough their fields with a sharpened stake.

Babylonia and Assyria.—If we go back to the earliest traces of man in the East, we find in the most ancient tombs—in "the First Age," as Professor Rawlinson expresses it—of Babylonia, "knives, hatchets, arrow-heads, and other implements both of flint and bronze, . . . chains, nails, fish-hooks, &c., of the same metal, . . . leaden pipes and jars, . . . armlets, bracelets, and finger-rings of iron"—showing the contemporaneous use in the dawn of Babylonian life of stone, bronze, and iron.[1]

[1] Smith's Ancient History of the East, vol. i. p. 210. Rawlinson's Five Great Monarchies, second edition, i. pp. 119, 120.

The flint and stone axes, knives, and hammers, says Professor Rawlinson, "abound in the true Chaldæan mounds," and they are, he tells us, exceedingly rude—(i. 95).

This fact is worth a volume of speculation. Why should those people, possessing a written language, erecting great temples, considerably advanced in agriculture and commerce, make use of stone knives and hatchets? Is it strange that in Western Europe stone should have been in use? and that at a time when iron was precious in Babylonia there should have been no metal on the coasts of Hampshire?

Had these Chaldæans passed through a Bronze Age? If so, where are the monuments? Had they passed, yet earlier than that, through a Stone Age? There are no traces.

But this is not all. Stress is laid on the form and "type" of the stone implements. There is, we are told, a "palæolithic" type. We are informed, however, by Mr. Tylor that "Mr. J. E. Taylor, British consul at Basrah, obtained some years ago from the sun-dried brick mound of Abu Shahrein, in Southern Babylonia, two taper-pointed instruments of chipped flint, which, to judge from a cast of one of them, would be passed without hesitation as Drift implements." M. Louis Lartet, in his work on the "Geology of Palestine," mentions also the finding of a flint implement in Babylonia (now in the British Museum), "in every respect similar to the finest types from our Quaternary beds of the Somme and those of England."

It was doubtless this palæolithic type which re-appeared in Europe when some of the ruder Turanian tribes migrated in that direction.

At a much later date, amid the ruins of the palace of Sargon (B.C. 715), at Khorsabad, near Nineveh, M. Place, in raising the great stone bulls, which weighed 15,000 kilogrammes, and which had never been disturbed, found beneath them a number of bracelets and necklaces of cornelian, emerald, amethyst, &c., and with these products of an advanced civilisation—some of them with Phœnician inscriptions—two knives of black flint.[1]

Layard found both bronze and iron spear-heads at Nimrud,[2] and Rawlinson tells us that the Assyrian arrow-heads are either of bronze or iron, while a few stone arrow-heads are also found.[3]

Persia.—The arrow-heads of this people, we are told by Rawlinson, are (like the Assyrian) either bronze or iron.[4]

Egypt.—If we pass to the other great contemporaneous monarchy of that primeval time, we find the stone axe constituting one of the hieroglyphical characters, and represented, as are also stone sickles, knives, and arrow-heads, on the bas-reliefs of Beni-Hassan (of the twelfth dynasty), and on other Egyptian monuments.[5] Stone-tipped arrows, as we learn from Sir Gardiner Wilkinson, continued to be used in Egypt "after the eighteenth dynasty."

Knives of flint have been repeatedly found placed in the mummy-cases of the Egyptian tombs. The fact was mentioned long ago by Rosellini, the companion of Champollion. Prism-shaped implements of flint were

[1] Congrès d'Anthrop. et d'Archéol., 1867, p. 118.
[2] Nineveh and Babylon, p. 194.
[3] Five Ancient Monarchies, second edition, vol. i. p. 454.
[4] Ibid., vol. iii. p. 175.
[5] Archiv für Anthrop., Januar, 1876, s. 250.

also obtained from the tombs by Passalacqua and Lepsius.[1] At the meeting of the Institut Égyptien, May 19, 1870, M. Mariette-Bey expressed himself as follows: "The fact that there are found [in Egypt] flints worked by the hand of man cannot be contested. . . . The flints in question do not go back to the age of stone. They belong to the Historic Age of Egypt, and their great number on the plateau of Biban-el-Molouk simply shows that, in all historic antiquity, even to the time of the Ptolemies, flints were worked on this plateau on account of its proximity to Thebes, in order to supply the demand for instruments of this material, which have been always used. There are found in the tombs of Gournah, which date back to the eleventh dynasty, arrows in great numbers, made of reeds, and armed either with a point of wood hardened in the fire, or with the bone of a fish, or with a point of flint. Sometimes also the point is formed from the reed itself; but what is particularly remarkable is that in all antiquity *pharaonique*, and even in the tombs of the Greek epoch, there are no arrow-heads of metal. The Greek tombs alone yield points of bronze.[2]

"With the flints they made knife-blades, which they fixed in handles of wood. One finds them even among the Greeks. These knives are also sometimes *toothed* in the form of a saw.

. . . .

"In a geological point of view, it remains to be ob-

[1] There is a lance-head in the Berlin Museum.

[2] Observe that *bronze* was used for weapons in Egypt as late as 300 B.C.; and such a fact plays havoc with the Bronze Age.

served that the worked flints up to this time have always been found on the surface of the soil. This is their position on the plateau of Biban-el-Molouk; in another *gisement* situated at the entrance of the same valley; in another, which is found at the entrance to the turquoise-mines of Mount Sinai; and in a fourth at Monfalont. It is the same with those which are found in the quarries. But, on the contrary, if the flints were truly pre-historic, it would happen that we would encounter them in certain beds in the interior of the soil, which has never yet occurred."[1]

Troy.—If we take another step, and come down to about 1500–700 B.C., on the Asiatic side of the Hellespont we find, in the relic-beds at Hissarlik, stone and bronze continuously used together, from the lowest (pre-Trojan) bed up to the Historic or Greek bed (700 B.C.) To this we shall recur. At present we desire only to note the fact that stone implements abound in these successive beds, and in the lowest beds, along with the remains of an advanced civilisation, beautiful pottery and elegant jewellery.

In the third bed, counting upwards from the bottom —that is, in the bed immediately succeeding the Trojan bed—the implements are almost exclusively of stone.

Greece.—The same facts are presented in Greece. Axes and knives of flint, obsidian, and compact quartz have been taken from the tombs of Attica, Bœotia, Achaia, and the Cyclades.[2] Arrow-heads of flint and

[1] Reported in Matériaux, 1874, p. 17.

[2] Lenormant, Ancient History of the East, trans., vol. i. p. 33.

of bronze were found on the plains of Marathon,[1] and the only question is whether they belonged to the Greeks or the Persians. "Small knives and saws of flint are found in numbers," says Dr. Schliemann, "in the Acropolis of Athens, and they appear to have been used up to a very late period."[2] The excavations of this same distinguished archæologist at Mycenæ have revealed, in the beds of what may be called the Middle Period—that is, later than the so-called tombs of Agamemnon and his companions—stone, bronze, and iron, in use at the same time; while those royal tombs, in which was obtained such wealth of gold, contained both bronze and flint weapons.

What was the condition of Gaul or of Britain at this time? They were in their Stone Age, of course; and the metals did not reach them, in fact, until much later. It is safe to say that these regions were five hundred years behind the coasts of Asia Minor; and if so, the introduction of the metals—even bronze—must have been late indeed. And when introduced, it was precious, and beyond the reach of the common people. Stone continued to be used, doubtless, in retired districts, long after the Christian era.

There is no trace of iron in the relic-beds at Hissarlik (excepting the surface bed); it is all bronze and stone, and the stone implements are much more numerous than the bronze (or copper) implements; and Homer is therefore right in equipping his heroes with arms of bronze rather than iron. Hesiod expressly tells

[1] Evans, Ancient Stone Implements, p. 328.
[2] Troy and its Remains, p. 274.

us that there was no such thing as iron in those ages:—

Τοῖς δ'ἦν χαλκεα μὲν τεύχη, χαλκεοι δέ τε οἶκοι
Χαλκῷ δ' εἰργάζοντο, μέλας δ' οὐκ ἔσκε σίδηρος.

Pausanias undertakes to prove this by a number of instances; and it is stated by Plutarch that when Cimon, the son of Miltiades, conveyed the bones of Theseus from the isle of Scyros to Athens, he found interred with him a sword of bronze, and a spear-head of the same metal. And Sir Gardiner Wilkinson, in his "Manners and Customs of the Ancient Egyptians," has pointed out that the offerings of iron in the temples of Greece in the early period of her history shows the value of that metal.[1]

The Etruscans.—Bronze seems to have been chiefly used for cutting implements among the Etruscans, and iron was probably rare among the Romans during the kingly period.

Ethiopia.—The Ethiopians of the Upper Nile, it is well known, had attained a high degree of civilisation centuries before the invasion of Greece by Xerxes; and yet we find the contingent of soldiers furnished by this nation towards this expedition, as we are told by Herodotus, pointing their arrows with sharpened stones instead of iron, and using antelope's horn for the heads of their javelins.[2] In the same work we are told the Libyans were dressed in skins, and had the points of their spears hardened in the fire.

The Massagetæ.—Later than this, the Massagetæ, a

[1] Vol. ii. p. 153

[2] Book vii. § 70.

powerful Scythian tribe, are described by Herodotus as using weapons of bronze. "They have both gold and brass," he tells us, "but neither iron nor silver." "Their spears, the points of their arrows, and their battle-axes are made of brass."[1] These are the people who encountered and defeated Cyrus the Great. Strabo mentions them about the beginning of our era, and confirms the statement of Herodotus, remarking that "they have abundance of gold and bronze," but "no silver, and little iron."[2]

Palestine.—The Abbé Richard examined the so-called tomb of Joshua, at Gilgal, on the banks of the Jordan, and found within great numbers of knives, saws, and fragments of flint.[3]

At the village of Bethsaour, or Beit Sahur, near Bethlehem, in Judæa, the Abbé Moretain found a number of worked flints and articles of worked bone. They were picked up on the surface of the ground, and found in certain grottoes. In one of the grottoes the Duke de Luynes found a specimen of pottery (which may be later) made on the wheel.[4]

A number of Neolithic flints were obtained also by Captain Burton from the same locality (Beit Sahur). These were found, together with human bones, in certain jug-shaped cisterns pierced in a ridge of chalky

[1] Book i. § 215. Herodotus tells us that Ariantas, a king of the Scythians, in order to number his people, levied an arrow-head from each, all of which were afterwards collected and melted into an enormous bronze vessel (iv. 81).

[2] About A.D. 180 Pausanias writes that the Sarmatians have no knowledge of iron (i. 21).

[3] Comptes Rendus de l'Acad. des Sciences, Juil.-Déc., 1871, p. 541.

[4] Matériaux, 1873, p. 179.

limestone, which are used at the present time for storing grain.

India.—At the International Congress of Archæologists at Brussels (1872), M. Leemans called attention to an ancient Buddhist temple in the island of Java, the walls of which are covered with many bas-reliefs, forming a complete illustration of the life of Buddha. This temple was erected by architects from the Continent in the seventh century of our era. On the reliefs are figured perforated flint tools furnished with handles of wood, and also pile-dwellings. These sculptures illustrate the life of India, rather than that of Java, in the seventh century, and show that pile-dwellings and stone implements were both well known at that time.

China.—It appears from the statement of Mr. E. B. Tylor, that stone weapons are still in use in some parts of China. The same writer mentions that it is stated in a Chinese work, that the inhabitants of the province of Kwang-tong, in Southern China, "find in the mountains, and among the rocks which surround it, a heavy stone, so hard that hatchets and other cutting instruments are made from it."

In the annals of the Song dynasty (A.D. 964–1279), in the life of Tchang-sun, soldiers are mentioned armed with arrows, having stone points, probably Tatars.

In the annals of Northern China, composed under the Thang dynasty (A.D. 619–907), it is said that in the country east of Fo-ni all the arrows had stone points. In these same annals mention is made of stone axes (*chi-fon*), a stone knife (*chi-t'ao*), a stone sword (*chi-kien*), and an agricultural implement of stone (*chi-jin*).

Japan.—Mr. Franks has a paper entitled "Stone Implements in Japan," in the Norwich volume (1868) of Pre-historic Archæology, in which he quotes from Dr. O. Mohnike, formerly a physician in the Dutch East-Indian Army, who presented a report on this subject to the Society of Northern Antiquaries in 1853. Dr. Mohnike states, that "though the useful metals may have been known in Japan before the commencement of our era, I believe they were first imported from China, and employed but rarely in Japan before the seventh or eighth century after Christ, when copper mines were discovered." Before this, stone was used, and perhaps until the ninth or tenth century. In the well-known Japanese historical work, "Niponki," written in 720 A.D., it is stated that in the spring of the year 27 B.C., "a ship went to Japan from Sinra in Corea, with a son of the King of Sinra on board, who brought to Japan presents for the Mikado, including spears of stone" (Siebold, French edit., liv. v. p. 138).[1]

The Ichthyophagi.—These people (to whom we have already referred), living in the time of Strabo on the north coast of the Arabian Sea, between India and Persia, knew nothing at that late period of iron, and used darts of wood hardened in the fire; but the civilisation of Southern Arabia, the great Persian Empire, the arts of India, and—separated only by the Persian

[1] See Proc. Internat. Cong. Anthrop. and Archæol., 1868, pp. 261, 262.

Gulf—the cities of the Chaldæan plain, had in turn shed their light within their borders.

The Tatars and Mongols.—From the valley of the river Kama in Eastern Russia to Lake Baikal, "there is not," says "Matériaux pour l'Histoire de l'Homme," "among the great Uralo-Altaic race the least trace of a Stone Age." Stone implements occur in the region of the Altai, but they are found in association with implements of copper.

On the other hand, iron appears to have been always rare in Southern Siberia. We have spoken of the Massagetæ, who occupied, according to Herodotus, the region east of the Caspian Sea (Turkestan and the Kirghis Steppe), and whose weapons were of bronze. They continued, as we know from Strabo, to use bronze (and to be without iron) four centuries later.

These people belonged to the great Mongol race, which under Tscenghis Khan and his successors conquered nearly the whole of Asia (including Siberia) in the twelfth and thirteenth centuries; and to these belong, no doubt, those "Strangers' Graves" which abound throughout Southern Siberia, and in which are found such numerous relics of bronze and gold. "The arms, swords, arrows, daggers, and the like, dug out of these graves," says Strahlenburg, "were not forged, but cast of copper, especially swords, which were shaped much like our bayonets" (p. 367). Iron is also found with these burials, but bronze is apparently the prevailing material.

It would appear, therefore, that in all this vast region there has been neither an Age of Stone nor an Age of

Iron down to the thirteenth century of our era. Bronze reigned supreme; and it was the same race, no doubt, which carried the use of copper and bronze into those regions of North America where the Toltecs and Aztecs (and perhaps the Mound-Builders) established their empires.

Africa.—As there is little trace of a Stone Age in the whole continent of Asia, the same may be affirmed with yet greater emphasis of the continent of Africa. We have stated on p. 41 that the Stone Age still exists in Africa, but this is only true in the loose sense that some of the African tribes still use stone implements. These, however, are used by them in conjunction with iron.

Stone implements are found in the North of Africa; but there is no evidence to show that they were used without metal. They are found in association with metal in some instances, and apart from metallic objects in some others. Of Egypt we have spoken.

In South Africa, Dr. Livingstone states that there are no flints to be found in the regions examined by him, and that there is no trace of a Stone Age. On the contrary, he found a rude furnace for smelting iron at every third or fourth village which he entered; and the iron prepared they preferred to the English, which they declared was "rotten" in comparison.[1]

He also informs us that pottery like that now used in the country was found in a bed of gravel in the delta of the Zambesi, along with bones of the hippopotamus, wild hog, buffalo, antelope, crocodile, hyæna, &c., all of

[1] Expedition to the Zambesi, pp. 561, 562.

which animals now inhabit the country. Similar remains were found again in another gravel-bed of the Zambesi in 1856, and in 1863 in the sand on the shore of Lake Nyassa. But no implements of flint occurred.[1]

As far back as we have any knowledge of the tribes of Middle and South Africa, they seem to have been acquainted with iron. There is no trace of the use of bronze for cutting implements. Iron appears to have been the metal in universal requisition in these parts of Africa, as bronze was the prevailing metal in Egypt, Babylonia, Assyria, and Northern and Central Asia. There seems to have been one uninterrupted Iron Age in Africa (south of Egypt), as there was one uninterrupted Bronze Age north of the Hindoo Koosh, the Kuenlun Mountains, and the Yellow River, and south of about 60° north latitude.

And notwithstanding the existence of this Bronze Age in Northern Asia from time immemorial, stone implements are even to this day in use among the Kamstchadales;[2] and notwithstanding the existence of this Iron Age among the Central and Southern tribes of Africa from the earliest times known to us, stone implements and implements of bone are still (along with iron) in use among the Bushmen, the Hottentots, the Damaras, the Kaffirs, and the Coast Negroes.[3]

The Canary Islands.—The inhabitants of these islands are believed to have belonged to the Berber race of Northern Africa, and were at one time no doubt ac-

[1] Expedition to the Zambesi, p. 560.
[2] Descriptive Sociology, Herbert Spencer, Asiatic Races.
[3] Ibid., African Races.

quainted with the metals; but in the fourteenth century they had only hatchets, knives, and spear-heads of obsidian, and axes of green jasper, or spears pointed with horn. And yet, we are told that, although unacquainted with iron, "they had advanced to a considerable degree of civilisation—cultivating music and poetry with success, and having a kind of hieroglyphic writing." After they were visited by the Spaniards, they made swords of pitch-pine, the edges of which were hardened in the fire, until they cut like steel.

The Mexicans and Peruvians.—If we pass now to the American continents, when they first became known to the Europeans, we find a striking resemblance to the state of things revealed to us by the excavations at Hissarlik—the absence of iron, and stone and bronze in contemporaneous use. "The tools of the Peruvians," says Mr. Prescott, "were of stone, or more frequently of copper. But the material on which they relied for the execution of their most difficult tasks was formed by combining a very small portion of tin with copper. This composition gave a hardness to the metal, which seems to have been little inferior to that of steel."[1] With these tools the Peruvian not only hewed into shape porphyry and granite, "but by patient industry accomplished works which the European would hardly have ventured to undertake."

The Mexicans had the same bronze tool, an alloy of tin and copper, and with this they cut not only metals,

[1] Conquest of Peru, vol. i. p. 152.

but, with the aid of a silicious dust, such substances as basalt, porphyry, amethysts, and emeralds.[1]

The Peruvian edifices were usually built of porphyry or granite, sometimes of brick.

Besides their bronze tools, the Mexicans, we are told, used others of *itztli*, or obsidian, a dark transparent mineral, exceedingly hard, found in abundance in their hills. They made it into knives, razors, and their serrated swords.[2]

It is for the archæologists to explain this fact, in consistence with their theory. The Stone Age is not only seen in full operation in the sixteenth century among these highly-refined and ingenious nations in America —and the inhabitants of Central America, as well as the Mexicans and Peruvians, used stone weapons—but they all used obsidian knives, swords, spear-heads, and axes along with implements of copper and bronze. At the battle in the district of Tlascala between Cortez and the Mexicans, the Indians are described as "having their naked bodies gaudily painted," and carrying "spears and darts tipped with points of transparent *itztli*, or fiery copper."[3]

If it be suggested that these people were *in transitu* from the Stone Age to the Bronze Age, we reply: But 1. It is evident (however that may be) that the Stone Age, or the use of stone for implements, does not necessarily involve any very great *antiquity;* the Stone Age may be found in recent times, and spread over two con-

[1] Conquest of Mexico, vol. i. p. 139. [2] Ibid., p. 140.
[3] Ibid., pp. 140, 441, 442.

tinents. 2. The Peruvians and Mexicans were not savages just emerging from the use of stone to that of bronze; they had made astonishing progress in architecture and in the useful and ornamental arts. The aqueducts of the Peruvians, formed of large slabs of freestone nicely adjusted together, carried for hundreds of miles through rivers and marshes, and not unfrequently tunnelled through the solid rock; their terraces constructed for the purposes of agriculture on the steep sides of the Cordilleras; the great roads which traversed the kingdom (as that, for example, from Quito to Cuzco, and thence southwards towards Chile), 1500 or 2000 miles in length, built of heavy flags of freestone, in some parts covered with a bituminous cement—conducted over pathless sierras covered with snow—with galleries cut for leagues in the living rock—the rivers spanned by bridges suspended in the air—crossing profound and broad ravines filled up with solid masonry;—which Humboldt describes as among "the greatest and most useful works ever executed by man;"—these, and the ruins of their magnificent palaces and temples, exclude, of course, the idea of the use of metal having just dawned upon the subjects of the Incas. It was an old civilisation when the Spaniards were introduced to it.

The roads of Mexico also are described as extending great distances from the capital, and as constructed, like the Roman military roads, of large squared blocks of stone. Cortez, describing the city of Mexico to Charles V., represents it as surpassing in grandeur and beauty the ancient Moorish capital of Cordova. The population of the city he estimated at 300,000, and its streets and canals were illuminated at night, he says, "by the blaze from the sacred altars of numberless teocallis that reared their pyramidal summits in the streets and squares of what Prescott fitly calls 'this city of enchantment.'"

Many of the statues, we are told, found at Otumba, Mitlan, Jochichalo, and the magnificent flower-temple of Oajaca, are sculptured in a purely classical style, whilst vases rivalling those of Egypt and Etruria have been discovered in sepulchral excavations.

If we look out from the coast of Mexico into the Pacific Ocean, a curious fact is presented to us in connection with the theory of the "Three Ages," in the island-world between America and Asia. The inhabitants of Polynesia, when first encountered by Europeans, were using "beautiful stone implements," but had no metal. We find, however, on these islands, traces of an anterior and superior population—ruins of temples and fortifications, constructed of hewn stones, as in the Marquesas Islands, Navigator's Islands, Tahiti, Hawaii, Asunsion, Strong's Island, Easter Island, and others. The inference from this is that the Stone Age on these islands *has succeeded* the Metal Age.

The North American Indians, as is well known, were in their Stone Age when the country was occupied by the European settlers. Some of the tribes of the Pacific slope are still in their Stone Age. Arrow-heads and knives of obsidian from Mexico or west of the Rocky

Mountains, and carvings in stone representing the manatee of South America or the Antilles, the jaguar, the toucan, the cougar, and the paroquet, have been found in the Ohio mounds, and obsidian, we believe, in Indian graves in Georgia, showing relations on the part of the aborigines of the Ohio Valley and the Gulf States with Mexico and South America. And if this must be accepted, the inquiry presents itself, why did not the stone-using people of the Ohio Valley or of Georgia, who procured obsidian and the carved figures of the South American animals and birds, obtain also *metal* from the same sources?

A significant circumstance as regards the distinction usually made in Europe between the Palæolithic and Neolithic Ages, is the fact that all over the United States we find stone implements belonging to the Red Indians, which show that the polished and unpolished specimens were in use at the same time, while on the surface and in the mounds, as we are told by Professor Rau, "flint implements of the European 'drift type' are by no means scarce." Professor Rau mentions particularly in this connection, that in one of the "sacrificial" mounds of Clark's work, on the North Fork of Paint Creek, Ross County, Ohio, Messrs. Squier and Davis found more than 600 oval or heart-shaped implements, clumsy and very roughly chipped, averaging six inches in length by four inches in width, which bear "a striking resemblance to the flint 'hatchets' discovered by Boucher de Perthes and Dr. Rigollet in the diluvial gravels of the valley of the Somme."[1]

[1] Smithsonian Report, 1872, pp. 398-400.

Professor Rau adds, that "there is no sufficient reason to refer the implements of this type found in North America exclusively to the Mound-Builders, as they occur on the surface, and in deposits below it, in regions where the people designated as Mound-Builders are not supposed to have left their traces."

Dr. Charles C. Abbot has described in the "American Naturalist" (March and April 1872), a number of stone implements (of Indian origin) found in the State of New Jersey, on the Delaware River, on or near the surface of the ground. Dr. Abbot expresses himself greatly surprised to find that implements differing so widely in their workmanship should occur together, and concludes that the polished specimens belonged to the Indians who lived on the Delaware River a few centuries ago, while the ruder forms he refers to the "autochthones" who inhabited the country in the Palæolithic Age. But this, of course, is purely arbitrary as there is no doubt that the implements are all of one date. The following cuts represent some of these implements, and are taken from Dr. Abbot's paper.

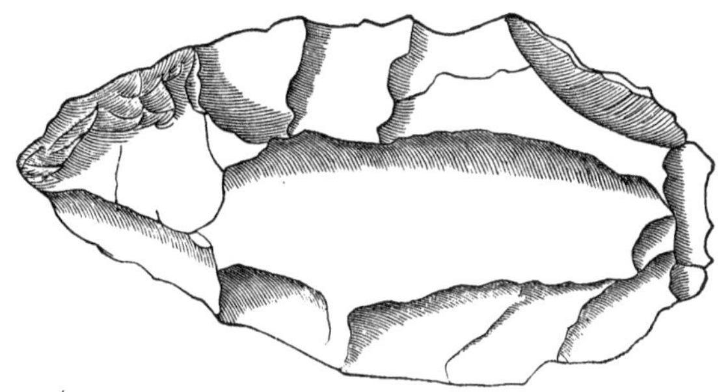

One-half natural size.

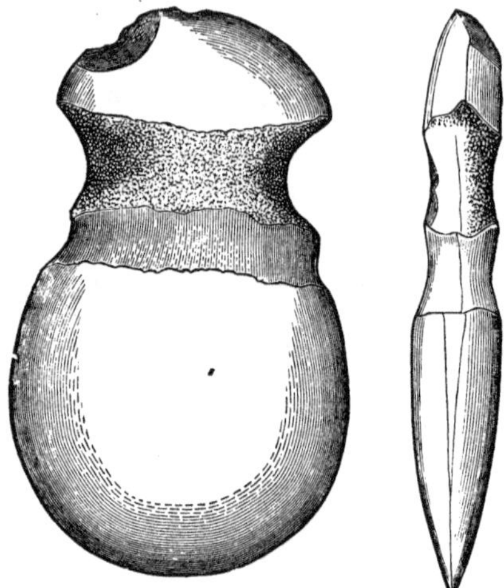

One-half natural size (side view).

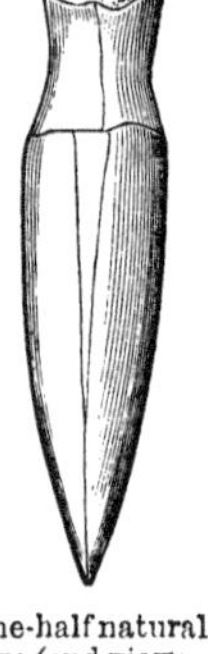

One-half natural size (end view).

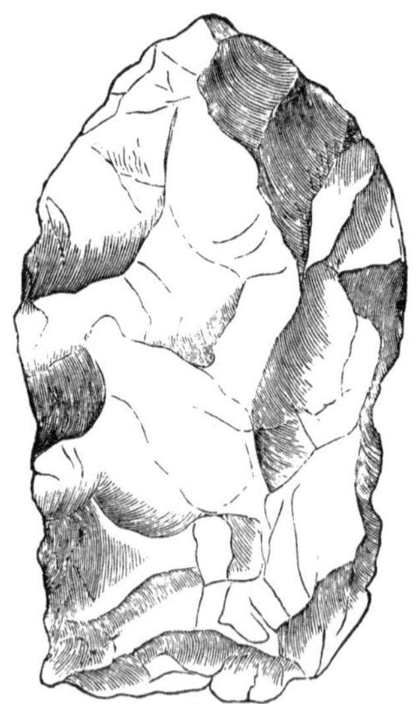

Natural size.

It is important to note the occurrence of these so-called "drift" forms among the Indian implements of

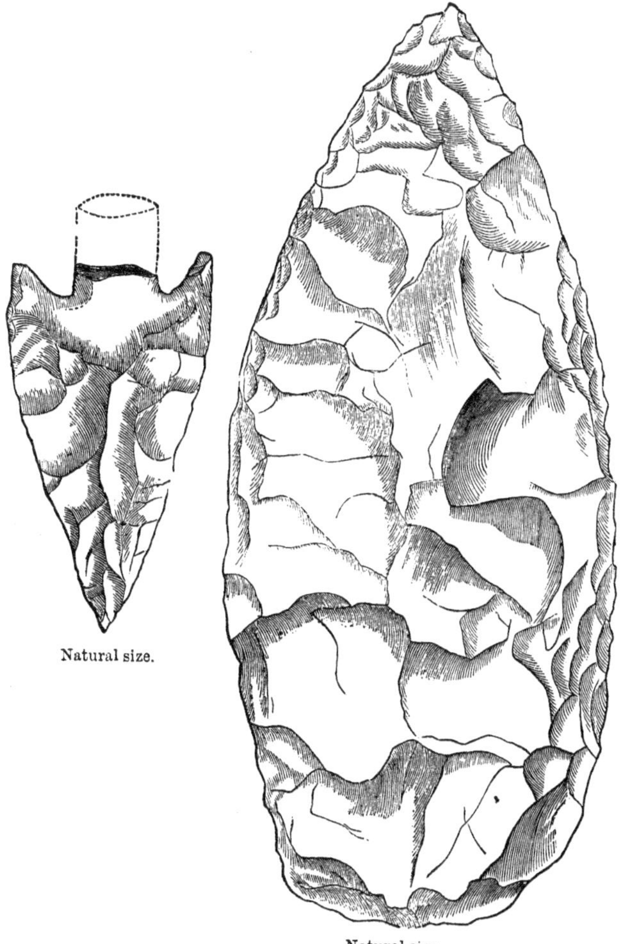

Natural size.

Natural size.

America, because the archæologists lay great stress on what they term the *palæolithic type*, and it is asserted that it is entirely different from the neolithic forms. In fact, M. de Mortillet's chronological scheme is based on the different types of implements which characterised the different periods of the Stone Age.

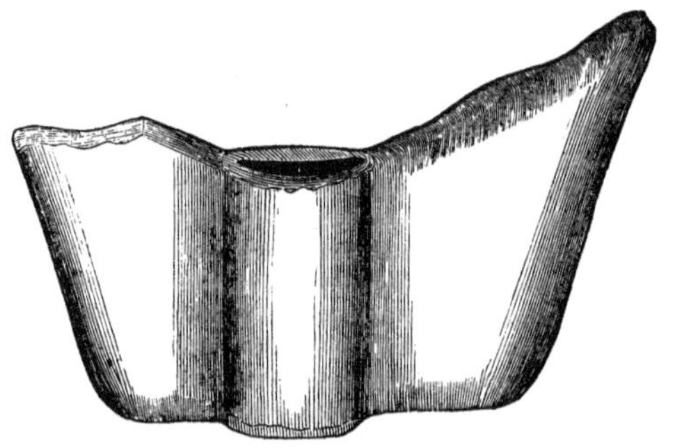

Natural size.

The American Indians and the Polynesians are by no means the only races who have been in their Stone Age within the past century. The Australians are still making use of stone, and, their implements being for the most part unpolished, they may be said to be in their Palæolithic Age.[1]

One hundred years ago, the Woguls, on the Obi River, and the Tchouktchis, in Eastern Siberia, were living *precisely* as the cave-dwellers of Europe lived in the days of the mammoth. The Tchouktchis lived in caves. They had no instruments of iron or any other metal; their knives were of stone; their pincers or punches of bone. They used the sinews of animals to sew with. Not far from these people, on the petty islands east of Kamschatka, there lived other tribes yet more

[1] Matériaux, liv. 5e et 6e, 1873, p. 279.

savage, who had no domestic animals, not even the dog.[1]

And even in Europe, the inhabitants of Scandinavia, in the province of Nordland, Norway, as was stated by Professor Rygh at the Stockholm Congress of Anthropologists (1874), "although they lived for many centuries in communication with people who used iron, remained themselves in the practice of the Stone Age till the beginning of the eighteenth century." The same was true a hundred years ago of the Finns.

NO GAP BETWEEN THE PALÆOLITHIC AND NEOLITHIC AGES.

This was touched just now in our remarks on the occurrence of implements of the palæolithic type among the Indian implements found in America. We had something to say about it also in our chapter on the caves (p. 85). These observations were based on the character of the stone implements found in the palæolithic and neolithic stations. There are, however, geological indications that there was no gap between these periods.

The peat of the Somme Valley, containing the relics of the Neolithic Age, rests directly on the implement-bearing gravels. The Palæolithic Flood closed the Palæolithic Age. We have seen that it is the opinion of M. Belgrand that the change from the large rivers of the palæolithic times to the small rivers of the present

[1] Déscription de toutes les Nations de l'Empire de Russie. St. Petersburg, 1770. Cited in Matériaux.

times was not gradual, but "must have taken place rapidly" (see chap. ix. p. 134).

The ordinary theory on this subject is, that there was a great and mysterious *lacuna* or gap between the Palæolithic and Neolithic Ages. The first is supposed to have closed 100,000 or 200,000 years ago; the latter is believed to have an antiquity not exceeding 6000 to 10,000 years. There is an interval, therefore, between them—a chasm—of one or two hundred thousand years. But how can this be, when the peat invariably follows directly upon the gravel?

At Brixham Cave, as stated by Mr. Evans, there are two beds: 1. Cave-earth, from two to thirteen feet thick, containing worked flints, and bones of the mammoth, reindeer, &c.; 2. Above this a stalagmitic floor, from one to fifteen inches thick, which contained "in and upon it" antlers of reindeer, the humerus of a bear (probably *Ursus spelæus*), and bones of the rhinoceros and other animals. There is no deposit above the stalagmite. The bear and the reindeer lie, locked in the stalagmite, on the surface. Can 100,000 years have passed without the formation of a stratum of some kind over this floor of stalagmite?

The observations of M. Dupont on the Belgian caves are, however, the most instructive on this point, because he found a distinct vein of demarcation between the Palæolithic and the Neolithic Age, the mud or loess deposit of the Franco-Belgian Deluge. Below this mud or *terre à brique* he found human skulls, the palæolithic flints, and the palæolithic animals. Above it he found a different presentation; neolithic implements and objects of metal, medals of the Roman emperors, mediæval relics, &c. The Palæolithic Age is suddenly terminated by the deluge which M. Dupont found traces of in all these caves. It is followed at once, without any intervening geological formation, by the neolithic relic-bed.

Another example of this sort is pointed out by M. Piette in his description of the cave of Gourdan, mentioned by us in Chapter VI. Here the neolithic bed is superimposed, says this experienced archæologist, *directly* on the palæolithic bed. "One will observe," he says, "that between the bed which represents the age of the reindeer and that which corresponds to neolithic times, no deposit formed by the inflow of the waters, or by the operation of other natural causes, is found intercalated. The hearths of one epoch succeed those of the preceding epoch, without our being able to seize between them any trace of a geological disturbance."[1]

MM. Louis Lartet and Chaplain Duparc remark on the same immediate succession of the beds in the Grotto *Duruthy*, near Peyrehorade, in the department of Landes, France. "In this grotto," they say, "after having encountered man at the bottom of the beds, in his artistic period, in company with a bear, a lion, and the reindeer, we find him still represented in sepultures superimposed on the hearths of this first epoch, with arms which appear to inaugurate the era of polished stone."[2]

We will give only one additional illustration.

[1] Matériaux, 2e liv., 1874.
[2] Ibid., 3e et 4e liv., 1874, p. 101.

The coast of Cheshire, from the mouth of the Dee to that of the Mersey, consists of hills of loose shifting sand, which rests on a layer of marshy deposit, of little depth and no remote date. In or under this have been found human bones estimated to be about three hundred years old.

Beneath this comes a much thicker bed of fine drift sand, containing mediæval objects.

Then, below this, a still thicker bed of bog and sand, containing also mediæval objects of about the twelfth or thirteenth century.

Beneath this bed is another thinner stratum of blue marl or silt, with Norman and Anglo-Saxon coins.

Then, under this, a thicker bed of forest bog soil, filled with trees and shrubs, and many stumps of large trees. Here we find deer, ox, horse, boar, &c., with shells; and Roman objects, and a few Saxon relics, including a Saxon coin; and, finally, in lower portions of the bed, a few arrow-heads of flint, stone, and shell.

Then, lastly, under this bed there is a bed of some thickness of blue marl, containing the remains of the urus, the great Irish elk, and cetacea, and a few "primeval flints."[1]

This sequence speaks for itself, and takes us from the Palæolithic through the Neolithic Age, and, in succession, through the Roman, the Saxon, the Norman epochs, down to the age of Elizabeth.

[1] Intellectual Observer, vol. vii. p. 390.

CHAPTER XV.

STONE, BRONZE, AND IRON—continued.

Consideration of the use of stone implements in Europe—Continued among the barbarians down to period of the Roman Empire, and even to Saxon and Merovingian times—Metal traced in oldest pile-villages, and found with bronze and iron, and even Roman relics, at many stations—Date of the Stone Age in Denmark—Of the Iron Age—Of the Bronze Age in Gaul—No Bronze Age in Germany—Alleged "overlapping" of the Ages—Examples to prove the confusion of the Three Ages, and the recent date of the use of bronze and stone—The trenches of Alise—La Bruyère—All three materials found in same army—Kingston-on-the-Thames—The Iberians and Lusitanians—Examples from the Swiss lake-dwellings—Examples from the tumuli and dolmens—Cumarola—Cave of the Bats, in Spain—The cemetery of Hallstadt—Other miscellaneous examples of the presence of stone and metal together—Late use of bronze in Ireland, as shown by ancient Irish poems—Examples from Germany—Instances cited where stone implements were found with Roman objects—Evidence of use of stone in Saxon and Merovingian times—Caranda—The Three Ages in Russia—Late use of stone and bronze—Stone implements in use in every one of the continents within past hundred years—Survival of primitive customs in certain countries of Europe and Asia.

HAVING in the preceding chapter passed in review in connection with our subject the various parts of the world, excepting that part of Europe with which we are most immediately concerned—namely, the countries north of Italy and Greece—we shall proceed now to show that, recognising a non-metallic period for this region during the *Palæolithic* Age, the divisions of the archæologists into the Polished Stone Age, the Bronze

Age, and the Iron Age have little value, and that the use of stone continued in these countries down to Roman, Saxon, and Merovingian times.

Even in the very oldest Swiss Lake villages, as at Robenhausen, as we are told by Dr. Keller—a fact already adverted to,—"traces of copper and bronze are met with in the lower beds."[1] These Stone Age people, too, we are informed, practised agriculture, and fertilised their fields with the carefully preserved sweepings from the stalls of their cattle. They made use of beautiful vessels and utensils of wood, and manufactured fringed and embroidered cloths. At Wangen, Allensbach, and Markenfilgen, on the Lake of Constance, and at Locras—all Stone Age stations—perforated stone axes were found, and these, as we are told by Sir John Lubbock, "are generally found in the graves of the Bronze period, and [he proceeds] it is most probable that this mode of attaching the handle was used very rarely, if at all, until the discovery of metal had rendered the process far more easy than could have been the case previously."[2] At Wauwyl, another of the most ancient stations, a glass bead was obtained, but no metal. Glass beads hardly reached Switzerland a thousand years before the Christian era. At Meilen, on the Lake of Zurich, another Stone Age settlement *par excellence*, a bronze armilla, a bronze celt, Baltic amber, and a beautiful perforated stone hammer were found, while some of the piles had been sharpened with a metal axe. At four of the oldest stations—Meilen, Moosseedorf, Roben-

[1] The Lake-Dwellings of Switzerland, English trans., p. 57.
[2] Pre-historic Times, p. 91.

hausen, and Wangen—the explorers obtained several varieties of wheat and two varieties of barley.

It is evident from these facts that at the remotest period of the Polished Stone Age in Switzerland, the lake-dwellers had access to metal, and occasionally procured it from the countries bordering on the Mediterranean.

If we turn to the peat-mosses of Scandinavia, the date of the Stone Age in Denmark is fixed by Professor Worsaae at about 3000 years ago,[1] or about 1100 B.C.; and by Professor Leemans at 3000 or 4000 years ago as the extreme limit in Sweden.[2] Professor Worsaae also states that in the Stone Age strata of the Danish peat, leather-shoes or sandals made of a single piece of hide sewed together behind, and remnants of *woollen cloth*, have been found.

The *close* of the Stone Age in Denmark Professor Worsaae fixes at about 500 or 600 B.C.[3]

On the other hand, M. Oscar Montelius, in his beautiful work on the "Antiquities of Sweden," remarks that "the Age of Bronze was probably ended in Sweden a short while after the beginning of the Christian era." Professor Worsaae makes it last even to the fifth century.[4]

We have already mentioned that, according to the observations and deductions of M. Boucher de Perthes, in the peat at Abbeville, the Bronze Age in Gaul must have been about 200 or 150 B.C., as determined by the

[1] Primeval Antiquities, p. 135.
[2] Stockholm volume of Pre-historic Archæology.
[3] Primeval Antiquities, p. 135.
[4] Ibid., p. 147.

Gaulish coins which he found in the same beds with the weapons and implements of bronze (see chap. x. p. 146).

But if these facts are so, what colour is there for the association of the Polished Stone Age, or the Bronze Age, in Western and Northern Europe, with a high antiquity? There is none: such ideas have proceeded rather from the imaginations than the sober judgment of the antiquaries and the archæologists. As we have pointed out, the Stone Age in these countries must be a recent affair, because Switzerland, Denmark, and France were five or ten centuries behind Asia Minor, where we find stone in use down to 1000 and even 700 B.C.

In Germany, as was declared by M. Bertrand (one of the editors of the "Revue Archéologique") at the Stockholm Congress of Anthropologists, "the Bronze Age prevailed to the fourth century after Christ;" and the Iron and Bronze Ages, he declared, not only overlapped one another, but "they had positively been contemporaneous." In the same discussion M. Desor stated (therein concurring with Professor Worșaae), that "as far as the First Iron Age was concerned, it belonged in Scandinavia to the fourth and sixth centuries after Christ."[1]

It is exceedingly strange, therefore, that Sir John Lubbock and Sir Charles Lyell should fix the date of the Neolithic Age at 5000 to 7000 years ago, and that of the Bronze Age at 3000 to 4000 years ago; as does also M. Figuier in his "Primitive Man;" and which

[1] Academy, August 29, 1874.

are about the figures of Messrs. Evans and Dawkins also.[1]

The use of stone implements, as we have said, continued in Western and Northern Europe after the Roman period—in Ireland and Scandinavia down, perhaps, to mediæval times; and the stone and the metal implements were often in use at one and the same time at the same place; and, in other cases, stone was in use in one part of a country, while metal was in use in another district of the same country. The evidence for this is overwhelming, and strengthens as investigation has proceeded. The difficulty is not to name instances in proof, but to select from the mass of material which has accumulated within a few years.

The relics of the "Three Ages" are found commingled in many instances in the ancient dolmens and tumuli, in caves, on battle-fields, in river-beds, in peat-bogs, in the pile-villages, and in the shell-mounds; and, finally, in Roman, Saxon, and Merovingian graves.

It is customary, as already remarked, to evade this evidence by alleging, first, that the ages "lapped;" and, second, that the relic-beds, or the graves, have been disturbed. As to the latter, the instances are too numerous for the explanation to be accepted, and in many cases it is plain that there has been no disturbance: as to the former, the allegation, namely, that the ages have *lapped*, it might do to say that the stone had lapped the bronze, and the bronze the iron; but we often find the stone in association with iron, and the suggestion that the ages have "lapped," involves in

[1] Of course they are considered as merely approximate.

such a case a leap *across* the Bronze Age from Stone to Iron.

Selecting from the mass of instances now on record, we shall proceed to establish the declarations which we have made.

Alise.—Let us begin with the trenches at Alise—the ancient Alesia—where Cæsar besieged and captured Vercingetorix and his great army, after much hard fighting. In the ancient trenches before this city, which were excavated by order of Louis Napoleon, as we are told by M. Desor, "The arms of the Three Eras were found in the same foss, arrows of stone with those of bronze and iron."[1]

Similar facts appeared, as we learn from Napoleon III.'s "Life of Cæsar,"[2] at the excavations carried on in 1862 between Trévoux and Riottier, on the plateaux of La Bruyère and Saint Bernard; which, the historian remarks, leave no doubt of the place where Cæsar defeated the Helvetii on the Saône. There are found here numerous sepultures, Gallo-Roman and Celtic. The tumuli furnished vases of coarse clay, and many fragments of arms of flint, ornaments of bronze, iron arrow-heads, fragments of sockets, &c. The sepultures were by incineration and inhumation.

This is precisely what we should have expected in an army of Gauls at that period. The rich had iron, and the chiefs were no doubt in some instances very completely equipped with metal armour, offensive and defensive. No doubt picked bodies of soldiers had

[1] Palafittes of Lake Neufchâtel, trans., Smiths. Report, 1865, p. 400.
[2] Ibid, ii. p. 65.

metallic weapons. Iron was superseding bronze, but bronze was still in use. Thousands, at the same time, had, it is to be presumed, rude weapons of stone and bone, or, as Tacitus informs us, stakes hardened in the fire. We saw that the same diversity of equipment characterised the host of Xerxes in his invasion of Greece. Numbers of ancient bronze and iron weapons were found in the bed of the river at Kingston-on-the-Thames, the point where Cæsar is believed to have fought with the Britons. This discovery is mentioned in one of the early volumes of the "Archæological Journal," and was made before attention had been greatly drawn to the use of stone implements in primitive times. It is not unlikely that stone as well as bronze would have been found if it had been sought for. Among the objects obtained here were bronze celts, a bronze sword, iron spear-heads, an iron hatchet, and an elegant object in bronze, which appeared to support a standard, or Roman eagle.

At the beginning of our era, Strabo informs us that the Iberians and the Lusitanians used spears "pointed with brass."[1]

STONE AND METAL FOUND TOGETHER IN THE LAKE-DWELLINGS.

At the Iron Age lake-station of La Tène, on the Lake of Neufchâtel, already noticed by us, and where numerous relics (including coins) of Roman manufacture were obtained, we are told that the surface was strewn with

[1] Book iii. chap. iii. § 6.

flint flakes, which, as we learn from Mr. Evans, were used during the Stone Age for various purposes—sometimes for cutting, sometimes as scrapers, and again as saws.

At Unter-Uhldingen, on the Lake of Constance, we have a station (noticed in a previous chapter) which is referred to the Bronze Age. This is warranted, apart from the numerous objects of bronze obtained here, by the distance of the station from the shore—1000 feet.[1] We are told by Dr. Keller that a large number of bronze tools and weapons, "showing that bronze was both manufactured and used on the shores of Constance," were obtained here—a number of celts, six lance-points, twenty-five knives, sickles, armlets, &c. Sundry implements of iron were also found—an axe, two iron swords, two chisels, twelve knives, two pruning-knives, a ring, a fibula, a clothes-pin, &c. The iron objects seem nearly as numerous as the bronze. There were found also eleven bottoms of glass goblets, and a smooth glass slab, which are synchronous with the introduction of iron, and imply Roman influences.

At this station there were found, in addition, arrow and lance-heads of flint, 300 stone axes and chisels, besides stone hammers, net-sinkers, mealing-stones,

[1] M. Desor, in his paper on the Palafittes of the Lake of Neufchâtel, remarks :—"There exists a notable difference between the palafittes of the Age of Stone and those of the Age of Bronze. The latter, which are at once more extensive and more numerous, are found at a greater distance from the shore; their depth is, consequently, more considerable, generally from three to five metres below mean water. . . . In a letter of M. A. Senoner to M. de Mortillet it is said: 'There is a great difference between the stations of stone and those of metal; the former approach the shore more or less nearly, while the latter are distant from it about 330 metres' (1100 feet)."—Smiths. Report for 1865, p. 367.

fruit-crushers, &c.; the axes, for the most part, unperforated.

We have here stone, bronze, and iron. The bronze and the iron have not been introduced subsequently at a station dating from the Stone Age; this cannot be alleged; for, as we have said, the Stone Age stations were built near the shore; and here the stone implements, greatly outnumbering all the bronze and iron objects together, were brought to the bronze or iron station, and used contemporaneously with these metals.

Sipplingen, one hour's walk from Unter-Uhldingen, is 1200 or 1500 feet from the shore. It, too, is assigned to the Bronze Age. There were obtained here sixteen objects of iron (including a sword and a Roman key), one object of bronze (a celt), and 350 stone axes, hammers, &c. There were also specimens of glass. It will not do to refer this to the Stone Age, because, like Unter-Uhldingen, it is too far from the shore. It is hardly proper to refer it to the Bronze Age, as only one specimen of this metal (or copper) was found here. It really belongs to the Iron Age; and the stone implements were the implements chiefly in use.

Stone, bronze, and iron were found again at *Les Roseaux*, on the Lake of Geneva. The piles, we are told, were sharpened by "bronze axes"—though why not *iron*, we do not see. In any case, the village was built with metal tools, and stone continued in use after it was built.

A striking example is the pile-village near Lubtow in Pomerania, noticed in our chapter on the Lake-Dwellings. There are two relic-beds. In the lower, objects of flint and bronze occurred together; in the upper, objects of flint, bronze, and iron were found associated. These are only a few of the examples that might be given from the Lake-Dwellings.

IN THE ANCIENT GRAVES.

The Tumuli and Dolmens abundantly illustrate the same fact. The instances in which metal and stone are found associated are *legion*. The dolmens of the departments of Lozère, Aveyron, and Gard, in the South of France, contain, as a general rule, objects of flint and bronze, as do those also of Charente, in the West of France.[1]

In the Forest of Carnoët, Finisterre, in a round tumulus, faced within with hewn walling-stones, were found a number of "flint arrow-heads, a sword, and three lance-heads, one of silver."[2] The sword, we presume, was of iron, but this is not stated. The silver, however, fixes the date.

In a tumulus, opened by M. Sengensse, in the canton of Uzerche (Corrèze), five rude blocks of stone (forming a sort of dolmen) were encountered at the depth of a metre, and beneath these stones M. Sengensse found a flint arrow-head and a flint knife, a bronze bracelet, and two fragments of iron, conjectured to have belonged to a lance-head and a bracelet.[3]

An iron axe and an iron ring were found with a great

[1] Matériaux, 1e Série, tom. iii. p. 29; v. p. 326; 2e Série, 1873, pp. 345, 365.

[2] Eclectic Magazine for January 1844, quoted from "Athenæum."

[3] Matériaux, 1876, p. 362.

number of flint flakes in a tumulus on a hillock called the *Mané Bodegade* at Carnac, in Brittany.[1]

In a cairn at Lough Crew, Ireland, flint and bone implements, and implements of iron, were found together.[2]

In a virgin tumulus at Crubelz, France, Dr. de Closmadeuc found a number of flint arrow-heads in the chamber, and he refers in triumph to the "absence de toute trace des métaux." "Aucun doute," he says, "n'est donc possible. Ce dolmen appartient bien à cette classe de monuments primitifs de l'age de pierre." The enthusiastic archæologist then very naïvely adds, "Nous tenons peu de compte des débris de tuiles antiques rencontrées à la superficie du tumulus, *et même sur les tables du dolmen*"—it is reasonable, he says, to suppose that they have "accidentally penetrated into the interior."

The Baron de Bonstetten opened another tumulus near this; at the depth of one foot from the surface he met with the usual flint implements; and two feet below this he encountered two statuettes of Latona, in terra-cotta, and a coin of Constantine II.[3]

In a cist in the well-known tumulus of Gib Hill, was found a vase containing a stone celt, a flint arrow-head, and a small iron fibula, which had been enriched with precious stones.

Mr. Bateman found in a barrow on Cross Flatts (Derbyshire), an iron knife and a spear-head of flint;

[1] Matériaux, 1872, p. 63.
[2] Fergusson's Rude Stone Monuments, p. 218.
[3] Ibid., pp. 337, 339.

in Galley Low a gold necklace, a coin of Honorius, and (towards the outer edge) a flint arrow-head; in Boerther Low, a flint arrow-head and a bronze celt; in Rolley Low, a coin of Constantine, two flint arrow-heads, &c.; in a barrow on Ashford Moor, an iron arrow-head and flint implements; in Stand Low, stone implements and flint chippings, and at the centre an iron (Saxon) knife, a bronze box, silver, glass, &c.; at Moot Low, six rude instruments of stone, a bronze lance-head, iron knives, &c., &c.

M. Féraud found in a dolmen in Algiers, at the foot of the skeleton, the remains of a horse and an iron bit, a ring of iron, objects of copper, worked flint implements, and a coin of the Empress Faustina.[1]

In the Derbyshire barrows, about one-third of those which yielded remains of any sort contained metal, which implies that metal was in common use along with the stone. The flint is more common in these barrows for the very obvious reason that it was *cheaper*, and doubtless (from the same sentiment which prompted the Hebrews to use flint knives in circumcision) it was deemed more suitable for the realm of shades than the more modern metal.

In the Wiltshire barrows, the proportion of metal found in the graves was even greater than in Derbyshire.

[1] Of these African cromlechs, M. Bertrand remarks, that "stone, bronze, and iron are found mixed up in their contents."—*De la Distribution des Dolmens.* Cited in the Proceedings of the Society of Antiquaries of Scotland, vol. vi. p. 131.

Dr. Bleicher describes in the issue of "Matériaux" for May 1875, certain grottoes in Morocco, in which he found in the same bed worked flints, wheel-made pottery, and bronze nails (p. 209).

Mr. John Evans and Sir John Lubbock admit that stone continued in use in the Bronze Age; indeed the latter cites the fact that out of thirty-seven barrows, among the explorations of Mr. Bateman in Derbyshire, which contained objects of bronze, twenty-nine of them contained at the same time implements of stone. Nothing could be more conclusive. But Mr. Evans doubts whether the stone continued to be used along with iron.

If the reader will look back, he will observe that most of the instances which we have cited above, are instances in which stone was found with *iron*. We selected on purpose that class of cases. As for bronze, in the tumuli the bronze dagger and the flint arrow-head are habitually found in association.

Cumarola.—One of the most striking instances of the contemporaneous use of bronze and stone weapons was met with at Cumarola, near Modena, in Italy, where forty skeletons were discovered in 1856, buried in the earth three feet deep. Each had on its right side a socketed lance-head of copper [bronze?], and on the left side a flint arrow-head; while some of them had in addition, on the right side, a lance-head of very hard serpentine, and others a perforated stone-celt placed at the head. The certainty that there has been no disturbance, and the number of the skeletons, give especial value to this example; whilst it is also evident that the objects of stone were not deposited from any superstitious sentiment, which, it is alleged, prompted these ancient people to deposit flints in the grave long after stone implements had ceased to be used; the perforated celt was manufactured for the living, and not for the dead.

Cave of the Bats.—An equally graphic illustration of the co-existence of these ages—of the commingling of the currents of civilisation and barbarism—may be drawn from Spain. In the *Cueva de los Murciélagos,* or Cave of the Bats, in Andalusia, Señor Don Manuel de Gongora y Martinez informs us that a number of human skelėtons (eighteen) were found, and alongside of them various weapons of flint—knives, hatchets, and arrow-heads; bone knives and pickaxes; spoons of wood; baskets; and vessels of clay. The bodies were reduced to the condition of mummies, and "were covered with flesh." They were clothed in short tunics of *esparto* (Spanish broom), and some of them had sandals and caps of *esparto,* several of the former being elaborately worked; around the skull of one of the skeletons was a diadem of pure gold of twenty-four carats, valued at twelve pounds. The dresses and baskets still retained their original colour. The vases were rude, but had spouts and handles.

We cannot fix the date of these remains, but they seem to be comparatively recent, and we perceive that these stone-using troglodytes were in communication with some other race which must have been far advanced in civilisation.

HALLSTADT.

Near Salzburg, in Austria, nearly a thousand ancient graves—a great cemetery of the Pre-historic Age—

were discovered by M. Ramsauer. The date of these graves cannot be definitely determined, but as they contained various objects of *glass, wheel-made pottery*, and *African ivory*, Hallstadt must be later than the imperial era of Rome. Glass was unknown during the so-called Bronze Age, and Sir John Lubbock makes the same statement as regards the potter's wheel.[1]

In these graves the explorers obtained a number of stone implements, 109 weapons of bronze, 510 weapons of iron, 182 "vessels" of bronze, 3215 ornaments of bronze, 270 ornaments of amber, 73 objects of glass, 1242 specimens of pottery, &c. We have stone, bronze, and iron in use at the same time, and associated with numerous objects of amber, glass, ivory, and wheel-made pottery. Some of the bronze "vessels" delineated in M. Figuier's "L'Homme Primitif" are nearly three feet high, while others indicate a superb workmanship. The predominance of iron weapons clearly shows that we are in the "Iron" Age; but, on the other hand, there are more than 100 weapons of bronze, and several thousand ornaments and vessels of bronze; while there are also implements of stone—how many is not reported—but these were probably about as numerous as the cutting implements of bronze.

It is a favourite idea with the archæologists that *cremation* was specially characteristic of the Bronze Age, while the extended skeleton is supposed to have been the mode of burial in the Iron Age. At Hallstadt about one-half of the bodies have been burned, while the other half are represented by extended skele-

[1] Pre-historic Times, p. 16.

tons. But with the first half, which ought to belong to the Bronze Age, there were found 349 weapons of iron, and 91 weapons of bronze; and with the second half, only 161 weapons of iron, and 18 weapons of bronze. The distinction obviously fails, and it is equally plain that all the graves belong substantially to *one* era.

ADDITIONAL EXAMPLES OF THE CO-EXISTENCE OF STONE AND METAL.

These examples would seem to settle the question, and to nullify, for all practical purposes, the argument drawn from the "Three Ages" in favour of a vast lapse of time since the Neolithic or Second Stone Age. Other examples are numerous; and as the matter must ultimately be decided by *facts*, and not by unsustained assertions, we proceed to mention still farther the following discoveries illustrative of our position.

In the well-known work of Mr. Wright, entitled "The Celt, Roman, and Saxon," it is mentioned that at old Toulouse, in France, a stone axe was found in the place where it had been originally deposited, "which was surrounded with a band of iron, that had evidently fixed it to the handle." "Instances might be adduced," Mr. Wright remarks, "of the continued use of implements of stone down to a much more recent date."[1]

Four bronze swords, and two iron swords, and two iron spear-heads, mentioned by Sir W. R. Wilde in his "Catalogue of Bronze Implements, &c.," were found at

[1] Third edition, p. 98.

Kildrinagh Ford, on the river Nore, in Queen's County, Ireland.[1]

On the other hand, he mentions the finding at Toome Bar, in the river Bann, at the depth of three feet, of a stone celt and a bronze celt together.

This distinguished archæologist also shows that stones were used as missiles in battle, in Ireland, as late as the tenth century. He quotes for this purpose from the "Book of Lismore," that in a battle fought near Limerick by Callachen Cashel against the Danes, about A.D. 920, "their youths, and their champions, and their proud, haughty veterans, came to the front of the battle to *cast their stones*, and their small arrows, and their smooth spears on all sides." Sir W. Wilde states that naked stone celts, without handles, were used as missiles in battle at this period.

This last statement settles the meaning of the Latin quotation from William of Poictiers with regard to the use of stone by the Saxons at the battle of Hastings. This chronicler wrote: "Jactant cuspides ac diversorum generum tela, sævissimas quasque secures ac lignis imposita saxa."

Mr. Evans attempts to evade the more obvious meaning of these words, and suggests that the stones were projected as missiles from some kind of engines; but from Sir William Wilde's statement it appears that the naked stone celts, about the same time, were thrown from the hand in this way by the Irish.[2]

[1] Page 444.

[2] While on this point, we may mention that in the Saxon Glossary of Ælfric (A.D. 1000), the Latin *bipennis* is translated *stan-æx*, showing that the stone axe was still in use.

The late use of bronze weapons in Ireland is illustrated by Major-General J. H. Lefroy, R.A., F.R.S., in connection with the discovery of a bronze battle-axe of the ninth or tenth century in a tumulus at Greenmount, Castle Bellingham, Ireland. General Lefroy takes occasion, in commenting on this discovery, to remark that there are passages in the ancient Irish books which prove that bronze weapons were used in Ireland long after the Christian era. He gives the following examples:—

"Whoever wishes for a speckled boss
And a sword of sore inflicting wounds,
And a *green* javelin for wounding witches,
Let him go early in the morning to Ath-Cliath."
—*Four Masters*, A.D. 917.

"This day, Brinde fights a battle for the land of his grandfather,
Unless the Son of God will it otherwise, he will die in it;
To-day the son of Ossery was killed in a battle with *green* swords."
A.D. 704, *Three Fragments translated by O'Donovan*, 1860, p. 111.

In another passage from "The Battle of Magh Rath," A.D. 637, the poet speaks of "the expert *blue* sword" and the "broad *green* spear."

The "green" weapons are evidently bronze, while the "blue" is iron.

Mr. Evans states that he has in his own collection a stone celt found in Ireland, with a hoard of Anglo-Saxon coins of the tenth century.

Sometimes we can approximate the date when certain stone implements were in use. Near the hamlet of Cernois, in a region called *Le Bâtardeau*, France, M.

Morlot discovered beneath the soil five slabs, which he regarded as originally constituting a box designed to cover a sepulture. He found below the slabs a polished hatchet (broken) in diorite, two knives, one of them of a beautiful red flint, fragments of pottery, and finally, "chose embarrassante," *a very small Gaulish medal.* This medal was hardly older than the Gaulish coinage, which goes back to about 300 B.C.

Continuing his explorations, M. Morlot, a few days afterwards, found close by flint lance-heads, and the fragment of a bronze hatchet.[1]

In another instance, the Abbé Croizet found axes of stone and Celtic medals in certain ancient dwellings excavated in the sandstone, near the village of Neschers, Puy-de-Dôme. They had been covered by a flow of volcanic matter, which had been laid open by the river Couze.[2]

Polished stone hatchets and bronze hatchets occurred together in Sicily, at the sepulchral grotto of Porco-Spino.

In the *Caverna del Re Tiberio*, in the Apennines, near Imola, in the North of Italy, M. Scarabelli found in the upper bed fragments of zinc, bronze, and iron; and at one metre below this upper bed, wheel-made pottery, Roman and Etruscan vases, worked bones, and three flint knives.[3]

In Germany the stone axes have been frequently found with objects of iron. On the island of Rügen, famous for its large megalithic monuments, there was

[1] Matériaux, 1873, p. 465. [2] Ibid., 1876, p. 346.
[3] Ibid., 1872, p. 192.

found in 1793, near Banzelwitz, a long stone chamber sixteen feet in length. It contained ten sitting skeletons (a posture characteristic of the Stone Age), and in the clay beneath these were nine urns, on a layer of loose flints. Under each of the three largest urns was found a flint axe, besides which there were also found an amber bead and a rusted fragment of iron. There was no trace of a secondary interment.[1]

Another find of this sort is mentioned by Hünefeld and Picht as occurring in a large stone-grave near Stubnitz, which contained, in addition to a sitting skeleton, twenty or more cinerary urns, and on one of the burnt bones a firmly-adhering iron slag.[2]

In Westphalia M. Schaaffhausen found, near Wintergalen, in a passage-grave packed full of skeletons, a perforated wolf's tooth, implements of flint, two pieces of iron, and a band of copper.[3]

A stone-grave, twenty to thirty feet in length, near Wersahe, in Hanover, entirely undisturbed, contained flint axes, urns, and burnt bones, and two small pieces of iron.

It is well known that the *Hunebeds,* as they are called, of Altmark, frequently yield iron implements.

Of the stone-graves of Mecklenburg, Lisch remarks, that although the predominant material is flint, yet

[1] Archiv für Anthropologie, Januar 1876, s. 283.

[2] Ibid., s. 284.

[3] Ibid. Sir John Lubbock says these 'passage'-graves are the oldest of all these monuments, and that they (and the long barrows) "seem always to belong to the Stone Age." To the same purport the 'British Quarterly Review' (October 1872) declares, that "in no authenticated instance have these passage-graves furnished articles of bronze or iron where they have not been previously disturbed."

traces of iron are found in them; this metal, he observes, in most instances having perished. The same writer states that a battle-axe of iron, iron rings, &c., were found in stone chambers near Greven, Rosenburg, and Schlemmin, along with stone implements.

Iron was found again in the chamber of a large galleried mound near Jägersprùs, in 1834, along with arrow-heads and splinters of flint.

In 1838 Professor Worsaae found, in a very large stone chamber, in the parish of Veibye (district of Frederiksborg), a great many stone wedges, knives, and hammers, arrow-heads of flint, and a piece of iron that had been bent, and which had a hole through the middle. The same archæologist opened another large gallery-grave in the same district in 1839, which contained skeletons and implements of stone. Near the skulls lay a flint knife, and a piece of iron having the form of a knife, which was fastened with a nail to a piece of wood.[1]

The late Dr. Pruner-Bey gives an account of the discovery of iron and flint arms in the same tumulus, at the village of Minsleben, district of Wernigerode, Prussia. Forty-six skeletons were found in this barrow, lying side by side, along with urns filled with ashes and ornaments. By the fragments of pottery there were great numbers of flint knives and arrow-heads, and with them two knives of iron, one by the skeleton of a child, and the other by that of an adult. The only animal bones occurring were the head of a horse. We are obviously in the Iron Age.[2]

[1] Archiv für Anthropologie, Januar 1876, s. 285.
[2] Matériaux, 1e Série, tome i. p. 400.

The presence of iron in the stone-graves of Sweden can admit of no reasonable doubt, since we have the testimony of Nilsson, that "he had found in most of the passage-graves investigated by him one piece, but rarely two pieces, of iron."[1]

STONE IMPLEMENTS IN ROMAN TIMES.

The use of stone in Roman times for implements, is implied by the discoveries of stone in association with iron; but we propose, in order to put this matter beyond all dispute, to mention now a number of instances in which the stone axes, flint arrow-heads, and the like, have been found in direct association with objects of unequivocal Roman origin. The examples are numerous, and we can only select.

In the Roman cemeteries opened by the Abbé Cochet (so well known for his archæological studies), in Normandy, "he found," we are told, "*as the usual accompaniment* of the urn-interments, pieces of chipped flint, generally formed into the shape of wedges."[2]

Five polished stone celts were found with Roman remains at Kastrich, near Gonsenheim; a case mentioned by Mr. Evans.[3]

Stone implements were found again with Roman remains at Ash, in Kent; at Leicester; at Great Whitcombe, Gloucestershire; at Ickleton, Essex; at Alchester, Oxfordshire; and at Eastbourne. A fibrolite hatchet was found with Gaulish coins of the time of Augustus at Mont Beuvray.[4]

[1] Archiv für Anthropologie, Januar 1876, s. 285.
[2] Essays on Archæological Subjects. By Thomas Wright, vol. i. p. 28.
[3] Ancient Stone Implements, p. 98. [4] Ibid., p. 130.

Flakes and rudely chipped pieces of flint are "a very common occurrence on the sites of Roman occupation," as at Hardham, Sussex; at Moel Fenlli; at Reculver (Regulbium); at St. Albans (Verulamium), &c. (See "Ancient Stone Implements.")

At Stonham, in Suffolk, in 1869, great quantities of iron, lead, pottery, glass, querns, flue-tiles, Roman coins, and other objects were found, and with them "many flint implements, such as celts, arrow-heads, spear-heads, scrapers," &c. The coins were chiefly third brass of the Lower Empire, belonging to Claudius Gothicus, Diocletian, Carausius, Constantine I., Constantine II., Magnentius, and Valens.[1]

Colonel A. Lane Fox describes two other cases in the "Journal of the Ethnological Society of London," in 1869, occurring in Oxfordshire and the Isle of Thanet. He reports to the society of which he was the honorary secretary, that he found in the districts named worked flints (very rude) with Roman pottery; and he draws this conclusion: "There is now good reason for supposing that flint implements continued in use among the Britons during the Roman, and perhaps during even the earlier part of the Saxon period."[2]

M. Grewingk, in his Memoir on the Archæology of the Baltic Coasts and Russia (Braunschweig, 1874), states that in the tombs of the eastern Baltic region we find arrow-heads of iron of the same form as the arrow-points of flint, and with them implements of stone and Roman coins of the first and fourth centuries. "The

[1] Student and Intellectual Observer, vol. ii. p. 152.
[2] Journal of the Ethnological Society, N. S., vol. i. p. 1.

beautiful axes of stone," he says, "remained in use a long time after the introduction of iron, which, as appears, took place in the first century of our era."

In France the examples (apart from Normandy, already alluded to) are as numerous as in England.

In the Bologna volume of the International Congress of Archæology, M. Roujou gives an account of finding flint knives, arrow-heads, scrapers, &c., at the station of Champsperlard, in the environs of Choisy-le-Roi, department of the Seine. With these were found a Gaulish coin, objects of bronze, and Roman pottery.

M. Beauvais mentions some excavations on the site of a Roman villa at Corberon, Côte-d'Or, where a polished stone axe was found with Samian pottery, and a sword, key, &c., of iron.[1] They belonged to the second or third century.

In the commune of Monsempron, department of Lot-et-Garonne, M. Combes, as reported in "Matériaux," found a polished flint hatchet side by side with a pruning-knife, a gimlet, and a third object of iron. He represents it as a grave. The objects all lay at the depth of a metre.[2] These relics are very probably post-Roman.

Without wearying the reader with details, it will suffice to add that in a Gallo-Roman sepulture at La Souterraine (Creuse) there was found an arrow-head of flint; in the Gallo-Roman necropolis of Varennes-sur-Allier, flint arrow-heads; in the funeral pits of Beaugency (Roman), stone axes; in the Gallo-Roman sepultures of Luneray (Seine-Inférieure), stone axes; in a

[1] Matériaux, 1e Série, iii. p. 487. [2] Ibid., p. 63.

Gallo-Roman grave of the third century at Saint-Privat-d'Allier, three worked flints; in the ruins of the Gallo-Roman villa of La Touratte (Cher), stone axes; in a Roman *sacellum* near Conches (Eure), stone axes; in another *sacellum* near the Château des Roches (Sarthe), stone axes; in the sarcophagi of Bray (Oise), stone axes; in an ancient iron mine near Guéret (Creuse), flint flakes and tiles; in the *Caverne de Condere* (Hautes-Cévennes), a polished stone hatchet, &c., with Gallo-Roman relics; in cinerary urns of the Gallo-Roman epoch, at Corsac (Haute-Loire), chipped flints; at the camp of Catenoy (Oise), numbers of flint implements, along with Roman coins, potteries, and tiles; in the *terramare* of Regona de Seniga, to the south of Brescia, stone implements and objects of Roman origin; at the necropolis, or settlement, of Marzobotto, Italy, dating about 500 B.C. (as proved by works of art and a coin), objects of stone, bronze, and iron; at the cavern of Velo (Italy), flint arrow-heads and knives, and wheel-made pottery; in an artificial grotto explored by M. Foresi, in the Isle of Pianosa (Italy), stone implements and wheel-made pottery; in the Romano-British cemetery at Seaford, Sussex, flint implements, bronze fibulæ, and iron nails."[1]

These facts prove that the use of stone and bronze continued to the North of Italy, in Europe, after the

[1] Matériaux, 1871, pp. 339–41; for 1872, p. 260; for 1874, pp. 215–217; for 1875, pp. 141, 362, 371; for 1876, p. 265. Academy, November 25, 1876.

The following case is cited in Dr. Smith's preface to the English translation of Dr. Schliemann's "Troy and its Remains:"—"A mound recently opened at the Bocenos, near Carnac (in the Morbihan), has disclosed the remains of a Gallic house of the *second century* of our era, in advance of the Roman arms and Roman civilisation into those regions.

There was a point or a period in the history of most, perhaps all, of the European nations, when they went *bare-footed;* and when they became civilised, this Bare-footed Age was doubtless succeeded by an Age of Shoes (or sandals). But this Bare-footed Age is still in existence in some parts of the world, and, in ancient times, after the Romans had reached Britain, doubtless the two ages co-existed, the rich wearing shoes, and the poor going bare-footed; the coast tribes being shod, and the inland tribes (in general) unshod. It was so with stone and metal. Stone is the more primitive, the more abundant, the cheaper; it continued in use a long time, and, strange as it may appear, it is in use at this time in some parts of Europe. It was certainly much more extensively used in ancient times than had been conceived of by modern students; and archæology is entitled to the credit of having brought out this fact. But the mere use of stone for cutting implements, throws no more light on the *antiquity* of the stone-using race than the want of shoes does on the age of a bare-footed race.

STONE IMPLEMENTS IN SAXON AND MEROVINGIAN TIMES, AND IN THE MIDDLE AGES.

We propose now to show yet further, that in various parts of Europe the stone weapons did not cease to be

which *flint implements* were found intermixed with pottery of various styles, from the most primitive to the finest examples of native Gallic art, and among all these objects was a terra-cotta head of the *Venus Anadyomene.*—Academy, January 9, 1875."

used until the fourth, fifth, and even as late as the tenth and eleventh centuries.

The burial-place at Ash, in Kent, which we have mentioned as containing Roman objects along with objects of stone, is really of Saxon date. We mentioned also that a stone celt is said to have been found in Ireland with a hoard of Anglo-Saxon coins of the tenth century. "A club or axe armed with stone," says Mr. Boyd Dawkins, also already noticed by us, "was used even at the battle of Senlac," and "a cargo of stones for missile purposes," he adds, "formed an important part of a Viking's equipment."[1] "Small nests of chipped flints," it is stated by Mr. Evans, "are not unfrequent in Saxon graves."[2]

The most remarkable confirmation, however, of the use of flint at this date, is afforded by the recent excavations of MM. Moreau and Millescamps at the Merovingian cemetery of Caranda in the department of Aisne, France. The epoch of the interments is not questioned; the contents of the graves prove them to be Merovingian—indeed, M. de Mortillet thinks that some of them touch the Carlovingian period.[3]

Twelve or fifteen thousand rudely-worked flints were found in these graves. "The soil," we are told by M. Millescamps, "in which the tombs are dug, has never been disturbed."

The fact seemed so astounding to M. de Mortillet

[1] Journal of the Ethnological Society of London, vol. ii. p. 145.

[2] Ancient Stone Implements, p. 255.

[3] Matériaux, 1875, p. 108. The Frankish battle-axe of iron, the pottery, the jewellery, &c., establish the date.

that he published an article in "Matériaux pour l'Histoire de l'Homme" to explain it, and he took the ground that ordinarily the flints found in Merovingian graves were either "strike-a-lights" (pierres à feu) or *amulettes;* but, in this case, he argued that the number of the flints in the graves is explained by supposing that there had been an *atelier* or flint-implement *factory* on the spot which the Franks afterwards selected for their cemetery. Finding here a dolmen, they established around it a vast cemetery. They saw the earth strewn with flints, that kind of stone from which fire proceeded. Moreover, the regular forms of the stones struck their imagination; they attributed to them magical properties. When they dug a grave, they gathered up the flints which they had encountered, and laid them by the dead.

This is really very well conceived under the circumstances, and does credit to the genius of the most brilliant of the French archæologists; but M. de Mortillet misrepresents the facts. The facts on which he rests his explanation do not exist. M. de Millescamps (who replied to him in the same journal) states that there is no trace at Caranda of any *atelier* or *factory;* that he ascertained by examination that "this soil does not contain any flints, and only presents very few of them at the surface." "Il faudrait," proceeds M. Millescamps, "prouver le fait que n'admet jusqu'ici aucun de ceux qui ont été sur les lieux et qui n'y ont rien vu de ce qui caractérise l'emplacement d'un atelier. En effet les débris rencontrés à la surface du sol sont rares, et dans les tombes on ne trouve qu'un petit nombre de silex recouverts de cette patine blanchâtre qui dénote une longue exposition aux intempéries de l'atmosphère."

We are farther told by M. Millescamps, that while the cemetery of Caranda is the richest depository of funeral flints [of recent date] which has yet been signalled, it is far from being the only one. "À l'époque romaine, les nècropoles de la Normandie en ont offert à M. l'Abbé Cochet, et les fouilles d'un temple de Mercure, au Mont-de-Sene (Côte-d'Or), à M. Bulliot. Il y a vingt ans, M. Bandot, dans ses belles fouilles de Charnay, constatait le même fait que j'ai moi-même verifié l'automne dernier dans les sépultures Mérovingiennes trouvées a Suzarches, près de Paris."[1]

Axes of stone were found at another cemetery, of Merovingian date, at Labruyère (Côte-d'Or); an arrow-head and a lance-head of flint in the Merovingian sepultures of Puxieux (Moselle); and the stone hatchets in a tumulus of the tower Sainte-Austrille (Creuse), of the sixth or seventh century,[2] as well as in other tumuli of the same period in this district of France.

M. Millescamps has the statement that stone axes were used in the year 1298 by the soldiers of Sir William Wallace; we are not informed of his authority for this fact.

Implements of stone, which must have been of the eighth century, were found in the tumulus raised over Harold Hildetand, at Lethra, in Zeeland, by his nephew Sigurd Ring, after the battle in which the former was killed.

Stone axes with Runic inscriptions have also been

[1] Matériaux, 1875, p. 221.

[2] Ibid, 1872, pp. 341, 346.

found, as, for example, one now in the Museum of Upsala, on which is written "Oltha owns this axe."

THE THREE AGES IN RUSSIA.

Within a few years past, great numbers of the tumuli or *kurgans* of Russia have been opened, and the result has been rather surprising to those who, in the first place, remand these monuments to a very remote age; and, in the second, cherish the idea of a very high antiquity for the implements of bronze and stone which have been found in similar mounds in other parts of Europe.

M. Louis Leger, in a letter to M. Bertrand, published in the "Revue Archéologique,"[1] describes three of these kurgans near Kiev, at the village of Gatnoje, which were opened during the session of the Third Congress of Russian Archæologists at the city of Kiev in 1875.

Count Ouvaroff has published at St. Petersburg an account of the exploration by Count L. Pérouski and himself of 7729 kurgans in the government of Novgorod (south-east of the government of St. Petersburg). The results of these investigations are summarised in an article in "Matériaux" for 1876.[2]

The kurgans of Little Russia—on the banks of the Dnieper, the Desna, and the Sëim—have been explored by M. Samokwascof, and are also described in "Matériaux" for 1876.[3] These explorations were made under government authority, and were carried on in the provinces of Tchernigov and Kharkov (and also in Koursk,

[1] Vol. xxx. (Nouvelle Série), 1875, p. 291.
[2] Page 210.
[3] Page 241.

Great Russia), to the east of the province of Kiev. More than three hundred of the kurgans had been opened when the account before us was written.

A general review of the Russian kurgans is furnished in an article by Dr. Heinrich Wankel (giving an account of the Russian Archæological Congress at Kiev) in the *Mittheilungen der Anthropologischen Gesellschaft in Wien*, for 1875.[1] Among others, he describes those of the departments of Kiev, Podolia, and Volhynia.

It appears from these various accounts that the tumuli of Russia date about the tenth century of our era, as is proved by the coins and other objects obtained from them. It will be observed that the explorations cover a considerable part of Western Russia:—the government of Novgorod, adjoining that of Petersburg, and not far from the Baltic coasts, and extending into Central Russia; the government of Kiev, in the south-west, and to the west of this, the Polish governments of Podolia and Volhynia; and east or north-east of Kiev, the governments of Tchernikov, Kharkov, and Koursk.

Beginning with Novgorod, we find the tombs in question referred to the Merians, and learn that this people in their burials practised at the same time both inhumation and incineration, as is proved by coins found in the two kinds of graves. This sets aside the statement common among archæologists, that the extended corpse always characterises the Iron Age, and the burning of the dead the Bronze Age. In the graves were found pendants of metal, representing ducks, horses, and birds; bears' teeth; claws of metal; the

[1] Skizzen aus Kiev, s. 1.

cyprea moneta, or shell-money; engraved amber; German and Anglo-Saxon coins; and coins of the Caliphs and other Asiatic dynasties, "of which the greater number is not posterior to the eleventh century—some going back to the eighth century."

"The surprising fact," says the editor of "Matériaux," "is the presence of *arms of stone* in the midst of these objects, which belong incontestably to the Age of Iron, and even to the second half of it."[1] These arrow-heads and knives of flint and battle-axes of stone belong to the tenth and eleventh centuries.

The tumuli or kurgans of the eastern departments of Little Russia (the Ukraine) belong also, we are told, to the tenth century, and were constructed by the Severiani, a Sclavonic tribe. We find here, as in Novgorod, burials by both incineration and inhumation. Among the contents of the graves were arms of iron, vases of copper and iron, bucklers of copper, ornaments in silver and bronze, bits of tissue in gold and in silk, and a Byzantine coin, containing the image of Jesus and the inscription JUS. XRS. REX. REGNANTIUM.

The kurgans of the departments of Kiev, Volhynia, and Podolia, have yielded weapons of iron, bronze, and stone of post-Christian date, silver crosses, glass balls, &c. Great numbers of arrow-heads of gray bronze are found in them. On an island in the Dnieper, near Krementschuk, thousands of these arrow-heads have been found, and with them glass beads, arrow-heads, and other objects of iron, and a silver plate.

Speaking of the tumuli at Gatnoje, visited by the

[1] Matériaux, 1876, p. 214.

Congress from Kiev (six in all), Dr. Wankel sums up with regard to them as follows: "It is evident that all of these kurgans belong to the Metallic Period, notwithstanding the fact that in some of them no metals were found. In support of this opinion the perfect relationships and the presence of like objects are a conclusive proof. Further, that they probably belonged to one and the same people, the similar vessels, and their perfectly similar *céramique* seem to indicate. I say *Metal Period*, because, so far as I know, it has not yet been shown that there was a distinct bronze period in Russia; for bronze has been constantly found with iron, silver, or gold, or at least found under such circumstances as to allow of the supposition of yet another metal. Hence a separation of the Bronze and Iron Periods has no justification certainly for great districts of Russia. We know, moreover, from the investigations of Professor Pryborovsky in Warsaw, that among the people who lived on the shores of the Vistula, a Bronze Period did not exist at all, and that the Stone Period of these people continued into the Iron Period, and continued to exist with the same a considerable time." [1]

RESULTS.

The facts of this chapter appear to us to show conclusively that the archæological division into the "Three Ages" does not deserve the importance which has been attached to it; and that, at all events, the attempt to rear upon it a high antiquity for the Bronze and Stone Ages is entirely unwarranted.

[1] Mittheil. Anthrop. Gesells. in Wien, 1875, s. 29.

There is not, indeed, one of the continents on which the Stone Age has not been in existence within the past hundred years. It was in existence in North-Eastern Asia a hundred years ago. It was in progress in the valley of the Missouri within the last half-century. It is in existence to-day among some of the Indian tribes of the United States, and in South America. In Africa, at the present time, the Bushmen use harpoons pointed with bone, and hammers of stone, along with iron; the Hottentots, while acquainted with iron, use awls made out of the bones of birds, and spoons made out of shells, and pound their food with stones; the Damaras dig roots with pointed sticks, and have knives of both iron and stone; the Kaffirs pursue their game with sharpened stakes, cultivate their land with wooden spades, and have hammers of stone, along with knives of ivory, and smelt iron in holes dug in the ground; the Coast Negroes have axes of stone, and weapons of iron. In the Sinaitic peninsula the Arabs still make use of flint knives to scrape their sheep after shearing. In Europe, stone weapons were used in the North a hundred years ago; and to this day, in the South of France, ploughs and other farming implements, pointed with flint and horn, are to be met with.[1]

In Australia the natives use not only stone for their implements, but for the most part use unpolished stone —and we find here, therefore, at the present time, the Palæolithic Age in progress.

In the islands of the Mid-Pacific the Stone Age was

[1] Matériaux, 1876, p. 170.

in full operation a century ago—apparently following an age of metal.

Knives of stone are said to have been in use in the Shetland and Orkney Islands within the present century. Stone hammers were used by tinkers in Ireland up to a very recent date; and perforated stone mallets, with wooden handles, are still used in Iceland for driving posts and other heavy work.

And so the Basque population of the Pyrenees still make pottery with the hand, and the Syrians and the Turks (as already mentioned) plough their fields with a sharpened stake; in Palestine (also noticed) they drive carts with *stone wheels;* in Portugal (also noticed) they have farm-carts with solid wooden wheels, the axle of which revolves with the wheel.

Bows and arrows (who does not remember the scorn of Captain Dugald Dalgetty?) seem to have been used as weapons in the Scotch Highlands as late as the time of Cromwell.

CHAPTER XVI.

WAS THERE A BRONZE AGE?

It is difficult to name any country where bronze weapons were used independently of both stone and iron weapons. In Chaldæa bronze seems to have been more largely used than iron (unless this has in many instances perished); but, as we have stated, in the oldest tombs, stone, bronze, and iron occur together. In Egypt stone and bronze appear together, *possibly* before the employment of iron;[1] then all three materials were used—bronze, however, being preferred to iron for a long period. At Hissarlik we have stone and bronze together, from the lowest bed up to the Greek bed. At Mycenæ, Dr. Schliemann reports all three materials in the post-Agamemnonian bed. The Etruscans and their kinsmen of the Altai mountains give stronger indications of a Bronze Age than any other people, although it is by no means certain that other materials were not used by them for cutting implements.

[1] M. de Mortillet affirms that iron was known in Egypt from the most remote times. The hieroglyphic for iron has been recognised in documents of the Third Dynasty. Painters of the Fourth Dynasty represent instruments of a red colour, that is, of copper, and of a grayish-blue colour, which can only be iron. In these same paintings one sees wild animals brought to the Pharaohs, lions and tigers, in cages, the grayish-blue bars of which would be too thin to resist these animals if they had not been of iron.—*Meeting of the French Association at Clermont-Ferrand*, 1876.

The testimony of the Egyptologists and Assyriologists, and of some of the most eminent archæologists, is decidedly adverse to the theory of the "Three Ages." Mariette-Bey, as we have seen, declares that stone implements were in use among the Egyptians during the entire Pharaonic Period. Sir Gardiner Wilkinson informs us that their falchions were of iron or bronze, and their battle-axes of bronze, and sometimes steel. All the adzes, saws, and chisels found at Thebes are of bronze, although iron was well known.[1]

In the Assyrian ruins, we learn from Professor Rawlinson that both bronze and iron spear-heads occur, while arrow-heads are found also of both metals, and sometimes of flint.[2] And it is the same in Persia.

M. Chabas rejects the distinction of the Three Ages for Egypt, as well as for a Pre-historic Period.

M. Oppert, speaking of Babylonia and Assyria, asserted at the Stockholm Congress of Archæologists, that these countries had no Iron Age and no Bronze Age.[3]

M. Lenormant observes on the same point: "The distinction between the Age of Bronze and the Age of Iron has been from the first too much exaggerated, from an observation of the special facts in the Scandinavian North, and it tends to be effaced. In the greater number of countries the two metals were known at the same time, and it was local circumstances, facilitating rather the working of bronze, which made it at

1 Wilk., Anc. Egyp., vol. ii. pp. 113, 153; vol. i. pp. 360, 363.
2 Ancient Monarchies, i. 456.
3 Comte-Rendu, M. de Baye, p. 54.

first predominant among certain peoples, whilst the fabrication of iron was developed in preference among others from an extreme antiquity."[1] The negroes of Central and Southern Africa, he observes, "appear to have passed at once from the exclusive use of stone to that of iron;"[2] (but see chap. xiv., p. 230).

M. Alexandre Bertrand, already cited by us, spoke very emphatically in rebuke of the prominence given to a Bronze Age at the Stockholm Congress. He declared that "not only did the Bronze and Iron Ages overlap one another, but they had positively been contemporaneous," and that "in Germany the Bronze Age prevailed to the fourth century after Christ." "In Italy," he said, "objects in bronze are rare, and are only met with in small quantity in the terramares." "There was, in reality, no Age of Bronze in Italy and Gaul. At the epoch when the Druids civilised the Gauls, iron was in use, and it was the same in Italy."[3]

At the same Congress, M. Leemans, Director of the Museums of Archæology and Ethnology at Leyden, declared that there was no distinction between the Age of Bronze and the Age of Stone in Holland; and at the same meeting Mr. John Evans made the state-

[1] See *Les Prémières Civilisations*, by this author.

[2] Matériaux, 1874, p. 82.

[3] See Stockholm volume of Internat. Cong. Pre-hist. Archæol., and also "Revue Archéologique" for 1875, p. 334. In the latter it is remarked: "On s'est, en effet, beaucoup trop hâté de professer qu' ailleurs que dans le Nord se retrouve, en Europe, *un âge du bronze* correspondant à l'âge du bronze scandinave et distinct à la fois de l'âge de la pierre et de l'âge du fer. Cette doctrine absolue de la succession des trois âges, dont on a fait une loi sans exception, est, selon nous, le contraire de la vérité."

See also Comte-Rendu of Stockholm Congress, by J. de Baye, Paris, 1875, p. 66.

ment that, as to England, the bronze swords found in that country are invariably hilted with another metal.

Mr. Roach Smith and Mr. Thomas Wright both express the opinion—and none are better qualified to speak on the subject—that the bronze swords, axes, chisels, &c., found in England, are all *Roman;* and Mr. Llewellyn Jewitt is inclined to entertain the same opinion.[1]

Mr. Wright adds that this was also the opinion of M. de Caumont, who is of equal authority with Mr. Wright himself, in the archæology of the Roman period. (See *Cours d'Antiquités Monumentales*, i. p. 233.)

In proof of this view, it may be mentioned that a bronze sword was found with the skeletons of a man and horse, in 1801, in a peat moss at Heilly, France, and with these four coins of the Emperor Caracalla. Another bronze sword was found in the peat at Picquigny, near Abbeville, in a large boat, which appeared to have been sunk, and in which were several skeletons, with some coins of the Roman emperor Maxentius (A.D. 306–312). A bronze helmet and another bronze sword lay outside of the boat.

We gave in the preceding chapter the declaration of Dr. Wankel that it has not yet been shown that there was a distinct Bronze Period in Russia, while (he adds) Professor Pryborovsky, of Warsaw, has shown that on the banks of the Vistula "a Bronze Period did not exist at all."

[1] Trans. Ethnolog. Soc., N. S., vol. iv. p. 176, paper on Bronze Weapons, by Thomas Wright, M.A., F.S.A., &c. Grave-Mounds, by Ll. Jewitt, F.S.A.

The same is substantially true of the basin of the Upper Danube. M. de Pulsky, President of the Congress of Buda-Pesth, declared that "in ancient Pannonia, so rich in objects of the Age of Polished Stone, the Age of Bronze fails almost entirely," while M. Virchow, at the same Congress, remarked that, "there is a very marked difference between Northern Germany and Southern Germany, as whilst in the first the Scandinavian theory of the Age of Bronze is fully admitted, in the second, the archæologists protest that one does not find there bronze without iron."[1] At the same meeting it was stated as to Hungary, by Dr. Romer, that it must be admitted that the implements of obsidian which occur in that country "are often found with objects of bronze."[2]

Such is the testimony of Egyptologists, Assyriologists, and some of the highest authorities in Archæology, against the existence of a Bronze Age. That their opinion seems on the whole to be correct, appears from the following facts.

1. Mr. Dawkins informs us that, "up to the present time, all the pre-historic caves discovered in Britain belong either to the Age of Stone or of Iron."[3] But if there was a Bronze Age, lasting 1500 or 2000 years, there ought to be caves belonging to this period. The caves were inhabited during the Roman period, as late indeed as the fifth and sixth centuries, as is proved by the discovery of late Roman coins. The Victoria cave,

[1] Matériaux, 1876, pp. 419, 449. [2] Ibid., p. 425.
[3] Macmillan's Magazine, December, 1870.

for example, was occupied as late as the fifth century. The Albert cave (near by), the Kelko cave, the Kirkhead cave (on the shore of Morecambe Bay), Poole's cave, Derbyshire, Thor's cave, Staffordshire, and others, belong to the same period. Why, then, are there no caves of the Bronze Age? The answer is, that there was no Bronze Age in Britain. And this, as we have indicated, is the conclusion reached by Mr. Thomas Wright and Mr. Roach Smith, pre-eminently the English specialists in the archæology of this period.

2. If there was such an age in Britain, we ought to ascertain the fact from the barrows and other ancient graves.

The BRONZE AGE is defined by Sir John Lubbock to be "that in which bronze was used for *weapons and cutting instruments of all kinds.*" The ornaments of bronze of course continued to be used in the Iron Age.

In the "Pre-historic Times" of this writer he gives us the contents of some 250 tumuli and dolmens which have been examined in Great Britain and France (most of them in the former), and he constantly speaks of a large proportion of them as belonging to the Bronze Age. Now it appears that in these 250 graves the only bronze weapons or cutting instruments found were fifteen daggers (which were worn in the Middle Ages), two axes, and one spear-head. Are we to be told that this constitutes and represents one grand division in pre-historic chronology? It represents nothing, and it is unwarrantable to teach, with such materials as these, the theories of pre-historic archæology.

3. If, again, there was a Bronze Age, we ought to find it in the Lake-Dwellings of Switzerland; and Sir John Lubbock has given us here again the tabulated results from these stations which will enable us to decide this question, at least so far as Switzerland is concerned. On page 43 of his work, we find the following table of six principal stations (besides "other places") of the so-called Bronze Age in that country.

	Nidau.	Möringen.	Estavayer.	Cortaillod.	Corcelettes.	Auvernier.	Other Places.	Total.
Celts and fragments	23	7	6	13	1	6	11	67
Swords	...	...	...	...	...	...	4	4
Hammers	4	...	1	...	...	...	...	5
Knives and fragments	102	19	14	22	19	8	9	193
Hair-pins	611	53	239	183	237	22	22	1367
Small rings	496	28	115	195	202	14	3	1053
Ear-rings	238	42	36	116	...	3	5	440
Bracelets and fragments	55	14	16	21	26	11	2	145
Fish-hooks	189	12	43	71	9	2	1	248
Awls	95	3	49	98	17	...	...	262
Spiral wires	...	...	46	50	5	...	...	101
Lance-heads	27	7	...	4	2	5	2	47
Arrow-heads	...	...	5	1	...	...	...	6
Buttons	...	1	28	10	10	...	...	49
Needles	20	2	3	4	1	...	...	30
Various ornaments	15	5	7	18	3	1	...	49
Saws	...	...	3	...	...	...	...	3
Daggers	...	...	...	...	...	...	2	2
Sickles	18	12	1	2	7	1	4	45
Double-pointed pins	75	...	...	...	...	...	...	75
Small bracelets	20	...	...	11	...	...	...	31
Sundries	96	3	5	16	...	...	4	124
Total,	2004	208	618	835	539	73	69	4346

At Corcelettes, it will be observed, 539 bronze objects are reported,[1] of which only 29 are weapons and cutting instruments. At Estavayer, we have 618 bronze objects, and 11 weapons (including arrow-heads). At Cortaillod, the bronze relics number 835, and the weapons amount to 18.[2]

Contrast this with a station of the Iron Age—Marin—where 15 objects of bronze and 250 of iron were obtained. Here the weapons (of iron) amounted to 78, nearly one-third of all the objects of iron.

The entire number of bronze objects reported in our table is 4346; the weapons obtained from all these stations are 4 swords, 6 arrow-heads, 67 celts, 193 knives, 47 lance-heads, and 2 daggers. The number of weapons (which, omitting knives, is only 126) is entirely out of proportion to the iron weapons found at Marin, or to the stone weapons found at the Stone Age stations. At Wangen there were obtained 1500 stone axes; at Nussdorf there were 1000; at Moosseedorf there were 100 axes out of 400 objects of stone (arrow-heads, knives, &c.), besides 2300 flakes.

At the so-called bronze stations, unfortunately, the objects of stone are not reported, except at Nidau, where the objects of bronze amounted to 2004. Now at this, the greatest of all the bronze stations, *the stone axes obtained outnumber the bronze celts.*

At Unter-Uhldingen, another so-called bronze station, "300 stone celts were found, besides arrow-heads, chisels, stone hammers, &c."

[1] A Roman amphora was found at this station, and some implements of stone.

[2] Stone axes were found here.

There is some reason to speak of a Bronze Age in Denmark (and Sweden), and possibly, in Ireland. In these countries a great many bronze weapons have been found. In the Museum at Dublin there are 725 celts and chisels, 282 swords and daggers, 276 lance-heads and arrow-heads. In the Museum of Copenhagen, of swords alone there are 350.

As to Ireland, if there was a Bronze Age there, as we have shown, it continued down to the eighth and ninth centuries.

In Denmark, according to Professor Worsaae, the Bronze Age terminated about A.D. 200[1]—and, therefore, possesses no antiquity. The objects manufactured of bronze found in the Danish and Swedish peat and graves, are of a highly ornate and superior workmanship, and are associated with bracelets of gold, comfortable woollen garments, plank coffins, combs, and wooden cups *turned on the lathe.* The cuts on the following page will illustrate the character of the pre-historic industry in this region.

We observed that Professor Worsaae fixes the date of the Bronze Age in Denmark at A.D. 200. On this point the following remarks from this eminent Danish archæologist are important:—

"But if the people in the neighbourhood of Rome," he says, "and influenced by Roman civilisation, at the

[1] Mr. Valdemar Schmidt expresses himself to the same effect, stating that the First Age of Iron in Denmark corresponds with the Roman period, and fixing the close of the Iron Age in Scandinavia at the epoch of the Vikings. Matériaux, 1875, p. 352, 353.

So in the "Revue Archéologique" for 1875, p. 334:—"Les commencements de l'âge du fer en Suède semblent coincider avec le commencement de l'Empire à Rome."

commencement of the Christian era, generally possessed weapons of iron, it does not follow that the people of

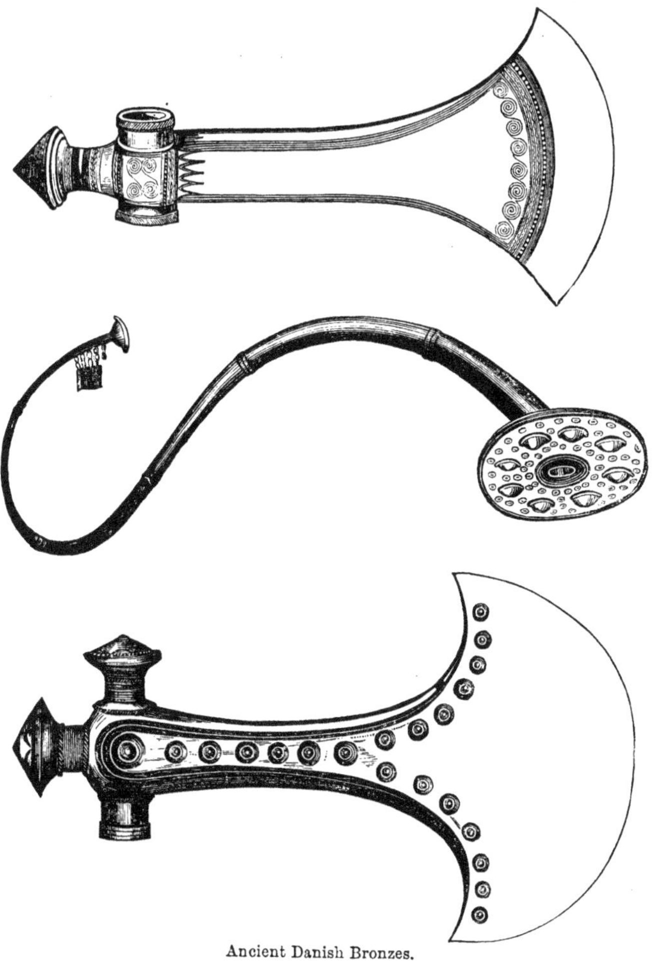

Ancient Danish Bronzes.

the North had also, at so early a time, plenty of that metal. Cæsar says distinctly that in Britain iron was only to be found at the coasts, and that in such small quantities that the inhabitants used imported bronze (*ære utuntur importato*). It must also be remembered that he speaks of their using iron rings as money. A century after Christ, the Britons seem to have got a great deal more iron, but the Germans had so little of it that they very rarely had swords, or large lance-heads, of that metal. It was when the Romans got colonies in Hungary, Germany, Gaul, and Britain, or about from the third century of the Christian era, that their civilisation first got some influence in the northern part of Germany and in Scandinavia, where, however, it had a hard struggle with the old civilisation."[1]

It appears to us that the tendency among the German archæologists is to a more conservative line of thought than has characterised the archæologists of France, Scandinavia, Italy, and England. The "Archiv für Anthropologie"[2] reviewing Dr. Hans Hildebrand's "Das heidnische Zeitalter in Schweden," discusses a great number of cases, and draws from them the following conclusions:—

1. The system of the Three Ages set up by the Danish archæologists is to be rejected as scientifically unfounded.

2. A Northern Bronze Realm has not existed; hence the bronzes of the mound-graves are to be regarded as only objects of traffic from Southern countries.

3. All the pagan graves of North-Western Europe fall

[1] Primeval Antiquities, pp. 139-142, English translation.
[2] Januar 1876, s. 310.

in the time of the burning of corpses and working in iron. The differences, in general, rest only on the gradually changed customs of one and the same people.

On the whole, it is evident that the matter is exceedingly mixed, and there is no good line of demarcation.

As between bronze and iron, some nations appear to have preferred bronze, and some to have preferred iron; but where was *bronze alone* used? In the Trojan beds and at Mycenæ (in the royal tombs) we find bronze, but we also find stone. In Mexico and Peru we find bronze and no iron, but we also find stone. In Africa (outside of Egypt) we find iron and not bronze, and no stone age. The Massagetæ, at the beginning of our era, used bronze, and the Ichthyophagi used stone, while all their neighbours used iron. The Danes used bronze when the Romans and the Gauls and Germans used iron. The inhabitants of Russia used iron and bronze alike—and continued to used stone. The Chaldæans and the Egyptians knew iron from the earliest period, but bronze was chiefly used down to (apparently) 1500 and 1200 B.C. There is no trace of iron at Troy down to 700 B.C. Either they *preferred* bronze, or the iron has rusted away.

CHAPTER XVII.

EXCAVATIONS AT TROY AND MYCENÆ.

A REVIEW of the "Three Ages" would not be complete without some account of the remarkable discoveries of Dr. Schliemann in the relic-beds and tombs of these ancient cities, which, however, in conformity with the plan of this work, must necessarily be brief.

At Hissarlik, the site of the Homeric Troy, this explorer dug down fifty feet below the surface to the virgin rock, and passed through five distinct relic-beds. These excavations were carried on in the most thorough manner, and extended through the years 1871, 1872, and 1873. Beginning at the bottom, the beds exhibited the following results:—

1. *Remains of the Oldest Settlement.*—At the depth of from 10 to 16 metres (33 to 52 feet) he found thousands of terra-cotta whorls, and on the virgin soil he found a number of copper (or bronze) pins, and a few knives, a nail, and some bracelets of the same metal; a silver dress-pin; and needles, a ring, a knife, and a plate of ivory. At the same time he found hammers and axes of diorite, weights of granite, beautifully polished wedges of transparent greenstone, flint saws, hand mill-stones of lava, punches of bone, a lamp in the form of a bowl, boars' teeth, sharks' bones, and great quantities of

fine pottery. There were black urns with Assyrian ornamentation, shining black bowls with a tube on each side, small black pots representing the human face, &c., &c., bespeaking "the opulence and fine taste" of the primitive settlers and predecessors of the Trojans. There were found also numbers of immense hewn and unhewn blocks of stone, which cover the pottery in layers from four to six metres thick.

2. This race was succeeded by what Dr. Schliemann identifies as the Trojan settlement. On the ruins of the old city these settlers erected buildings whose foundations consisted of small stones held together with clay; the walls being constructed of unburnt brick. This is at the depth of seven to ten metres. In this stratum the weapons were of stone and bone and copper (or bronze)—the stone being more abundant than the metal. The stone implements were hammers, millstones, wedges, pestles, weights, mortars, discs, saws, &c. Many and various specimens of pottery were found: drinking-cups, fantastic red goblets, a great profusion of finely-burned but uncoloured pottery, terra-cottas representing the priapus, &c.

In this bed he discovered a tower forty feet in diameter, the foundations (as he believes) of the Temple of Minerva; a house with eight rooms, adjoining the tower; and many human bones, among them two skeletons wearing copper helmets. The implements of copper (or bronze) included fourteen weapons, which he believes to have been battle-axes; seven double-edged copper daggers, a copper knife, and the fragment of a sword. There were found also a large copper dish, forty-nine centimetres (about twenty inches) in diameter, probably a shield; a copper kettle, and a copper vase; a round bottle of pure gold; a heavy gold goblet; and a drinking-vessel of gold in the form of a ship; five silver vases, a silver goblet, and a silver bowl; in one of the silver vases two magnificent golden head-bands, one frontlet, and four splendid golden ear-pendants; fifty-six golden earrings, and thousands of very small rings, pendants, dice, buttons, &c., all of gold; six golden bracelets, &c., &c. These treasures were found near the foundations of a large house in the vicinity of the tower, and Dr. Schliemann believes that it may properly be called the House of Priam. The pavement of a street, sixteen feet wide, formed of stone blocks, about four feet square, led from this house to a large massive double gate, the copper bolts of which were found among the rubbish.

The fashion of the jewellery is entirely original, and offers no resemblance to that of Assyria or Egypt.

Among other evidences of the destruction of this settlement by a fierce conflagration, Dr. Schliemann found "a layer of slags of melted lead and copper, in some places an inch thick, extending over the whole site of the city." With the exception of the stately edifice near the "Scæan Gate," nearly all the houses of Troy were built of unburned brick, with sills of hewn stone.

In this relic-bed occur the first traces of wheel-made pottery.

3. The next bed above this is at the depth of from four to seven metres, and the relics are still character-

istic of the same Aryan race, whose symbols (as, for example, those of the sun and the cross) are found in all of the beds.

The stone implements occur in this bed by "thousands," and there were also found a few copper implements. The implements of stone, moreover, are less highly finished than those below, giving evidence, as does the scarcity of metal, of a ruder people. The architecture has also changed, the walls of the buildings being no longer of brick, but of small stones and clay. The terra-cottas, too, are still graceful, but of inferior quality to those in the two preceding beds. Several of the terra-cotta discs found in Bed 3 are precisely identical in shape, size, and emblematic decoration, we are told, with those found in the Lake-Dwellings of Northern Italy. The emblems referred to, in both instances, point directly to India—"to the Sanskrit myths of *Pramantha*, the far earlier origin of the Greek Prometheus."

We learn thus that the date of the Lake-Dwellings of Italy is later than the Trojan War.

Many of the patterns on the discs of terra-cotta, and also on certain terra-cotta "bells," are well-known Vedic symbols, such as the hare (a symbol of the moon), the tree of life, the caterpillar, and the peculiar cross, of which we have already spoken, called in the Sanskrit *swastika*.

4. There was yet another epoch at Troy prior to the so-called "Historic" Period. This is represented by the bed at the depth of from two to four metres. The city was destroyed for the third time, and a yet ruder and poorer race succeeded the people represented by Bed

No. 3. They are still Aryans. The pottery is scarcer and ruder than in Bed 3. But we have here implements chiefly of copper; lances, knives, nails, &c. The implements of stone are rare, and include saws and knives of volcanic glass, &c.

5. Above these remains, that is, at the depth of from one to two metres, we reach the relics of the "Historic" or Greek Period. Here we find Greek architecture and works of art.[1]

Such are the revelations with regard to the Stone and Bronze Ages at Hissarlik. It appears strange that there is no iron. We know that this metal is far more perishable than bronze, and it may, possibly, have disappeared; but our impression is that it would hardly all have perished if it had been in use.

There was no Stone Age and no Metal Age at Troy. All of the settlers, up to the "historic" relic-bed, used stone and bronze together, and (excepting Bed 4) stone in greater abundance than bronze.

Mr. Gladstone, in his book entitled "Homer's Place in History," has shown that the date of the Trojan War was B.C. 1356–1206—perhaps about B.C. 1270, the date given by Herodotus.

If we suppose the race represented by the third bed to have occupied the site 200 years, then we find stone implements (with but little metal) used by the inhabitants of a *city* on the Hellespont during the period

[1] It is a strange fact that even in this bed only a few objects of iron were found, viz., a key and a few arrows and nails. The bronze, however, continued, and was represented by a half-dozen knives, a double-edged axe, two dozen nails, and a few lances and arrows—showing that even the historic Greeks used weapons of bronze.—Troy and its Remains, p. 31.

represented by B.C. 1270–1070. The people represented by Bed 4 still used stone, but chiefly copper or bronze, and no iron, *down to the Historic Period* (B.C. 650 or 700).

And, subversive of all archæological theories, we find Bed 3 representing a stone-using people above Bed 2 representing a bronze-using people.

The facts at Hissarlik are totally irreconcilable with the system of the modern science of Pre-historic Archæology, and we regret to observe that the expounders of this system studiously ignore them, and continue to teach in their works a scheme of the exfoliation of the human race in Europe, which must be mischievous so long as it is a false representation of the primitive life and habits of the early populations which occupied this Continent.

A most astonishing feature of the history revealed by the *culture-beds* (as the Germans call them) at Troy, is that we have here stone implements in use amongst the inhabitants of *a city;* and if they were used in the cities and towns, what must have been the case in the rural districts of the Troad and of Greece?

Dr. Schliemann, it ought to be noted, constantly speaks in his book of "copper" implements in these beds; but he should have known that great blocks of stone cannot be hewn with implements of copper or stone. An analysis of some specimens from the Trojan bed (No. 2), by M. Damour of Lyons, showed that some of the implements, at least, are of *bronze*—one specimen containing four per cent. of tin, and another nine per cent.

We have previously stated that among the vessels of pottery found here by Dr. Schliemann, was one representing in its form the hippopotamus. This object was found at the depth of six or seven metres, or in the relic-bed immediately succeeding the Trojan bed. Its date is about 1200 B.C.

On the handle of a sceptre, in crystal, found at eight metres, was found the carving of a lion's head, an animal no doubt perfectly familiar to the inhabitants of the Troad at that time.

SANTORIN.

The cliffs on this volcanic island consist of horizontal beds of black lava, alternating with layers of reddish scoriæ and violet-gray ashes, and, capping all, a stratum of pumice-stone of a brilliant white colour. In quarrying for this pumice, the workmen some years since discovered a buried city—traces of houses built of irregular blocks of lava (uncemented). Great quantities of pottery—jars with a capacity of several gallons,[1] containing chick-pease, barley, and coriander seed—broad basins with handles—cups, platters, &c.—a bright yellow vase with beautiful arabesques—were met with. They recognised also certain "stables," containing bones of the horse, and horse-troughs made of large blocks of lava, with shallow rectangular cavities cut in them. Outside of one of the house-walls there was found a set of large hewn stone blocks, laid regularly over each other, in the top

[1] "The counterpart of those in which the modern islanders store their grain."

For an account of this discovery, see Dublin University Magazine, 1870, article, "A Greek Herculaneum."

of which was a cylindrical cavity an inch in depth. Several implements of bronze were met with, and two gold rings, which were the links of a chain. There were found in addition a lava oil-press, hand-mills, weavers' stone discs, a stone knife or lance-head, a flint saw, and knives and arrow-heads of obsidian.

The hewn blocks and stone troughs imply, of course, iron or bronze tools. The pottery and the presence of the domesticated horse indicate a considerable progress in civilisation.

It is only necessary to remark on this buried city—overwhelmed evidently by a volcanic eruption—that it reveals a state of things parallel to what we have observed at Troy—metal and stone in use at the same time.

MYCENÆ.

Last year Dr. Schliemann carried on considerable excavations at this place, which is the site of the oldest city in Greece, with the exception of Tiryns. The walls of the Acropolis of Mycenæ have been built at different periods: a portion of them, like those of Tiryns, consists of huge blocks joined with small stones; another portion (and much the larger one) of carefully hewn polygonal blocks, fitting closely together; and, lastly, as seen near the Lions' Gate, there are sections of quadrangular blocks in horizontal layers, the joints not perfectly vertical.

The city covered a square mile to the south and south-west of the Acropolis, the site of which is marked by frequent traces of cyclopean walls, by the remnants of cyclopean houses, by fragments of archaic pottery, &c.

Dr. Schliemann began his excavations at the passage which led from the Lions' Gate into the Acropolis, where he opened a trench 113 feet long by 113 feet broad. At the surface there was a layer of rubbish of the Hellenic period, which went to the depth of three feet. As the terra-cotta figures and fluted vases are of the Macedonian period down to the second century B.C., Dr. Schliemann thinks that this relic-bed dates from the fourth century B.C. Below this comparatively modern Hellenic city he found thousands of fragments of beautifully painted archaic vases, made, for the most part, on the wheel; more than two hundred terra-cotta idols of Juno, in the form of a woman, or that of a cow; "two terra-cotta horse-heads, the figure of a lion, that of a ram, and that of an elephant, which seems to prove that the Greeks knew this animal many centuries before the Macedonian period."

At the depth of about ten feet he found a pearl and some objects in the shape of buttons of a glass-like substance; some iron knives and keys; two well-preserved knives of bronze; two arrow-heads of bronze; two beautifully polished hatchets of diorite or greenstone; a number of weights and hand millstones of trachyte; a large quantity of lead, and a small particle of gold. Also hundreds of whorls of a beautiful blue stone, fragments of a lyre and a flute, &c. At 10 to 11½ feet, and sometimes 6½ feet, he encountered "cyclopean houses," built of unhewn stones, whose foundations were at the depth of 20 feet. He discovered also traces of "small streets," cyclopean water-conduits of uncut stones, and numerous tombs, marked by upright slabs of limestone. On two of these slabs are bas-reliefs—on one, a warrior, armed with a lance, and standing in a chariot drawn by one horse, together with other figures; on the other, a warrior in a chariot, holding in his left hand a sword, and in his right hand a long lance, with which he pierces a fantastic animal, resembling the two lions above the great entrance door to the Acropolis. This animal, however, is represented with horns, and Dr. Schliemann raises the question whether the lions above the door (whose heads are missing) may not have been represented in the same way. He thinks these sculptures on the tombstones belong to the same period as the lions over the entrance door, that is, about 1200 B.C. He refers the Treasuries (he mentions nine) and the wall near the Lions' Gate to the same period. The oldest portions of the circuit walls he refers to about 2000 B.C.[1]

In his excavations, at another point, on the Acropolis, Dr. Schliemann discovered the foundations of "a cyclopean house," and, at the depth of about eighteen feet apparently, found "axes of a hard black or green stone;" many spindles of blue stone; and numerous vases, some of which "represent *crocodiles;*" all of the vases being covered with paintings of a dark-red colour, representing warriors wearing plumed helmets and breastplates and greaves.

Dr. Schliemann has discovered also at Mycenæ, at a

[1] Letter from Dr. Schliemann in London "Times," of September 27, 1876.

greater depth, five tombs hewn in the rock of the Acropolis—evidently the royal tombs—possibly, as Dr. Schliemann believes, the sepulchres of Atreus and Agamemnon, "and those who returned with him (to use the words of Pausanias) from Troy." He has found in these tombs immense treasure of gold and silver, of wonderful workmanship; numbers of bronze swords, lances, and knives; in one of them, "twenty-five arrow-points of stone;" and in another "thirty-five arrow-heads of obsidian."

We are further told that "in, on, and about these tombs a new world of splendid hand-made pottery comes to light, *and a vast number of obsidian knives.*"

We find thus at Mycenæ stone, bronze, and iron[1] all in use at the same time in the bed represented by a depth of ten feet; while in the tombs, still deeper down, we find the arrow-heads of stone and the obsidian arrow-heads and knives associated with swords of bronze and cups and vases of gold and silver and beautiful jewellery; this, too, in the *royal tombs.*

Among the objects of gold found in these tombs were three or four small square plates of exquisite workmanship "with lions engraved on them."

The Aryan *Swastika* or pre-Christian cross is also, as at Troy, stamped upon the pottery.[2]

The "Gate of the Lions," and the frequent occurrence of this figure in the relic-bed and tombs, shows

[1] No iron was found in the tombs, which are evidently older than the relics found at the depth of ten feet.

[2] One of the most striking facts mentioned is that some of the human bones in the tombs are said to be "*like the bones of giants.*" This recalls the statement that the coffin in which the bones of Orestes were found at

that this animal was a familiar one to the inhabitants of Greece at the time of, and after, Agamemnon.

We find the crocodile, too, represented, and we must fairly infer that this too was found at that day in the rivers of Greece.

But what shall we say of the terra-cotta image of the Elephant? Where did the Mycænians get their knowledge of this animal? We have found the Hippopotamus at Troy; and we have seen that the elephant was hunted in the Tigris valley about 1100 B.C.—was living, indeed, on the head-waters of this river in the ninth century B.C. We are compelled to believe that the elephant inhabited Greece *after* the tombs which we have described had received the mortal remains of the royal house of Atreus. The only possible alternative is to suppose that it is the Assyrian elephant, or that the Argives had imported the effigy from the north of Africa—and when we admit either of these hypotheses, it is equally easy to suppose that the animal lived in Europe."[1]

Tegea was ten and a half feet long (Hdt., i. 68), and the other statement that the skeleton of Theseus, which was brought to Athens by Cimon in 468 B.C., belonged "to a large body," by the side of which a bronze sword and spear were buried. Were there "giants in those days?"

[1] The only traces of foreign influence in Greece at this period are Assyrian or Phœnician. Prior to the Trojan War, Sidon had her ships in all these parts, and Mr. Gladstone believes that Phœnician artisans built the walls of Tiryns and Mycenæ.

CHAPTER XVIII.

FURTHER CONSIDERATION OF THE PEAT-MOSSES.

Extravagant estimates—The Danish peat—Represented by three strata; the pine, the oak, and the beech—These forests probably contemporaneous—Evidence that no great time has elapsed since the pine grew in Denmark—Statements of Rennie and Steele—Hatfield Moss—Roman axes, &c., found at bottom of, and trunks of the pine, oak, and beech—Earl of Cromarty on the growth of peat—Bog in Ross-shire—Kincardine moss—Roman road at bottom of—Irish Crannoge under fifteen feet of peat—Various other examples to show rapid growth of peat—Statements of M. d'Archiac as to peat of Somme Valley.

THIS subject was partially considered in our remarks on the peat of the Somme Valley; but we desire to call attention to some additional facts presented in other localities. The estimates of M. de Perthes, as we have seen, would require 30,000 years for the creation of the peat of the Somme Valley; and Mr. Hudson Tuttle, of Boston, believes that it took 120,000 years for its formation.[1]

We mentioned that a boat laden with Roman bricks was found at the bottom of this peat, and that another boat containing several skeletons, a bronze sword, and coins of Maxentius was found in a peat-moss at Heilly near Abbeville. We gave at the same time various other examples tending to show that this peat was in

[1] Origin and Antiquity of Man Scientifically Considered, p. 55.

many instances post-Roman, and that none of it could date very many centuries before the Christian era.

Sir Charles Lyell, Sir John Lubbock, and others have also much to say about the Danish peat, in which, we are told, the Three Ages are successively represented by a primeval stratum containing the remains of pines; a second stratum containing remains of oak forests; and a third containing remains of the existing beech forests of Denmark. The pine stratum, we learn further, contains the industry of the Stone Age; the oak stratum, implements of bronze; and the upper stratum, relics of iron. The pine, it is observed, has not been a native of Denmark "in historical times." When it had ceased to grow in Denmark, it was succeeded by forests of oak, and the oak has in turn been supplanted by the beech.

We would remark on this, first, that in Denmark "historical times" do not go beyond the ninth or tenth century; secondly, that as to the time required for one forest growth to succeed another, we know that in the United States the chestnut forests do not require a great time to be succeeded by the pine forests. The probability, however, is that these trees were all contemporaneous in Denmark. Mr. S. R. Pattison, F.G.S., in his reply to Sir C. Lyell, observes on this point: "The superposition of the oak timber in the bogs is easily accounted for, without calling in the aid of thousands of years. The process and its progress are matters of ordinary observation. A clump of pine trees grows with here and there an oak; the firs are the first to become old and feeble; some of them fall and begin to decay; the tiny streamlet meandering through the wood is dammed up; mosses grow; the firs all fall; the bog increases; the more hardy oak yields next; the birch and the alder survive on the driest spots; but these too are ultimately engulfed."

We shall give some evidence presently that the pine, oak, and beech *were* contemporaneous.

The peat deposits of Denmark, as we learn from "The Antiquity of Man," vary in depth from ten to thirty feet. Around the borders of them, says Lyell, lie trunks, especially of the Scotch fir (*Pinus sylvestris*), "often three feet in diameter." As we pointed out in treating of the Somme Valley peat, these fallen trunks could not have lain long in the damp air without decay, and they must have been covered up by the peat before they had time to rot. They would (uncovered) have rotted in fifty or seventy-five years; and, where they are three feet thick, the peat must have grown three feet in seventy-five years, which is four feet in a century. It is obvious, therefore, that the Danish peat, even where it is thirty feet deep, need not be very ancient.

Again: Sir Charles Lyell observes that "swords and shields of bronze have been taken out of the peat in which oaks abound," and M. Morlot is quite sure that the oaks belong to the Bronze Age, because in this layer were found "the magnificent bronze bucklers of the Museum of Copenhagen." These swords of bronze and "magnificent bronze bucklers," do not suggest to our mind the idea of a high antiquity, nor can we believe that such armour was used in Denmark before our era.

With regard to the antiquity of the pine stratum of the peat, characterised by the relics of the Stone Age, we learn from Professor Worsaae's "Primeval Antiquities," in his section on the "Antiquities of the Stone Age," that the apparel of the aborigines of Denmark consisted chiefly of skins, and that bodies clad in such skins have from time to time been dug up from the peat-bogs, "with some primitive leather shoes or sandals, made of a single piece of hide sewn together behind." He then adds, that "with these there have been found also remains of *woollen cloth*." We are, therefore, to understand that while the pine forests were flourishing in Denmark, the population clad themselves, in some instances, in woollen garments: which certainly could not have been true of Denmark 500 years before our era.

Rennie, in his "Essays on Peat," informs us that "many of these mosses of the North of Europe occupy the place of forests of pine and oak, which have, many of them, disappeared within the historical era." Mr. Steele, another writer on Peat,[1] gives us an instance of this at Hatfield Moss, in Yorkshire. The original forest here was cut down by the Roman General Ostorius, in the reign of Vespasian. Since this time the peat, which formerly covered an area of 20,000 acres, has formed, and "many feet deep at the bottom of the moss or fen mould," when the bog was drained, old "Roman axes and knives, and links of chains, and some

[1] Steele on Peat-Moss, pp. 282–285.

ten or twelve coins of the Roman emperors were found." In this peat, we are also told, trees of Scotch fir, oak, birch, beech, yew, thorn, willow, ash, &c., the roots standing in the hard soil at the bottom of the moss, were found in vast numbers. The pines were, some of them, ninety feet long, and were so firm and strong as to be sold for masts and keels of ships; while some of the oaks were 120 feet long, and were sold for from ten to twenty pounds, and were so hard and durable as to be fit for any purpose. Some of these trees had been burned; others had been chopped and squared; others riven with great wooden wedges and stones. We have here then the pine, the oak, and the beech all growing together in Yorkshire in the time of Vespasian.

We learn from Professor James Geikie that the Scotch fir does not now grow in England, nor south of the Forth.[1] It has disappeared from England, as well as from Denmark.

With regard to the rate of formation of peat, much has been already said, but we may add some farther illustrations of it.

The Earl of Cromarty makes the statement that "the frequent discoveries of mediæval objects low down in fen deposits, and the experience of those who have had to do with peat lands, lead to the conclusion that two thousand years constitute ample allowance for the growth of all the peat on the present surface of the globe." He gives an account, in the Philosophical Transactions of the Royal Society of London,[2] of an

[1] Great Ice Age (1874), p. 326.
[2] Vol. xxvii.

instance in which, within his own knowledge, the peat formed at such a rate that the inhabitants of the district dug it for fuel in less than half a century from the time when it began to grow. This was in the parish of Loch Broom, Ross-shire, and it was the period 1651–1699 over which the observations of the Earl of Cromarty extended. In 1651, on an elevated plain, he had noticed a forest or wood of fir trees, which seemed to be in a dying condition. About 1666 he came to the same spot, and the trees had all disappeared, and the plain was covered with a growth of green moss. He inquired what had become of the wood, and learned that the trees had been overturned by the wind, and, lying very thick, had been grown over by the moss. "Before 1699," he adds, "that whole piece of ground was turned into a common moss, where the country people are digging turf and peat."

The crannoges of Ireland, as is suggested by Sir W. R. Wilde, date probably from the ninth to the sixteenth century, and very few stone, or even bronze, weapons are found in them.[1] Sir Charles Lyell, however, informs us[2] that in one of these at Lagore, the relics, consisting of stone, bronze, and iron, were covered by fifteen feet of peat. Taking the extreme date suggested by Sir W. R. Wilde, it would appear that this peat must have formed in ten centuries.

The peat in Kincardine Moss, Perthshire, is from

[1] Proc. Soc. Antiq. of Scotland, vol. vi. p. 144; Proc. R. I. A., vol. vii. p. 152.

[2] Antiquity of Man, p. 30.

seven to fourteen feet in depth, and covers (at a point where the depth is eight feet) a Roman road twelve feet wide, formed of logs of wood laid across each other.

According to De Luc, the very sites of the aboriginal forests of Hercynia, Semena, Ardennes, and several others, are now covered by mosses and fens. A great part of these changes, he observes, has with much probability been referred to the strict orders given by Severus and other emperors to destroy all the wood in the conquered provinces.[1]

De Luc also tells us that a coin of the Emperor Gordian, A.D. 237, was found thirty feet deep in the peat at Groningen.

Degner states that the remains of ships, and nautical instruments, have been found in many of the Dutch mosses.

Sir W. R. Wilde, in his "Catalogue of the Antiquities of Animal Remains and Bronzes in the Museum of the Royal Irish Academy," mentions several instances in which vessels containing *butter* were found in the Irish peat at great depths. No. 37 of the catalogue was found, at the depth of nine feet, in Grallagh bog, near Abbeyleix, Queen's County.

No. 38 was found, at the depth of fifteen feet, in Ballyconnell bog, Donegal County. The butter is a hard, yellowish-white substance, like old Stilton cheese, and in taste resembles spermaceti. It was contained in a large square, thin "mether," apparently intended originally for a butter or milk vessel. This vessel is

[1] Lyell's Principles, vol. ii. p. 500.

nine inches high, and five inches across, is made of willow, and is double-handled.

No. 41 is another larger vessel of butter, found eighteen feet below the surface, in the county of Kilkenny.[1]

In the same work Sir W. R. Wilde mentions a shoe (No. 28 of the catalogue), found at the depth of twenty feet in a turf bog near Templemore, Tipperary. It is "a right," "thong-sewn, turned shoe," of thick, well-tanned leather, with a double sole.[2]

Now it is not to be entertained that these objects belong to a very remote date. Butter was not known to the Romans before the second century of our era (although the Germans are said to have known it before this); and a shoe like the one described above was hardly worn in Ireland fifteen centuries ago.

Sir W. R. Wilde mentions also that in 1824 a human body, completely clad in woollen garments, was found in a bog in the parish of Killery, at the depth of six feet. He refers it to the fifteenth century. A silver coin was also found, which was illegible.

In the bog of Lower Tyrone, Kerry, according to the same authority, a wooden candlestick of fir, 8½ inches high, was found at the depth of sixteen feet.[3]

Mr. Steele, in his work on "Peat Moss,"[4] states that a butter-kit, filled with butter, was found at the bottom of Cormaskae Moss, in Perthshire.

The same writer informs us that Dr. Plott, in his "Natural History of Stafford," mentions that "a parcel of coins of Edward IV. were discovered in a peat-moss

[1] See pp. 267, 268. [2] P. 292.
[3] Catalogue of Antiquities of Stone, &c., p. 218. [4] Page 11.

eighteen feet deep, which, supposing them to have been dropt on the surface in that reign, led him, by the latest date of the coins, to the arithmetical conclusion that the moss must have risen or grown upwards of an inch every year."[1]

"A very curious instance," says Mr. Steele, "of the growth of an extensive moss, viz., Cree, in the North of Scotland, was reported in 1785, as follows: About nineteen years before, a gentleman who lived near one side of it could, from a certain window of his house, observe the door of a cottage which was built on the opposite side of the moss; whereas then, from the same place, he could scarcely see the top of its chimney."[2]

Yet another instance cited by Mr. Steele is an extract from Mr. Vancouver's Agricultural Report of Cambridgeshire, which states that under peat twelve or fifteen feet thick in Ireland, there were seen ridges and furrows, the indisputable marks of a former cultivation, and at the bottom they found "the dash and lid of a hand-churn, and a large crane-necked brass spur, with a rowel a full inch in diameter."[3]

In excavating, some few years since, in the vicinity of London Wall, a bed of peat was reached which rested on a gravel similar to the Thames ballast. This peat was from seven to nine feet thick, and above this were the remains of London earth, composed of the accumulated rubbish of the city. In excavating the peat it was found to contain planks, Roman nails, red Samian pottery, bronze pins, iron knives, tweezers, shears, the leathern soles of shoes and sandals, thickly studded with

[1] Steele, p. 13. [2] Page 16. [3] Page 136.

hob-nails, the *caliga* of the Roman legions, &c. Roman relics occurred in it from top to bottom, showing that it had grown some eight feet in 400 years. We may add that among the animal bones occurring in it were those of the *Bos primigenius.*

Another instance, mentioned by Mr. Maxwell in his "Statistical Account of the Parish of Kilbarchan, Renfrewshire," shows that a peat-moss referred to by him has grown in depth at the rate of three feet per century. This is proved by the stumps of the trees, broken off three feet above the roots, standing erect in the peat. Mr. Maxwell suggests that this moss (which is eight or nine feet deep) cannot be very ancient, from the fact that there are places around it "still denominated by the Saxon name of *wood.*" "He might have added," observes Mr. Steele, "that a great proportion of the mosses in the Lowlands of Scotland retain the name of woods, though there does not now exist a growing tree in their vicinity."

The author of the Article on *Peat* in "Appleton's New American Cyclopædia," makes the statement that "an increase in the Irish bogs of *two inches a year* has been observed," which would be sixteen feet in a century! And this does not exceed the rate of formation in the instance cited by us from the observations of the Earl of Cromarty in Ross-shire, if it be true, as we have seen it stated, that the peat in that moss, in the fifty years mentioned, attained a thickness of eight feet! Nor does it exceed the rate of growth in some parts of the valley of the Somme, according to the testimony of M. A. d'Archiac, who says that "in some turbaries of the upper valley of the Somme, which we have described, it is estimated that a century is necessary for the reproduction of a bed of 3m 50 [11½ feet], which would give about 13 millimetres a year, a rate probably too great."[1]

This M. d'Archiac regards, however, apparently, as exceptional, for in the same connection he remarks that "according to a certain number of examples attentively studied, it has appeared that the first growth of peat was rarely less than 64 centimetres in a century [2 feet 2 inches], and that often it has been able to attain double this, or 1m 28 [4 feet 4 inches]."

[1] Introduction à l'Étude de la Paléontologie Stratigraphique, tom. ii. p. 394.

CHAPTER XIX.

NO PALÆOLITHIC REMAINS IN EGYPT AND BABYLONIA.

THE question of the antiquity of the human race must ultimately, we think, be laid at rest in the East. As we observed in the beginning of this work, all the migrations of men point to Asia, and even "the cradle of the Egyptian race," we are told by M. Brugsch, "must be sought in the centre of Asia." The palæolithic hunters of the Somme Valley did not *originate* in that inhospitable climate, but moved into Europe from some more genial region. The domestic animals also, and the cereals, as already stated, had their origin in Western or Central Asia, or in Egypt.[1] The nephrite of the palæolithic cave of Chaleux, and of the Swiss lake-dwellings, points in the same direction.

[1] M. Geoffrey St. Hilaire specifies some forty species of domestic animals; thirty-five of these, he says, such as the horse, goat, sheep, ox, dog, pig, &c., may be called cosmopolitan; and out of these thirty-five possessed by Europe, thirty-one appear to have originated in Central Asia or Northern Africa. Nearly all the forty are from a warm climate, which indicates that civilisation pertained to primeval Asiatic man.

The millet (two kinds), the six-rowed barley (*hordeum hexastichon*), the Egyptian wheat (*triticum turgidum*), the Cretan catch-fly, and the corn-bluebottle, are all found in the pile-settlements of the Swiss lakes.

Mr. Vicien stated at the British Association, in 1865, that no trace of the existence of the cereals can be discovered in geological formations that can be imagined older than six thousand years.

What, then, do we learn from the most ancient nations, according to tradition and monumental history? What does Egypt declare? What voice comes from the Lower Euphrates? What are the hints to be gathered from the first faint rays of the primitive Aryans?

The first glimpse which we get of "the happy Bakdhi (Bactria) with the lofty banner," is Zòroaster and the holy precepts of the Zend-Avesta. We find the Aryans in their primeval seat—before they crossed the Hindoo Koosh, or passed the Hellespont—in possession of the domestic animals, with a language of which the Greek and the Sanskrit are twin children, with fixed abodes, and dwelling in houses; tilling the soil, though by rude methods; contracting marriage with solemn ceremonies; with an organised, kingly government; fortifying their towns; with swords, and javelins, and helmets, and shields, and breastplates of metal.

This race has, however, left few or no monuments, and its life was not distinctly localised and confined to one spot, as was the case in Egypt and Babylonia.

It is, therefore, Egypt and Chaldæa that speak most distinctly on this subject. We can go back to the Great Pyramid, or to that of Sakkarah (doubtfully referred to the First Dynasty), and we find Egypt a thoroughly organised state, with a knowledge of letters, of the metals, of astronomy, anatomy, geometry, mechanics, agriculture, sculpture, of the useful and ornamental arts. The architecture and statuary of this period, as we took occasion to remark, are superior to anything in later times, even to that of the Second

Theban Monarchy, when, under Thothmes or Rameses, Egypt was at the acme of her power and glory. In Babylonia we encounter also a race of great builders, with the cuneiform characters, working in iron and bronze, and exhibiting an advanced civilisation.

We stated that behind the pyramids in Egypt, and the cities of Erech and Calneh, in Southern Babylonia, there is *nothing*—nothing to indicate the earlier presence of the human race. There was *no Palæolithic Age*—in fact, *no Stone Age*—in these countries.

If man, in the valley of the Nile, was originally a savage of the most degraded type—or if, indeed, he commenced life in Egypt only as rude and uncivilised as the cave-dwellers of Périgord—we ought to see some indications of the fact. If Egypt, like the Somme Valley, was inhabited by man one or two hundred thousand years ago, there ought to be monuments or relics of some kind—more or less rude—leading up to the splendid civilisation of the Fourth Dynasty. But we find in Egypt, and in the Mesopotamian Valley, nothing corresponding with the traces of man discovered in the river-gravels and caves of Europe, or the shell-mounds and pile-villages of Denmark and Switzerland.

Behind the Pyramids, and the ruins of the old Chaldæan cities, there is, as we have said, no human footprint. Man appears to have intruded upon the scene suddenly and abruptly, and his advent was at once signalised by the erection of those great tombs and temples, which are the first objects to betray the presence of a guiding and intelligent mind.

A writer in "Nature,"[1] over the initials "W. B. D." (believed to be Mr. W. Boyd Dawkins), has undertaken to reply to the affirmation (made in "The Recent Origin of Man") that there are no traces of palæolithic man or of a Palæolithic Age in Egypt or Babylonia. "The statement," he says, "that no traces of a rude and imperfect civilisation have been met with in the East[2] is refuted by the discovery of enormous quantities of flint implements in Egypt, and of neolithic axes in Asia Minor and India. In the river-gravels of both these regions palæolithic *hâches* have been found, of the same type as those of Amiens and Abbeville."

It is expressly stated in the work which "W. B. D." is criticising, that flint implements occur in the Nile Valley, and that palæolithic implements occur in India. This is not the point: the point is as to the *age* of the flint implements found in the Nile Valley; and the affirmation was that there were no traces of a Palæolithic Age in Egypt or Babylonia.

Stone implements, as we have shown, occur constantly in the old Chaldæan tombs, but they occur *with implements of metal:* they do not represent a Stone Age, and far less a Palæolithic Age.

So in Egypt (as M. Mariette mentions) they have been found at Biban-el-Molouk, at Monfalont, and at other points.[3]

All of these Egyptian implements, however, were

[1] Vol. xiii., No. 326, p. 245; also vol. xiii., No. 339, p. 510.

[2] This was not the statement.

[3] M. J. Delanoüe gives an account of his discovery of a number of flint implements on the summit of the hillock of Fatira, five kilometres from Djebel Salsile. He believes that they belong to the Palæolithic Epoch;

found *on the surface of the ground.* Numbers of them were found also in the old turquoise mines in the Sinaitic peninsula. They have also, as stated in a previous chapter, been found in the ancient Egyptian tombs—of both the Pharaonic and the Greek periods—arrow-heads, knives, flakes, &c.; and there are delineated on the monuments knives, hatchets, and lance-heads of stone.

There was not even a Second Stone Age—a Neolithic Age—in Egypt (any more than in Babylonia or at Troy).

But this, as just observed, was not the point: the affirmation was that there was no *Palæolithic Age* in Egypt or Babylonia. If man lived in Western Europe (as contended for by Mr. Dawkins) before the Glacial Age, we ought to find in Egypt and Babylonia something resembling, as regards geological horizon and fauna, the implement-bearing gravels of the Somme Valley; we say, *geological horizon*—that is, in beds of corresponding age.

In an article in the "Journal of the Anthropological Institute of Great Britain and Ireland,"[1] Sir John Lubbock gives an account of a visit by himself to the Nile Valley in 1873, and tells us that he found chipped flints at various points along the valley, especially in the Valley of the Tombs of the Kings, at Thebes, and at Abydos. He found them "on the slopes of the hills and on the lower plateaus, above the level of the inundation, wherever flint was abundant and of good quality."

but one of his cuts represents a beautiful specimen of polished white flint, which negatives the conjecture that the find belongs to the Quaternary Period. Cong. d'Anthrop., 1872, p. 314.

[1] Vol. iv., No. 1, p. 215.

Sir John adds nothing to what was previously known, excepting the discovery of several implements which, he tells us, "closely resemble" the St. Acheul specimens.[1]

That a few implements closely resembling those from the Somme Valley, should have been singled out from the multitude which occur, is what was to have been expected, and is in analogy to the few specimens of the same type which have been found in the Babylonian tombs. Our impression is that it was the earliest type, and we are rather surprised that more of them have not been found in Egypt and Babylonia.[2]

We may remark that implements of palæolithic type were found at the neolithic mines of Cissbury, explored so thoroughly by Colonel A. Lane Fox; and, guided by their resemblance to those of the cave of Le Moustier, Colonel Fox assigned the station to the Palæolithic Age. But the associated fauna fixes the date in the Neolithic Period, to which Mr. Evans and all others now refer it. We pointed out also (chap. xiv. p. 236) that implements of "palæolithic type" are found in the North American mounds, and among the relics of the Indian tribes, on the surface of the ground.

The only farther attempt by Sir John Lubbock to connect the stone implements of Egypt with the Palæolithic Age, is based on a single remark of M. Arcelin, of which Sir John Lubbock avails himself, and to which M. Arcelin also seems to attach some importance. The

[1] He seems to have been anticipated even in this by M. Arcelin.

[2] Professor Rawlinson informs us, however, that the stone implements found in the Babylonian tombs are very rude. Ancient Monarchies, i. 96.

remark is this: "Le gisement se prolonge sous les sédiments modernes; qu'il ne passe pas dans ces sédiments où je n'ai trouvé aucune trace de pierre taillé."

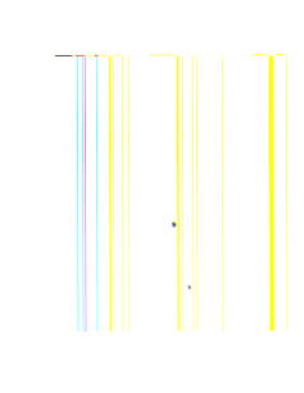

It appears to us that something more substantial than this is needed as a foundation for a Palæolithic or a pure Stone Age in Egypt. And it is as was to have been expected. The mud which covers (and which covered before the Human Period) the Nile Valley would, of course, spread in some places over the soil containing the native flint on the slopes of the valley. It would cover it and bury it up to a certain line. Where this mud deposit ceased, the flint stratum would appear to run under the mud, while the inhabitants of the valley would seek the native flint outside of these limits and up to the line where it ceased to be exposed. The worked flints—the refuse matter—would thus be found exactly where it has been found, on the plateaux and on the higher slopes of the valleys, and occasionally somewhat encroached on by the river silt.

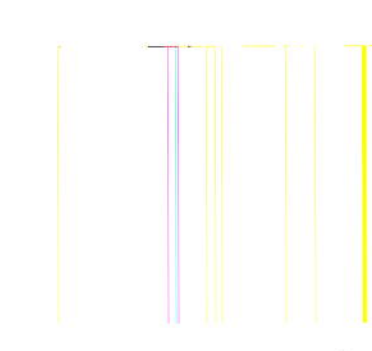

MM. Arcelin and Murard had previously explored the Nile Valley, "with the special view," says Professor Busk in his address, in January 1874, as President of the Society, before the Anthropological Institute of Great Britain and Ireland, "with the special view of ascertaining whether indications of a pre-historic Stone Age of the same kind as those which have been afforded in all parts of Europe, were to be met with in the valley of the Nile."

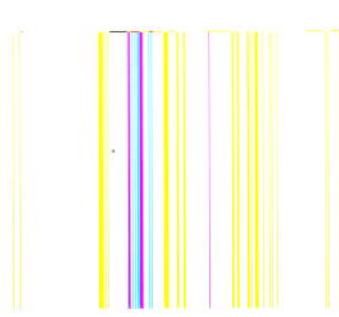

"The importance of such a discovery in Egypt in an ethnological point of view," he remarks, "could hardly be overrated." He goes on to tell us that the labours

of MM. Arcelin and Murard were soon rewarded by the discovery of abundance of flint implements, more especially in the neighbourhood of Gizeh, Sakkarah, Thebes, &c.

The implements were found either on the high plateau of the valley or beneath the fluviatile deposits of the river above the pliocene or quaternary beds, "at the extreme verge of the fluviatile beds where they thin out towards the desert."

But their researches in the ruins of the ancient cities, and in the disturbed ground where excavations had been made in the exploration of monuments, were less successful. In fact, according to their report, MM. Arcelin and Murard "discovered no traces of stone implements in inhabited sites belonging to the Historic Period." "Whence," says Professor Busk, "they conclude that implements of that nature have not been in use since the Historic Period."

Professor Busk adds: "But this appears to be hardly in accordance with the previous discoveries above alluded to, and with those of M. Rossellini and Professor Lepsius, who met with flint implements in mummy cases and tombs. Nor is it to be reconciled with the subsequent finds by MM. Hamy and Lenormant, who met with a very extensive collection of knives (flakes), cores, and rude implements, of the same character as found at Moustier,[1] in the neighbourhood of Biban-el-Molouk and at Deïr-el-Bahari.

[1] If these implements are really of the Moustier type, it shows that the palæolithic type of the oldest European caves was in use in Egypt in historic times.

The same observers, encouraged by these and other discoveries, pursued their search for stone implements with renewed zeal, which was followed by the discovery opposite Memphis [Lubbock found them in the Valley of the Tombs of the Kings at Thebes] of numerous flint flakes, glazed from their having lain long in the sand."[1]

In Babylonia, we repeat again, the "palæolithic" flints have been found in the tombs, along with objects of metal; but here, as in Egypt, no worked flints have been found buried deep in the soil, or in caves, in association with extinct animals.

Another question presents itself in this connection; for we are dealing with a *test* case: If Egypt and Chaldæa are as old as the cave-men of France and England, why do we not encounter, along with their civilisation, a palæolithic *fauna* — the elephant, the hippopotamus, the reindeer, the cave-lion, &c.?

The rapid settlement of these countries, and their advanced civilisation, tended, of course, to clear them at once of wild animals, and especially the larger ones.[2]

The northern animals we should not, of course, expect to see.

The hippopotamus, the lion, the tiger, the hyæna, the antelope, the leopard, we do find on the Egyptian monuments, and represented in hunting scenes, which show that they were found in Lower Egypt. The

[1] Journal of the Anthropological Institute, vol. iii., No. 3, 1874.

[2] The facts connected with the *antediluvians* have a bearing on this point. They may have cleared these regions.

Island of Elephantine, in the Nile, on the southern limits of Egypt, was probably, as we have remarked elsewhere, named from the elephant, the hieroglyphics AB, by which the name is expressed, signifying *Elephant-land.*

The representation of an elephant, carved in wood, is stated to have been found, along with chipped flints and a bronze finger-ring (set with turquoises), in the turquoise mines (dating from the Fourth Dynasty) of Wady Maghara, in the peninsula of Sinai. If this object is to be regarded as of the same date with the other objects found, it implies a knowledge of the elephant at a very early period in Egypt.[1]

In the Mesopotamian Valley the matter is less obscured. The facts already given by us in Chapter xii. show that the elephant and the lion abounded in this region, at least in Assyria, as late as the twelfth century B.C., as proved by the inscription on the prism of Tiglath-Pileser I. Three centuries earlier the Egyptian king, Thothmes III., in an expedition against Nineveh, captured on a hunting expedition one hundred and twenty wild elephants.

And yet there are no representations of the elephant on the Assyrian monuments, save on the Black Obelisk of Shalmaneser II., of the ninth century B.C., where it constituted part of the tribute brought to the Assyrian monarch by the *Muzri,* from the head-waters of the Tigris. But on this monument the rhinoceros also is

[1] The pottery representing the elephant found at Mycenæ shows unmistakably that the animal was found somewhere in the Mediterranean basin at this time.

among the animals delineated, and we may therefore infer that it too was found in Mesopotamia when the caves of Western Europe were inhabited by the palæolithic tribes. (See also p. 187, NOTE.)

We know it is fashionable to represent that "the higher civilisation is ever a growth and an outcome from a preceding lower state;" but, as Mr. Alfred Russell Wallace remarked before the British Association in 1876 at Glasgow, speaking of the Great Pyramid, "here we have a building which marks the very dawn of history, which is the oldest authentic monument of man's genius and skill, and which, instead of being far inferior, is very much superior to all which followed it." This is one of those things, which, as Sir John Herschel said, "according to received theories ought not to happen." But it does happen in Egypt, and [this early, in some instances this superior, civilisation] not only in Egypt, but in Chaldæa and among the primitive Aryans of Bactria, and at Mycenæ, among the ancient Malays, among the ancient Italians, among the ancient inhabitants of Siberia, among the inhabitants of the Mid-Pacific Islands, in Ashantee, and with the Mound-Builders of North America.

Is there anything in Greece older than the walls of Tiryns? Where is it?

The Europeans found the Isles of the South Pacific in their Stone Age; but they found the traces of a superior people and a departed civilisation.

CHAPTER XX.

SIBERIA.

Astonishing preservation of the tusks of the mammoth in Western and Southern Siberia, and of carcass of same in the East—The destruction of this animal in that country—Views of Erman and Murchison—Theory of Mr. Howorth—The destruction sudden—Proofs that a large portion of Siberia was formerly covered by the sea—The climate formerly milder—The Asiatic Mediterranean or Hyrcanian Ocean—No Glacial Epoch in Siberia—No remains of the reindeer or musk-sheep in the caves, and no palæolithic flints—Tula.

THE preservation of the carcasses of the mammoth in Siberia is referred to their being imbedded in the ice or frozen sand. The bones of the mammoth are found, however, in all the Lowland of Siberia—in the west as well as in the east, and from lat. 60° to the Arctic Ocean. They have indeed been found as far south as 56°, below the city of Krasnojarsk. The carcasses, on the other hand, are found ordinarily beyond the Arctic Circle, and in the east.

The bones and tusks of the animal are, however, like the carcasses, astonishingly preserved (the ivory being an article of commerce), and this can hardly be referred to the effects of cold, as the climate of Siberia is much milder in the west than in the east, and the summers at Krasnojarsk are very hot.

And, with regard to the carcasses, making ample

allowance for their being imbedded in the frozen soil, it is incredible that they have been locked in this embrace, undecayed, for several hundred thousand years. Palæontology furnishes no such example.

It is generally recognised now that when herds of the mammoth and rhinoceros were supported in Siberia, the climate was much milder than it is at present.[1] The destruction of these animals, and the wonderful preservation of their flesh, has given rise to various conjectures, but the views presented to the British Association, in 1869, by Mr. H. H. Howorth, strike us as more plausible than any that we have seen on the subject. He was, in some measure, anticipated by Erman and Sir Roderick Murchison.

Erman remarks that the alluvial deposits of Siberia, in which are found the bones of the mammoth, and leaves and twigs of the birch and willow, consist, to the depth of 100 feet, of strata of loam, fine sand, and magnetic sand, and that they have been deposited from waters "which, at one time, and, it may be presumed suddenly, overflowed the whole country as far as the Polar Sea." . . . "It is only in the lower strata of the New Siberian wood-hills (composed largely of drift-wood) that the trunks have that position which they would assume in swimming or sinking undisturbed. On the summit of the hills they lie flung upon one

[1] In 1810, Hendenstrom went across the tundra direct to Utsjouk. He says, "On the tundra, equally remote from the present line of trees, among the steep banks of the lakes and rivers, are found large birch-trees complete with bark, branches, and roots. At first sight they appear well preserved, but on digging them up they are found to be in a thorough state of decay. The first living birch-trees are not now found nearer than 3° to the South, and then only as shrubs."—Von Wrangel's Voyage.

another in the wildest disorder, forced upright in spite of gravitation, and with their tops broken off or crushed, as if they had been thrown with great violence from the south on a bank, and then heaped up. . . . So it is clear that at the time when the elephants and trunks of trees were heaped up together, *one flood extended from the centre of the continent to the farthest barrier existing in the sea as it now is.*"[1]

Sir Roderick Murchison observes that "the final destruction of the mammoth may have resulted from aqueous debacles dependent on oscillations of the mountain chains, and the formation of much local detritus."[2]

Mr. Howorth, however, has given the fullest expression to these views in the Report to the British Association to which we have referred. We have merely space for his conclusions, which are these:—

1. That the mammoth lived where its remains are found.

2. That a great portion of this area is now a moss-covered *tundra*, or an ice-and-boulder heap.

3. That no herbivore of the size and development of the mammoth could find subsistence in that area now.

4. That, although covered with wool, and therefore adapted to a more rigorous climate than that of India or Africa, neither the mammoth nor the rhinoceros could survive the present winter temperature of Northern Siberia.

5. That the remains of the food eaten by the mammoth, and found and examined by Middendorff and

[1] Travels in Siberia, Trans., vol. ii. pp. 378–380.
[2] Geology of Russia, vol. i. chap. xix.

Brandt, are remains of plants only found now in more southern latitudes.

Mr. Howorth concludes further, therefore:

That the climate and condition of things have changed very greatly in Siberia since the mammoth existed there. In support of this conclusion, he calls attention to the fact that the bed of the Arctic Sea, north of Siberia, is rapidly rising, and exposing banks of sand containing mammoth remains, the land rapidly gaining on the sea along the whole coast line.

The appearance of the tundra, says Mr. Howorth, seems to point to a not very distant submergence of the whole of Siberia, as far south as the highlands which roughly mark the present northern limit of trees.

What, then, has led to the extinction of the mammoth? The hand of man, says Mr. Howorth, is quite inadequate; and we must seek for the cause in the draining of the vast Mediterranean Sea which once extended from the Euxine to the Khingan Mountains. The drainage of this sea must have been sudden and overwhelming; for we find the mammoth remains aggregated in hecatombs on the pieces of high ground, and not scattered indiscriminately. This alone would account also for such an immediate change of climate (from an insular one to a continental) as should allow the bodies of the mammoth to be immediately frozen, and thus preserved intact.[1]

This is a bold conjecture, but some attention to the facts of the case renders it in a high degree probable.

Northern Siberia is one vast plain, sloping gradually

[1] Proc. of the British Association, 1869, p. 90.

to the ocean. Between the Obi and the Yenisei, from lat. 60° to the sea, and between the Yenisei and the Lena, from the Arctic Circle to the sea, the country consists of *tundras,* or mossy deserts, which have very recently been covered by the sea. This is proved by the thin coating of sand and fine clay which extends over these plains, and contains heaps of shells perfectly identical (at least in the high latitudes) with those of the adjacent sea.[1] (In this sand and clay the bones of the mammoth are found.)

M. Reclus remarks that "after Humboldt's profound investigations on Central Asia, we shall not, at the present day, show too great temerity in assuming that during some portion of the present period a vast strait, like that which once ran along the southern base of the Atlas, extended from the Black Sea to the Gulf of Obi and the Frozen Ocean."[2]

We mentioned in the chapter on "Recent Changes in Physical Geography," that skeletons of the whale have been found 800 miles up the Lena; and that Chinese documents report the land towards the north to have terminated at a remote period at no great distance beyond the mountain chain of Northern Tartary.[3]

[1] See Reclus's The Earth, p. 91. Lyell's Principles of Geology, vol. i. pp. 181, 183.

An idea of this region may be formed from the fact that Tobolsk, which is situated on the Irtisch, a tributary of the Obi, 525 geographical miles in a direct line from the mouth of the latter, is only 115 feet above the level of the sea. Bernaoul, on the Obi, 920 geographical miles from its mouth, is 383 feet higher than the sea. The Yenisei, after leaving the mountains, traverses a similar flat region for nearly 800 miles to the head of its estuary.

[2] The Earth, p. 637.

[3] See p. 205, and a memoir read at the Geographical Society, February 8, 1841; also Biblioth. Orientale d'Herbelot, tome iv. p. 171.

And now as to the reality of that ancient Hyrcanian Ocean of which the ancients speak: "Nearly in the middle of the southern border of the Great Plain," says M'Culloch in his 'Geographical Dictionary,' "on both sides of the hills of Mugodsharsk, and the countries lying south of it, between 45° and 64° E. long., occurs the most remarkable depression on the surface of the earth. A tract of country extending over an area of more than 300,000 square miles, exclusive of the Caspian Sea, is, according to the supposition of Humboldt, lower than the surface of the ocean. The lowest part of it is occupied by the Caspian Sea, which is . . . 116 feet below the surface of the Black Sea, the Lake of Aral being fourteen feet above the latter sea." "The Caspian Sea," he says, "there can be little doubt, was formerly much more extensive on three sides—the north, north-west, and east;" that "it has been observed that the present bed appears to descend in terraces;" and that "on the east and north-west the land presents also incontestable proofs of having formerly been covered with sea-water; being uniformly flat, except when it rises in sandy ridges to form the terraces before mentioned; being uniform in soil, which consists of sand combined with marine slime, without a trace of terrestrial vegetation (except the common desert plants), or the slightest indication of minerals; the substratum being clay, at a considerable depth from the surface; and the surface itself abounding in sea-salt, sea-weed marshes, salt-pits, and lakes, together with innumerable shells exactly resembling those of the Caspian Sea, and which are not found in any of the rivers. . . . Towards the east the whole country has the same appearance of a deserted sea-bed; and the conclusion therefore appears inevitable, that at comparatively no distant period the Sea of Aral, the Caspian, and the Black Sea, formed one body of water, uniting the present anomalous salt lakes of Asia with the ocean. This conclusion is further strengthened by the presence of the same species of fishes, seals, &c., in the three seas, a fact which it is impossible to account for on the supposition that they were always separated."

MM. Lenormant and Chevallier, in their "Ancient History of the East," alluding to the first appearance of man on the earth, tell us that at that time "in the north of Asia a vast mediterranean sea, which subsequent elevations of the soil have removed, occupied the whole basin of the Caspian and Sea of Aral, covered great part of the Steppes situated between the Ural Mountains and the Volga, as well as the country of the Kalmucks, and reached southward to the base of the Caucasus. Its eastern limits are uncertain; but according to the observations of travellers, and *indications drawn from the annals of China*, it seems to have occupied all the desert of Gobi to the north of Thibet."[1]

Herodotus, Strabo, Ptolemy, and all the authors of antiquity who allude to the subject, attribute to the ancient Hyrcanian Ocean an extent far greater than that of the Caspian of our day; most of them, indeed, considered this sea a prolongation of the Northern Ocean.[2]

[1] Ancient History of the East, Trans. (1870), vol. i. p. 26.

[2] Herod. Clio., 203, Strab., xi. 507.

May there not be an allusion to this Asiatic Mediterranean in the inscription of Rimmon-Nirari on a pavement slab from Nimrud, trans-

The existence of such an ocean can hardly be questioned, and it doubtless contributed to fix the character of the climate of Western Europe in the Palæolithic Age. At the Anthropological Congress of 1871, at Brussels, M. Dupont alluded to the singular conjunction of northern and southern forms in the fauna of the Belgian caverns—the reindeer, the musk-ox, the glutton, &c., on the one hand, and the hippopotamus, the hyæna, and the lion, on the other. He proceeded to observe: "It is evident that the hippopotamus proves the absence of rigorous winters, and the species of the north excludes very warm summers. It is necessary, then, to suppose at this epoch a climate more equal and temperatures less extreme than in our days. But it is the north-east wind which brings the cold in winter and the heat in summer, a double effect which seems to hold with the existence of a great plain in that direction. It is necessary, then, to seek the explanation of the climate of the Quaternary epoch in the absence of those lands, and the presence at that epoch *of a great sea to the north-east of Europe*."[1]

There was no Glacial Epoch in Siberia: there are, we are told, no traces of glaciation either there or in North-Eastern Russia.[2]

lated by the Rev. A. H. Sayce? The Assyrian monarch describes his empire as reaching "from the great sea of the Rising Sun to the great sea of the Setting Sun."—Records of the Past, vol. i. p. 3.

It was evidently, says Mr. Gladstone, in his *Juventus Mundi*, the idea of the Homeric geography that there was a great ocean to the north or north-east of Greece. Such notions as the Greeks of that period had on the subject were doubtless a tradition from the Phœnicians.

1 Matériaux, Janvier 1872, p. 35.

2 Geology of the Ural Mountains, by R. J. Murchison, pp. 554, 555. Sir R. J. Murchison, after stating that Siberia is perfectly free from

The Siberian mammoth and rhinoceros were, doubtless, living in Siberia and Russia when Northern Europe was covered with ice, and at the close of the Glacial Period they wandered into Europe. The climate of Siberia was then milder than it is now. The ocean advanced up to the Arctic Circle, and even beyond; while farther south a vast inland sea, covering 500,000 square miles, and communicating with the Northern Ocean, spread out like a second Mediterranean.[1]

In Siberia the cold set in after the Glacial Period—at the close of the Palæolithic Epoch probably. The draining of the Asiatic Mediterranean was connected, probably, with the change of climate in Europe after the Palæolithic Age, and with the change that took place in the climate of Siberia; and was a part of those general disturbances which took place at this time in Europe, in India, in the valley of the Mississippi, and in Montana, Idaho, Colorado, and the western territories of the United States, where are seen such recent traces of some extraordinary geological convulsion.

The severe cold in Siberia followed upon the elevation of the land, the destruction of the great inland ocean of Central Asia, and the retirement of the Arctic Sea; it was due, as Mr. Howorth says, not only to the eleva-

erratic blocks, remarks: "All lands, therefore, in the Northern Hemisphere, which are as void of such drift as large portions of Siberia on the one hand, and Siluria on the other, may have been, like them, for ages the habitation of the great extinct quadrupeds."

See also Congrès Internat. d'Anthrop., 1871, p. 128. M. Vogt observes: "L'époque glaciaire n'a pas existé dans l'Asie Centrale; on n'en trouve du moins aucune trace dans l'Altaï."

[1] There was in Africa at this time a third great inland sea, commencing at the Gulf of Syrtes, and joining the Atlantic opposite the Canaries.

tion of the land, but to the consolidation of the continental area of Asia, which had not previously existed.

The climatic change in Siberia must have been *sudden;* otherwise it is impossible to account for the preservation of the flesh of the mammoth and the rhinoceros. Sir Charles Lyell is correct in saying that the ice or congealed mud in which their carcasses are found "has never once melted since the day when they perished." And the paroxysmal character of the phenomena connected with the destruction of these animals is indicated again by the statement of Howorth, that "we find the mammoth remains aggregated in hecatombs on the pieces of high ground, and not scattered indiscriminately"—as if they had all fled to these eminences for safety when the waters spread around them. The same fact is further corroborated by the statement of Erman, that on the summit of the hills the trunks of the trees are not found in the position they would assume in swimming or sinking undisturbed, but "flung upon one another in the wildest disorder, forced upright in spite of gravitation, and with their tops broken off or crushed, as if they had been thrown with great violence from the south on a bank."

With regard to the climate of Siberia at the time when the mammoth lived in this region, we may remark that M. Brandt has published a work on the fauna of the bone-caverns of the Altai, from which it appears that while the remains of the mammoth, rhinoceros tichorinus, great Irish elk, hyæna, aurochs, urus, tiger, *sus scrofa*, &c., are found, those of the reindeer and the musk-ox do not occur. It is also the *Hyæna spelæa*, the spotted or African species, which is represented, and not the striped hyæna, which is now spread over Western Asia. The animals mentioned are associated with a number of others still inhabiting this region. No human remains have been met with, nor works of art.

This is a very striking fact: why are there no palæolithic flints in these caves? The answer may possibly be, that the human contemporaries of the mammoth in Siberia were a bronze-using people, and not troglodytes like the men of the same age in Western Europe—a branch of that great Turanian family which is identified with the earliest civilisation of Babylonia, and which spread doubtless into Siberia and China—of the same stock, perhaps, with that mysterious bronze-using people who preceded the Romans in Northern Italy—connected, perhaps, with the bronze-using races, undoubtedly of Asiatic origin, which the Spaniards found in America on the coasts of the Pacific.[1]

[1] It is a noteworthy fact that the tumulus is found alike in Siberia, Tartary, Etruria, and Mexico; while in the Etruscan, Peruvian, and Siberian graves we meet alike, among the relics, with *bronze mirrors.*

Atkinson mentions ancient earthworks and canals for irrigation on the River Bean, the boundary between the Great and Middle Hordes of Tartars—reminding us of the Mound-Builders.

The Toltecs called their capital *Tula*, after (as they said) their original home. No doubt the great convulsions in Asia, in the time of Tscenghis Khan and his successors, drove them from the banks of the River Tula, near Lake Baikal. Tula is also the name of a province of Russia.

The conquests of the Mongols, in the thirteenth century, extended from Germany to the Yellow Sea, and included all Asia except Arabia and Hindostan. To them belong the "Strangers' Graves" in Siberia, in which are found such treasures of gold and bronze. One of the sons of Tscenghis was named *Tuli*, and in the vicinity of the River Tula, Tscenghis was born.

CHAPTER XXI.

THE RECENT DATE OF THE GLACIAL AGE DEMONSTRATED.

No traces of palæolithic man in the North of Europe—Due to the continuance of the ice in that region—Man first entered Denmark and Scotland in the Neolithic Age—Inference as to date of the Glacial Age—Erratics found in Sweden on recently elevated beach—And in Scotland—Arctic climate in Scotland in Iron Age—Recent date of Glacial Epoch further argued from age of peat—The Aryan tradition of the Glacial Age—The Victoria Cave.

WE are informed by Sir Charles Lyell and other writers, that there are no traces of the Palæolithic Age in the North of Europe—that is to say, in Norway, Sweden, Denmark, Scotland, Ireland, and the North of England. When man entered these regions, the Neolithic Period had been inaugurated. Nor do we find in Denmark, Sweden, or Norway the remains of the mammoth or the rhinoceros. The oldest implements found in all of these northern countries all belong to the period of Polished Stone, and are found in the peat-bogs, or in the estuarine deposits of Scotland. "It has been estimated," says Sir C. Lyell, "that the number of flint implements of the palæolithic type already found in Northern France and Southern England, exclusive of flakes, is not less than 3000. No similar tools have been met with in Denmark, Sweden, or Norway, where

Nilsson, Thomsen, and other antiquaries have collected with so much care the relics of the Stone Age. Hence it is supposed that palæolithic man never penetrated into Scandinavia, which may perhaps have been as much covered with ice and snow as the greater part of Greenland is at present."[1] And again: "The occurrence of the mammoth and reindeer in the Scotch boulder-clay, favours the idea that the retreat of the glaciers of the Grampians may have coincided in time with the existence of man in those parts of Europe where the climate was less severe, as, for example, in the basins of the Thames, Somme, and Seine, in which the bones of many extinct mammalia are associated with flint implements of the antique type."[2]

To the same purport we read in the *Archiv für Anthropologie:* "Neither in Scandinavia nor in North Germany have we yet discovered the slightest trace of palæolithic man." "Scandinavia and North Germany were then covered by the ice."[3]

It is the same in Switzerland, and in the elevated portion of Carinthia and in Styria. Of these last Count Wurmbrandt observed at the Buda-Pesth Congress, that they exhibit traces of two periods of glaciation, but that the caverns never exhibit any proof of the existence of man during that time. . . . "The farther one recedes from the mass of the Alps, the greater is the chance of finding in the caverns traces of palæolithic man."

[1] Principles of Geology, vol. ii. p. 560.
[2] Antiquity of Man, 4th edit., p. 295.
[3] Archiv, August 1875, Correspondenz-Blatt, s. 18. Meeting of the Anthropological Society in Munich in 1874.

It is astonishing that our geologists and archæologists have not observed the significance of this fact.

We know approximately the date of the Neolithic Epoch; it is the date of the older Swiss Lake-Dwellings, of the lowest stratum of the Danish peat, and of the older Megalithic graves. No archæologist would, we presume, place the beginning of the period farther back than 10,000 years. That would be an extreme limit. The calculation of M. Morlot, repeated in Sir John Lubbock's work, based on the age of the cone of the Tinière, reaches an antiquity of about 6400 years for the stone implements found in this gravel formation. M. Gilliéron reached about the same figures from certain data presented at the Pont de Thièle, to which we have adverted. M. De Ferry fixes the antiquity of the Neolithic Age, from his observations on the valley of the Saône, at 4000 or 5000 years. M. Arcelin's calculation, from similar observations in the same valley, makes the date range between 3600 and 6700 years ago. M. Worsaae, in his "Primeval Antiquities of Denmark," remarks that "it is therefore no exaggeration if we attribute to the Stone Period an antiquity of at least 3000 years."[1]

This last, we think it probable, is about the true date, and we may venture to fix the epoch of the pile-villages, the shell-mounds, the peat, and the oldest Megalithic monuments about the time of the Trojan war; that is, about 1300 B.C. To be within the mark, let us make it 2000 B.C.

[1] Transactions, p. 135.

That is the date of the close of the Glacial Age in Denmark and Scotland.

We see no escape from this conclusion; the Neolithic folk of Europe, according to the archæologists, moved into these northern countries on the retirement of the ice; and if we ascertain the date of the Neolithic Age, we ascertain the date of the Glacial Age.

It is a beautiful illustration of the incidental revelations of science, and of the mutual light shed on one another by two independent lines of inquiry. It is an illustration of the correlation of all true science, and of the inter-dependence of all the members of the great body of truth. We have seen the astronomer contributing his knowledge to the interpretation of geology, and now the youngest of the sciences—Pre-historic Archæology—unexpectedly illumines one of the darkest points in the same record.

Pre-historic Archæology has rushed undoubtedly to some extreme conclusions; geology, in the enthusiasm of a new world of discovery, fell into the same mistake; but it may safely be said that the archæological investigations of such men as Boucher de Perthes, Lartet, De Mortillet, Lubbock, Evans, Thomsen, Nilsson, Fraas, Wurmbrandt, Keller, Desor, Gastaldi, Regnoli, have brought out from the palimpsest of the stones and sediments of the caves and valleys, the living characters in which were written the primeval annals of man in Europe. They have done for the ruder tribes of the human race what Champollion and Young, Rawlinson, Oppert, and Smith, and Schliemann, have done for Egypt and Babylonia, and Troy and Mycenæ. They have added a Book of Genesis to the Kings and Chronicles of Europe. Their discoveries have not only revealed the human life of Pre-historic Europe, but they have brought up before us as in a picture the climate, the physical geography, the vegetation, and the fauna of this continent, when snow, and ice, and rain, and volcanic fires, mighty floods of fresh water in the rivers, and great waves from the sea, were familiar spectacles to the palæolithic hunter—and yet more familiar the gigantic forms of the mammoth and great elk, the cave-bear and the cave-lion.

The men of the Mammoth and Reindeer Epoch in Belgium had advanced as far as the rigorous climate of the close of the Ice Age permitted them to go; as soon as the North was relieved of the ice-sheet or the icebergs, they moved into Denmark. But by this time the Palæolithic Age had closed; they carried with them the Polished Stone Implements which are found in the lowest strata of the peat-bogs.

It was the same in Scotland and the North of England: man pressed, as Sir C. Lyell says, upon the retiring ice, and the relics of his industry, which were buried in the estuarine deposits of Scotland, and the peat-bogs of Ireland, tell us exactly the epoch in pre-historic chronology when this occurred.

There are some other facts that tend to corroborate the conclusion thus reached.

It is recognised that the present Baltic shells are of dwarfish proportions as compared with those found in the Danish shell-mounds, and that the exclusion of the waters of the North Sea from the Baltic was the cause of this deterioration in the marine fauna on the east of Sweden; in other words, the dwarfish mussels and cockle-shells of the Baltic are of later origin than the shell-mounds. Now Sir Charles Lyell informs us that he observed in 1834, near Upsala, a ridge of stratified sand and gravel, containing a layer of marl evidently formed at the bottom of the Baltic, by the slow growth of the mussel, cockle, and other marine species, all of dwarfish size, like those now inhabiting the brackish waters of this sea,—the bed being 100 feet above the level of the Gulf of Bothnia. Upon the top of this ridge repose several huge erratics, which must have been brought into their present position, since the neighbouring gulf was already characterised by its peculiar fauna. We thus learn that the transportation of erratics continued after this region had assumed that physical conformation by which the Baltic became divided from the North Sea, and the Gulf of Bothnia lost the standard of saltness which characterises the waters of the ocean; and after the shell-mounds (one of the oldest of which contained bronze) had accumulated on the Danish islands.[1]

As a parallel case to this, we learn further from Sir C. Lyell that Mr. James Smith, of Jordanhill, found a large boulder on the lowest ancient beach of the West of Scotland, which, in his opinion, could only have come

[1] "I cannot doubt," says Lyell, "that these large erratics of Upsala were brought into their present position during the recent [*i.e.*, the present] period, not only because of their moderate elevation above the sea-level in a country where the land is now perceptibly rising every century, but because I observed proofs of a great oscillation of level which had taken place at Södertelje, south of Stockholm, after the country had been inhabited by man."—Antiquity of Man, 4th edit., pp. 281, 282.

there on floating ice. Lyell recalls in this connection the position of the whales found in the Carse of Stirling, some twenty feet above high-water mark. On this he observes: "The position of these whales, and their association with human implements, imply that at the time when they were cast ashore by a tide rising twenty or thirty feet beyond the present high-water mark, man was already an inhabitant of Scotland; and their great size indicating that they belong to the Greenland whale —which only frequents seas of floating ice—*would point to an Arctic climate*[1] in these regions before the last change of level occurred."[2]

The estuarine silt of this carse was deposited, therefore, beneath "seas of floating ice" and during the prevalence of "an Arctic climate;" and, as an *iron anchor* was found in this silt, and iron implements (character not stated) in the Carse of Gowrie, we must draw the conclusion that ships carrying implements of iron sailed upon this "Arctic sea."

We have already indicated another line of argument from which we may derive an approximate date for the close of the Glacial Age. The peat in Denmark and the Somme Valley rests directly on the post-glacial deposits; if we could fix precisely the age of the peat, we should, for all practical purposes, ascertain when the

[1] Italics ours.

[2] Antiquity of Man, 4th edit., p. 60.

To show that the Glacial Epoch in Scotland is of later date than the same period farther south, Lyell remarks: "But while in the Bridlington sand [at Holderness] no less than five out of the seventy species of shells are not known as living, every one of the long list of shells from the Scotch till belongs to living species. . . . The Scotch till is therefore to be referred to a later period than the Holderness boulder-clay."—Antiquity of Man, 4th edit., p. 287.

post-glacial gravels were deposited. But we have shown that several thousands of years will cover all of the peat deposits, not only by the objects and the fauna found therein, but from the undecayed stumps of the trees which they contain. We find here, therefore, a corroborative evidence that the antiquity of the post-glacial gravels cannot be very great. The traces of the pile-settlement found by M. Boucher de Perthes in the peat at Abbeville rested immediately on the so-called "drift."

The recognition of the fact that man appeared on earth upon the heels of the Glacial Age has had much to do with the belief in his great antiquity, for it has been quietly assumed that that epoch is removed by tens and hundreds of thousands of years from the present. Millions of years were the figures employed to describe the time which has elapsed since that great geological episode. In the tenth edition of his "Principles," Lyell estimated it to be about 800,000 years ago, which was moderate compared to the 1,280,000,000 years of some geologists.[1] But in the eleventh and last edition of Lyell's great work, he substitutes (based on the theory of Mr. Croll) 200,000 for 800,000.

Dr. Andrews's calculations, to which we shall refer, drawn from very careful observations on the North American Lakes, put 25,000 years as an extreme limit, and indicate in reality only some 7000 years.

The date of the Neolithic Age is, however, a more unerring index than even these lake beaches, and by

[1] World before the Deluge, Figuier, p. 22.

that we have arrived at a conclusion substantially the same as Dr. Andrews.

PERSIAN TRADITION OF THE GLACIAL AGE.

An echo of this great event comes to us from the traditions of the primeval Aryans. The original seat of this race—the Arianem Vaedjo of the Zend-Avesta—seems to have been the region between the head-waters of the Oxus (Djihoun = Gihon) and the Jaxartes, to the south-east of Samarcand. There was the centre of the world, the Holy Mountain Bezerat, from whose side flowed the sacred river Arvand.[1] Here there was no sickness nor death, frost nor heat, and men lived three hundred years. But, says the Zend-Avesta, "then Aura-mainyus, who is full of death, created a great serpent and winter"—"ten months of winter and two of summer." Driven from their Eden by the cold, the Aryans journeyed to the south-west, into Sogdiana—Margiana—Bactria, and other regions north and south of the Hindoo Koosh.

The cold that fell as a curse upon Arianem Vaedjo was the work of the "Daevas," and even the summer months, we are told, were "cold as to the water, cold as to the earth, cold as to the trees; after this to the middle of the earth, then to the heart of the earth, comes the winter; then comes the most evil." [2]

[1] M. Eugene Burnouf has shown that the Bezerat is the Bolor Tagh, and the Arvand the Jaxartes.

[2] Avesta, Vendidad, Fargard I., sections 5–12.

Lenormant remarks that when science shows us the first men living in the midst of ice, under conditions of climate analogous to those under which the Eskimo now live, "we are naturally led to recall the ancient Persian tradition, . . . which places in the first rank among the

Of course, any Persian tradition of the Glacial Period points to an event devoid of geological antiquity: it is very certain that the memory does not go back 6000 years; and that the event to which it refers (as appears from the Zend-Avesta) is connected with a civilised race.[1]

NOTE.—We have not thought it worth while to notice the "Preglacial Man of the Victoria Cave." It may be well, however, to state that this alleged evidence of the existence of man in England before or during the Glacial Period, relied on by Professor James Geikie and others, consists in the discovery of a human fibula under "stiff glacial clay" in the Victoria Cave, near Settle, in Yorkshire, associated with bones of the extinct animals. This clay, we are told, "occupies both the entrance and the inside of the cave;" of course, therefore, it had been washed into the cave, for glaciers do not enter caves to form the till or boulder clay which are said to have been the product of the ice-sheet. And if washed in by the floods and rains, this may have occurred at any time after the cave was occupied by man, and thousands of years after the Glacial Epoch.

It is only necessary to say that such is the opinion of Mr. Boyd Dawkins: "At the entrance of the cave," he tells us, "are ice-scratched Silurian grit-stones imbedded in the glacial clay." These, he thinks, were probably derived from the waste of boulder clay which has dropped from a higher level, which "appears the more likely, because some of the boulders have been deprived of the clay in which they were imbedded, and are piled

---

punishments which followed that fault [the fall], as well as death and sickness, the appearance of intense and permanent cold, which man could hardly bear, and which rendered the earth almost uninhabitable."—Ancient History of Earth, vol. i. p. 42. See also Bunsen's Work on Egypt.

[1] The belief in a universal deluge has been found nearly untenable; the theory of a partial deluge has been substituted, commensurate with the limits of the human race. But it is a serious difficulty of this last theory, that no good reason can be given why the race had not been dispersed over the face of the earth. Why should it have been localised? The answer may be that they were shut in by the ice and the seas of the Glacial Epoch. Europe, we know, was in large measure under water at this time, and the cold, perhaps, prevalent over the Continent.

on each other with empty space between them, the clay being carried down to a lower level and re-deposited."

The deposits of glacial clay above the cave earth, he adds, have been introduced by the rains, either through the entrance or through the crevices which penetrate the roof, and consist of a finer detritus washed out of the boulder clay on the surface at a higher level.

The laminated portions of the gray clay considered by Mr. Tiddemann to have been formed by the flow of water through the entrance, derived from the daily melting of the glacier which occupied the valley, Mr. Dawkins does not believe to be of glacial origin. He remarks that "similar accumulations are being formed at the present time at the bottom of pools in many caves." See "Cave-Hunting," pp. 121–123.

If, however, it were admitted that man had penetrated in a few instances the region of ice and snow to the north of the area hitherto marked out as the limit of the implement-bearing river-gravels, it would not be strange; we know how far north the Eskimo have advanced in Greenland; and, as we have pointed out, the glaciers were yet lingering in the North of England after the flood of the Palæolithic Epoch. The palæolithic hunter, whose weapons have been found abundantly in the valley of the Ouse, presumably wandered occasionally beyond that line—wandered, perhaps, into glaciated regions, as we know the animals of that epoch did.

Mr. Dawkins is, therefore, in error in considering this fibula in the Victoria Cave to be pre-glacial (in the sense that he gives to that term) on the ground of its association with the remains of the extinct animals. (See "Cave-Hunting," p. 123.) This ground is as untenable as the view of Mr. Tiddeman. (See *Addenda.*)

CHAPTER XXII.

FARTHER EVIDENCE OF THE RECENT DATE OF THE GLACIAL AGE.

Dr. Andrews on the great lakes of North America—The oscillations of level in the lakes—Lakes Michigan and Huron—Erosion of the bluffs by the waves, and the formation of beaches with the detached sand —The close of the drift in this region very sudden—The orange loam —Sudden retirement of the waters—Age of the lower beach—Soundings—The terrace of erosion—A calculation—Annual rate of erosion —The upper beaches—The amount of sand drifted—The beaches probably five thousand two hundred or seven thousand five hundred years old—Absolutely impossible, therefore, to allow such a period as one hundred thousand years for the antiquity of the Glacial Age—Another calculation—Even twenty-five thousand years an impossible admission—Changes of level in this region—Flexures and contortions in the strata—Rapidity with which the lakes fell and rose—Probable identification of the loess with the period of the middle beach—General results reached.

We have argued in the previous chapter that the Glacial Epoch has been erroneously assigned by the geologists to a remote antiquity. We have gathered this as well from the age of the estuarine beds in Scotland, and the peat-beds in Ireland, Denmark, and France, which followed the disappearance of the glaciers in those countries, as from the absence of all palæolithic remains in the North of Europe.

We shall now call attention to a remarkable and independent evidence of the same fact in America. These observations are due to Professor Edmund Andrews,

President of the Chicago Academy of Sciences, whom we have already had occasion to quote in connection with the phenomena of the Somme Valley, and the formation of the cone of the Tinière in Switzerland.

In the second volume of the "Transactions of the Chicago Academy of Sciences" is a paper by Professor Andrews on "The North American Lakes considered as Chronometers of Post-Glacial Time," which appears beyond all contradiction to be a complete demonstration of the error of the prevailing opinion with regard to the extreme antiquity of the Glacial Period; and, in contravention of this generally accepted opinion, to show that the true date of that period does not extend beyond a few thousand years ago. Dr. Andrews reaches the conclusion that "the total time of all the deposits [since the Glacial Period] appears to be somewhat between 5300 and 7500 years." This is a startling declaration—accustomed as we are to the 800,000 or the 200,000 years of Sir Charles Lyell.

The observations of Dr. Andrews were made on Lakes Michigan and Huron, which, he says, are hydrographically one sheet of water, with the same level, and connected by a strait several miles in width. Lake Michigan is 350 miles in length from north to south, and about 85 in width. Its outlet is at the north, the southern extremity being a *cul-de-sac.* Its waves are continually in motion, and rapidly erode the drift-clay of the shores. This erosion, taking place upon material nearly uniform in character, varies mainly with the violence of the waves, and hence, when long periods are taken, has a very regular rate.

In Lake Michigan the material washed down by the waves is sorted by the same agency into clay and sand; the clay floating about settles whenever it reaches deep water, where the wave action is too slight to keep it longer suspended, while the sand is carried by the currents along shore southward, and deposited in beaches and dunes on the low sloping plain around the south end of the lake. The *beaches* thus formed have mapped out on the country around the head of the lake every successive level occupied by its waters, and show, by their relative size, the length of time during which each one was deposited; while the same periods further north are indicated by the ancient *bluffs*, from the erosion of which the sands of the beaches were derived. It is by the combined study of the erosion and the beaches that the total post-glacial time can be deduced.

The elements of the calculation are the following:—

1. The average rate of erosion.
2. The width of the subaqueous plateau formed by the erosion since the lake stood at its present level.
3. The amount and direction of the sand movement.
4. The amount of sand in the several beaches.

It should be observed, says Dr. Andrews, that our lakes have existed ever since the close of the Drift Period, a time which is rather sharply defined, because the close of the drift in this region *occurred with a suddenness unusual in geological phenomena.*

The last member of the Drift in Wisconsin and Michigan is the Orange Loam, which is a well-stratified layer, covering all the Drift hills and valleys like a sheet, and usually only a few inches in thickness. It shows its relation to the rest of the Drift by displaying a few boulders, some of which are three or four feet in diameter; but their numbers are comparatively small. Disregarding, says Dr. Andrews, the dispute whether the heavy Boulder Drift below was laid down by glaciers, or by icebergs and water, it is evident that this upper sheet is a water deposit, and that this region was under water during its formation. Again, there is never any trace of peat or vegetable mould between it and the Drift, showing that no period of land vegetation intervened between the two. In short, *the Orange Loam is the closing member of the Boulder Drift.*

The waters, proceeds Dr. Andrews, which deposited the Orange Loam *retired suddenly to the south, closing abruptly the Drift Period.*

"I make this statement deliberately," says Dr. Andrews, "after several years of investigation. It is the unanimous testimony of civil engineers that no great body of water can retire gradually from a region without leaving numerous beaches and bluffs to mark the shore lines. Beaches form with great rapidity, ridges ten feet high being thrown up sometimes in a single storm; and all the sand and gravel tossed beyond the water's edge is left as it retires, a permanent monument of the former level. Now the waters at the close of the Drift fell with such abruptness, that outside of the basin of the lakes they have left no beach lines between the highlands of Wisconsin and the Ohio River, a fact attested by railroad engineers and geologists alike. . . . This recession, of course, left the basins of the great lakes like so many cups filled with water, and the waves being never still, must of necessity begin at once to erode their shores and cast up their beaches, as they have continued to do ever since. It follows, therefore, that the history of our lake-shores covers the whole period from the present time to the close of the Drift Period, meaning by that term the time of retirement of the waters that deposited the Orange Loam. From that time to the present the history of the lakes is mapped out on their shores, and may be read with more certainty than is usually possible in geological phenomena."

The waters of Lake Michigan have stood at three different levels, which are marked in the north by three bluffs which they have cut at different heights on the shores; and in the region around the southern extremity of the lake, where the vast amount of sand thrown in by the currents shielded the shores from wash, the three shore lines are accurately mapped out by sand beaches, which are on the same level as the bluffs with which they were severally contemporaneous.

Age of the Lower Beach.—The shores of Lake Michigan are nowhere stationary for long periods. The waves are continually either tearing down the clay, or else piling sand upon it, according to the situation, and both these processes go on with an energy and rapidity astonishing to one not accustomed to the investigation. Dr. Andrews's personal observations were mainly on the west shore of Lake Michigan. From Manitowoc southward to Evanston, a distance of about 180 miles, the waters are eroding the shores into drift-clay bluffs, which are caving down under the lashing of the waves. The sand and gravel resulting from the sorting of this material is swept southward and thrown into beaches and dunes about the head of the lake, so that the lower bluff and the lower beach are contemporaneous, and the latter is made of the sand derived from the former. Now we have, in the contour of the lake bottom, a ready means of determining approximately the original position of the shore, and consequently the distance which the bluffs have receded since the water occupied its present level. The waves of these great lakes cease to have any erosive power upon the bottom at the depth of about sixty feet; hence when the shores are worn back there is left under water a sort of shelf or terrace, the surface of which slopes gently outward to the depth of about sixty feet, when the bottom dips down more suddenly to the deep water, below the reach of wave action. It is obvious that this terrace is the product of wave action, and it will be convenient to denominate it the terrace of erosion. It exists almost everywhere along the lake-shores where the circumstances admit of it. . . . The existence of this terrace has long been known to some observers, and has been noticed by a part of the United States engineers engaged in Lake survey. It is shown very finely among the islands and shores of the northern part of Lake Michigan. The following figure shows the

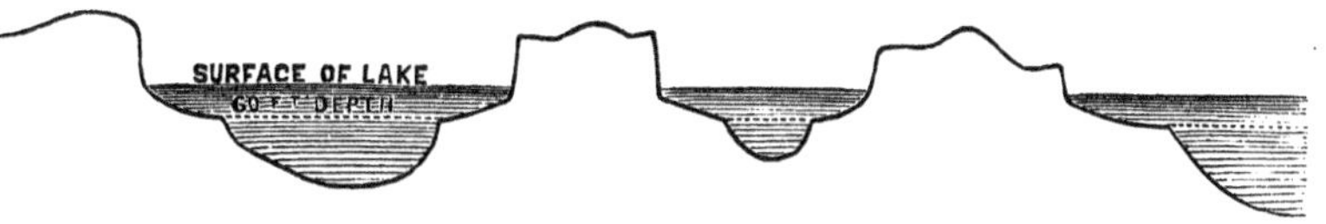

Fig. 1.

profile of the bottom from north to south across North and South Manitou Islands, and thence to the mainland near Sleeping Bear, Michigan. The terrace surrounds both islands, and skirts the mainland, and the sudden dip of the bottom from the plane of sixty feet depth is well illustrated.

Fig. 2, also derived from the soundings on the United States charts, shows the average contour of the terrace on the east shore of Lake Huron, from Brewster's Mills to Point Clark, a distance of fifty miles.

Where the shores are of drift-clay, the terrace has generally a breadth of from two to six miles, and occasionally more, but where it is of rock the width is much less. On some of the hard rocks of Lake Superior the terrace is scarcely 200 feet wide. Softer rocks frequently show a breadth of 1000 or 1500 feet. It is a curious and unexpected fact that the depth of the

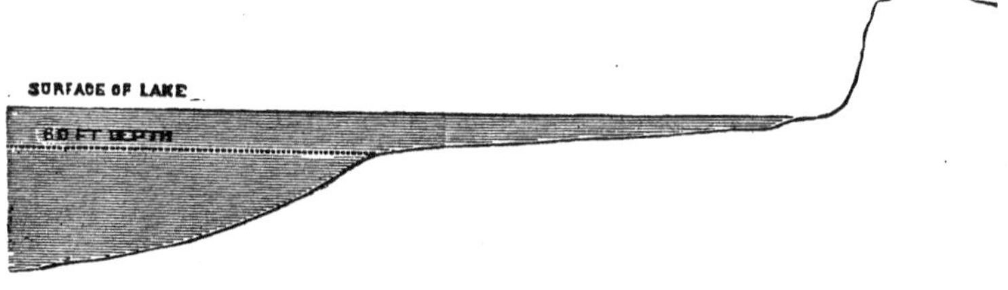

Fig. 2.

erosion is much less affected than the breadth of it by the hardness of the material. Even rock-shores often show the edge of the terrace to be sixty feet down.

Seven lines of soundings to determine the breadth of the terrace on the west shore of Lake Michigan, between Chicago and Manitowoc, a distance of 180 miles, were taken by an expedition fitted out by President Burroughs of Chicago University. Two more lines were taken by the United States engineers and others,—making nine observations of breadth between Chicago and Manitowoc. The edge of the terrace of erosion was found to average 3.98 miles from the present bluffs, and the position of the old shore about 2.72 miles. The latter figures, therefore, represent the total recession of the bluffs of the west shore of Lake Michigan during the period of the lower beach.

It is obvious, says Dr. Andrews, that the outer edge of the terrace represents the line where sixty feet of water was when the erosion commenced, and the old shore line must be somewhere between this and the present bluffs. The clue to the position of the old shore is found by taking the steepest part of the slope, just outside the edge of the terrace, and prolonging it upward till it meets the surface of the water. This of course involves some error, but on the average must approximate the truth.

Fig. 3 is the profile of the terrace averaged from the nine lines of soundings referred to. The dotted line represents the original surface of the clay, and O. S. the position of the old shore.

Annual Rate of Erosion.—The next point is to ascertain the annual amount of destruction of the bluffs. This varies considerably in single years, but, taking long periods, it appears to be quite uniform for the same region. The rate varies according to the exposure of the coast to the prevailing winds, and according to the hardness of the material. For shores of boulder drift, exposed to the full action of the waves, it appears everywhere to amount to from three to six feet a year, and often much more. At Cleveland, Ohio, for forty years it has averaged six feet per annum. On the

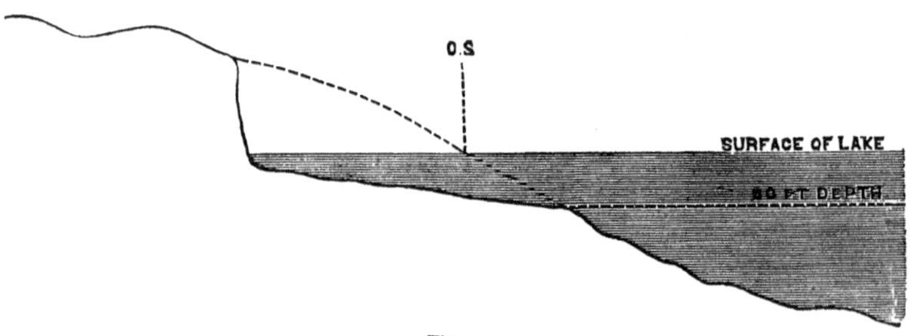

Fig. 3.

Canada shore opposite, it has been about the same. Rev. Thomas Hurlbut found that on Lake Huron it varied in different places from one to twelve feet,—an average of six feet per annum. A civil engineer at Goderich, on the same shore, found the erosion in front of that town to amount to eight feet per annum; but in the adjacent regions north and south about four feet per annum. The County Surveyor of Van Buren County, Michigan, judges the erosion to be about six feet a year.

Dr. Andrews, to determine the rate on the west coast of Lake Michigan, has through several years accumulated a large number of observations, of which he publishes a table, embracing twenty-three places. The greatest erosion was at Evanston, where it reached nearly seventeen feet a year. North of Milwaukee the erosion is less rapid than south of it, and the terrace of erosion is narrower. From Milwaukee to Manitowoc (about eighty miles) it averages four and one-third feet a year, while between Milwaukee and Evanston it averages six and one-quarter feet a year. The average of the two is 5.28, which is therefore the average erosion along the whole line. Numerous other less exact observations confirm this result.

We have seen that the total recession of the bluffs from the old shore line amounted to 2.72 miles, or 14,362 feet. Dividing this by 5.28, the annual rate of erosion, we find that the total age of the lower terrace is 2720 years. If we compare this with the same beach in Lake Huron, we find some variation, but still a confirmation of the general calculation. Taking the east shore, from Brewster's Mills to Point Clark (fifty miles), we find, from the United States charts, that the edge of the terrace is about six miles from the present bluffs, and the original shore line about 4.02 miles. The erosions there have been less carefully ascertained, but appear to be about five and one-half feet per annum, which would give 3859 years as the age of the terrace.

We must add to this result the amount of time covered by the periods during which the water stood at the higher levels.

The antiquity of the lower beach is of necessity the same as that of the lower terrace of erosion. The time required to form this terrace is the time which elapsed during the accumulation of the sand of the lower beach. It has been calculated that the amount of this sand is 1,747,570,000 cubic yards. We must refer the reader to Dr. Andrews's paper for the details of the calculation.

The total of the upper sands, that is, the sands in the upper and the middle beaches, is stated at 1,659,881,000 cubic yards.

That is, the total lower sands are to the total of the two beaches above nearly as seventeen to sixteen. The time of accretion of the lower beach has already been stated to be 2720 years; therefore the period required for the deposition of all the sands above must have been 2570 years,—making the combined periods for *all* of the beaches 5290 years.

If we take the results of the Lake Huron erosion as the proper estimate of the age of the lower terrace, viz., 3859 years, the total time for all the beaches would be 7491 years.

It is very evident that if we could ascertain the total annual sand-drift, we could make a third and independent calculation, by simply dividing the total amount of sands by the annual drift. To this we shall recur.

The body of water along the shores of Lake Michigan is in motion southward (the return waters passing northwards again along the middle of the lake), and every handful of sand lifted by the waves, as they lash the shore line, falls a few feet southward; and this process going on without cessation, the shore sands are in constant motion southwards, and the amount transported by the converging currents from the east and the west shores is enormous. Where piers are built out into the lake, they act as obstructions, which cause the sand to accumulate on the side from which the current comes. In the opinion of engineers, no pier stops more than a fraction of the sand, because the current is deflected, and passing around the end of the pier, carries most of the loose material with it. Captain Sanders, of the United States Army, in charge of the harbour works at Grand Haven, Michigan, estimates that the piers at that place (one of which, however, had a gap in it) stop only one-eleventh of the sand. There are piers also at Chicago and Michigan City, and Dr. Andrews estimates the amount of sand stopped by all of them at 129,000 cubic yards annually, "while probably five or six times as much passes into the head of the lake."

Now (as stated) the total amount of sand south of these two cities is 3,407,451,000 cubic yards. The annual amount of sand stopped by the piers is a very small proportion of all the drift-sand; but if we divide 3,407,451,000 cubic yards by 129,000 (the annual amount stopped by the piers), we obtain 26,000 years as a maximum and extreme limit of time for the accumulation of the 3,407,451,000 cubic yards of sand. It cannot be more than this. And as there is every reason to believe that the stoppage by the piers only amounts to one-fourth or one-fifth of the whole drift, we obtain 5200 or 6500 years as the probable period for the accumulation of the beaches. "This maximum," says Dr. Andrews, "is useful as showing that it is impossible to allow, even on the most liberal estimates, any such post-glacial antiquity as 100,000 years, such as has been often claimed. The narrowness of the terraces proves the same thing, for had the erosions gone on as they do now for 100,000 years, the lower terrace would have been *forty-nine miles* wide, which, counting the terrace of both shores, is actually more than the whole breadth of the lake, and the places where our west shore towns now stand would have been *in sixty feet of water, and forty-six miles from the nearest land.*"

"Another calculation will illustrate the same idea. If we estimate the total annual sand-drift at only twice the amount actually stopped by the very imperfect piers built—which, in the opinion of engineers, is setting it far too low—and compare it with the capacity of the clay basin of Lake Michigan, we shall find that had this process continued 100,000 years, the whole south end of Lake Michigan, up to the line connecting Chicago and Michigan City, would have been full, and converted into dry land 25,000 years ago, and the coast line would now be found many miles north of Chicago. It is needless to say no such enormous quantity of sand exists in this region."

It is proper to add to this that no sand in the south part of Lake Michigan (according to Dr. Andrews) is ever washed out into deep water, nor is any ever brought up from it. Beyond thirty-six feet, in the region of the beaches, the bottom is always of a smooth, impalpable clay. The waves here cease to have power to move sand at the depth of from twenty-four to thirty-six feet.[1]

[1] This assertion may seem to conflict with the previous one, that boulder clay is eroded sixty feet deep. But we are informed by Dr. Andrews that the reason of the difference is that in the southern section of the lake, where the beaches lie, the water is shallow and the waves act less deeply, but further north they erode to sixty feet. Dredgings, nevertheless, show that in neither region is beach-sand ever carried into deep water. The sands sometimes brought up on the greased lead from greater depths is different, and consists of gravel left in the boulder clay by the washing away of the clayey particles, at depths where the waves were

It follows that the sand in the beach lines around the head of the lake all came from the north, along the sand-bearing currents of the shores, there being no other possible source for it. Conversely, it follows that as the sand cannot pass out into deep water, it has no avenue of escape, and must lodge in the bight at the end of the lake, being caught in the *cul-de-sac.*

The sand deposits, as we have stated, are at the southern extremity of the lake; and they have a curved length of one hundred miles, and a maximum breadth of ten miles. The subsoil is boulder drift, which has here a gently sloping surface of remarkable uniformity. On this smooth incline the sands lie for the most part in three concentric beach lines. The uppermost beach or ridge was the first formed, and must have commenced immediately after the close of the Drift Period. "It is interesting," says Dr. Andrews, "to remark that this upper beach, which appears all around the lakes where not worn away by subsequent erosion, and which originally must have been level, has now been thrown *into a sinuous form, showing that the country has undergone changes of level since that time.*" Around the south end of Lake Michigan, and for a hundred miles north on the Wisconsin shore, it is everywhere about fifty-two feet above the present level of the water, while on the east side of the lake, south of Grand Haven, it is shown by the survey of Captain Sanders, of the United States Army, to be at the elevation of only twenty-one feet. On both

unable to stir the pebbles, thus leaving them on the surface. They differ from the beach sand by the angular form of the grains and their larger average size.

sides of the southern front of Lake Huron, which then was continuous both of Lake Michigan and Lake Erie, it presents an elevation, where cut by the Grank Trunk Railway, of about 140 feet. The western beach there makes a wide détour into the State of Michigan, and then sweeps around the southern shore of Lake Erie into Ohio, where, according to Professor Newberry, it has an elevation of 250 feet above the present water, or about 235 feet above Lake Michigan. As this old shore line must have been originally level, its present distorted grade can only be due to flexures of the strata of the continent occurring since the beach was laid down.[1] The fall of the waters from the line of the upper beach, which probably occurred at the time of this disturbance of the strata, appears to have been *very sudden.* This is shown by a peculiarity in the contour of the deposit, which is uniform in all the sand-shores

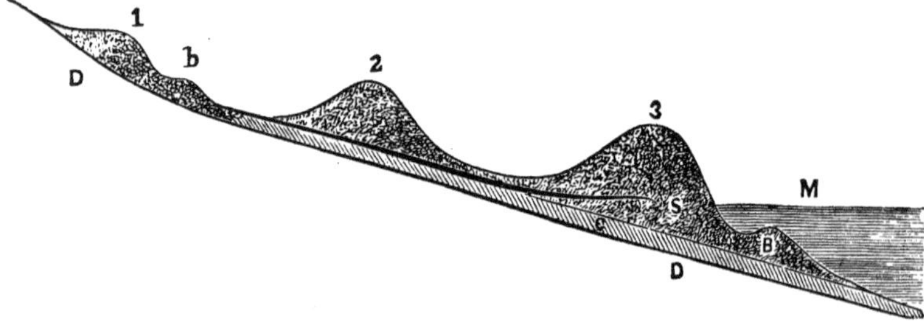

Fig. 4.

of this part of the coast. As you go out into the lake, the bottom gradually descends from the water line to

[1] This throws light on the positions in which the river-gravel in the east of England is found, and which sometimes seems to be dissociated altogether from the present lines of drainage.

the depth of about five feet, when it rises again as you recede from the shore, and then descends toward deep water, forming a subaqueous ridge or "bar" parallel to the beach, and some ten or twenty rods from the shore. This is shown at the point marked B in the section, Fig. 4.

The upper beach preserves its old bar perfectly (marked *b* in the cut), as if the lake had left it but yesterday. The quickness of the change is obvious to any one accustomed to lake-shore action, for had the water occupied even two months in receding from the bar, the waves would have torn it in pieces and covered it with new sand, leaving nothing distinguishable of its form. Another proof of the suddenness of the retirement is, that there are no sand ridges between the upper and middle beaches. The ground is bare clay, just as the waters left it, and the valley between the two beaches, which is generally about two miles wide, is absolutely continuous for a hundred miles, surrounding the head of the lake. . . . The waves of Lake Michigan act upon their shores with tremendous force, and are always engaged in either piling up the sand or tearing down the clay. There is no possibility that they could effect a slow retreat down such a slope without leaving marks which no time could erase. We have on this shore examples both of slow and rapid recession, and the comparison of the two establishes the above conclusions.

Singularly enough, says Dr. Andrews, this subsidence was at first not to the middle beach, but to the lower one. . . . The waters fell from the upper beach to about the present level so suddenly that they not only left the subaqueous "bar" almost undisturbed, but they did not throw up a single intermediate beach line, which, at the rate of sand deposit prevailing in this region, would have been visible, if there had been a pause even of six months. The waters remained here long enough for a thin stratum of peat to form, and then rose again over the soil-bed and deposited the middle beach upon it. . . . From the upper edge of the middle beach the water receded very slowly, occupying probably 2000 years or more in falling a few feet, and throwing up, where the sand supply was most abundant, numerous parallel ridges. It then fell perhaps ten feet more pretty rapidly, to the upper part of the present beach, leaving a continuous valley between the middle and the modern sands. This last recession, however, was not so sudden as that from the upper line, as shown by the fact that the subaqueous bar was demolished by the retiring wave action, and a considerable amount of sand was left between the middle and lower beaches.

One of the most important results of this investigation is *the probable identification of the high water of the middle beach with the more general submergence of the Loess.* The Loess is not a continuation of the Boulder Drift, as is often supposed (says Dr. Andrews); on the contrary, it is separated from the true Drift by a stratum of vegetable mould, marked with subaerial denudations, showing that a period of dry land and vegetation intervened between the close of the Drift and the submergence called the Loess. . . . The following sections will show the relations of the deposits on the lakes and on the Mississippi:

SECTION OF THE MISSISSIPPI.

Modern Soil. (Water at its lower level.)
Loess. (General submergence near the rivers.)
Ancient Soil. (Water at its lower level.)
Boulder Drift.

SECTION OF THE LAKE SHORES.

Modern Soil. (Water at its lower level.)
Middle Beach. (Extensive submergence about the lakes.)
Ancient Soil. (Water first at upper and then at lower beach.)
Boulder Drift.

It appears, therefore, that the general order of events on the lakes and on the Mississippi has been identical, and that the high water of the middle beach occupies exactly the same place in the series as the high water of the Loess near the Mississippi. There can hardly be a doubt, therefore, that the two were contemporaneous.

Dr. Andrews sums up the history and chronology of the lakes as follows:

1. The upper beach began to form immediately after the Boulder Drift period, and continued to accrete for about 900 years. No animal fossils have yet been found in it.

2. The waters then fell suddenly to about their present level, where they remained till a thin bed of peat accreted on the marshy slope vacated by the waves. He has not been able to collect data for a calculation of this first low-water period, but from the position of the soil-bed in the eastern dunes, inclines to think it lasted 500 or 1000 years.

3. The water rose again, submerging for a short time the upper beach, but soon fell to the line of the middle

one, where it remained about 1600 or 2000 years. This period appears to be contemporary with the Loess.

4. The water, which had already slowly fallen some feet, now retired more rapidly to near its present level, which it has maintained with only moderate fluctuations ever since.

5. The total time of all these deposits appears to be somewhere between 5300 and 7500 years.

This result corresponds with the conclusions we have reached on other and independent evidence.

NOTE.—We learn from Dr. Andrews that Dr. Lapham, of Milwaukie, suggests that the lakes may have stood for long periods at lower levels than the present one, and that he (Dr. Andrews) has not allowed anything for such lower level periods. In support of this Dr. Lapham calls attention to the fact that the channels of the rivers running into the lake are often much deeper than the adjacent bottom of the lake itself, indicating ancient lower channels. To this Dr. Andrews replies: That rivers, like brooks, cut deepest where the current is swiftest, and that the ancient greater size of the streams, as well as the modern spring floods, would cut out these deeper places, while at the point of entrance into the lake, the motion is checked, and the channel is either cut less deeply, or, if cut, is filled again by the waves. There is a narrow, swift place in Wisconsin River which is 100 feet deep, yet two miles lower down the stream the rock bottom rises nearly to the surface, though the descent of the surface itself is very slight.

Furthermore, numerous borings and deep-water dredgings, as well as a regular shaft sunk in the bottom of the lake two miles from shore, and a tunnel dug from the shore to the shaft, fail to show any traces of the submerged beaches which ought to exist under the lake if it ever had a much lower level than the present.

Dr. Andrews also writes us that since he wrote his article on the lake beaches, he has discovered that the deluge of the middle beach, which went temporarily much higher, deposited a stratum of muddy gravel over the black soil which had accumulated on the upper beach; and the higher part of the inundation is probably, he now thinks, the true analogue of the Loess deluge. The water remained at this upper limit for a very brief period —not long enough to lay down a definite shore-line.

CHAPTER XXIII.

THE FALLS OF ST. ANTHONY.

ANOTHER attempt to fix the date of the Glacial Age has been made very recently by the State Geologist of Minnesota, United States—Professor N. H. Winchell—in his Fifth Annual Report (1876) on "The Geological and Natural History Survey of Minnesota." This is based on the recession of the Falls of St. Anthony, on the Mississippi river, since the "Second Glacial Period," from Fort Snelling, where the cataract originally commenced—a distance of eight miles. Fort Snelling is on the Mississippi, at the mouth of the Minnesota. Professor Winchell seems to have studied the subject with great care, and his report goes far more into detail than can be done here.

There are two distinct glacial or hardpan deposits in this region—the red hardpan, which is referred to the First Glacial Period, and the gray hardpan, which is referred to the Second Glacial Period.

From the Falls to Fort Snelling the gorge between the rock-bluffs is about a quarter of a mile in width, and the rock has a freshly-broken appearance, the large fragments thrown down by the action of the water, as the falls receded, still lying in the talus along the bluffs.

Throughout this distance (eight miles) the rocks lie horizontal, showing that the recession, so far as it depends on this element, has been of uniform rate. The relative length of time during which the rocks of this gorge have been exposed to atmospheric forces, compared to the period of exposure below Fort Snelling, is indicated by the depth to which they have been weathered, or stained. Exposure to long weathering increases the depth to which the rock is stained; and this coloration may extend to the depth of several feet.

The Lower Trenton limestone, through which the river runs, when quarried, is blue within, at fresh exposures; when weathered, the stone is of a rusty buff or dirty-yellowish colour, resulting from the oxidation and hydration of the iron which it contains. The marked difference in the depth of this weathering above and below Fort Snelling indicates when the river began to form the gorge.

"Besides the aspect of greater age," says Professor Winchell, "as indicated by the greater change of colour in the rock below Fort Snelling, the bluffs themselves are smooth, and the rock hid by drift and loam, since the action of the river ceased. The top of the rock along the gorge above the fort is surmounted with a thickness of drift, gravel, and clay, which shows a section, as cut by the river, continuous perpendicularly with the rock-bluff itself. This thickness of drift (the gray hardpan) is nearly uniform from the Fort to the Falls, and indicates the spreading of the drift before the recession of the Falls; but below Fort Snelling (with a single exception) the rock-bluff is generally hid by a subsequent accumulation of drift. The same is true of the bluffs of the Minnesota above the Fort."

Professor Winchell then points out that, prior to the last glacial epoch, the Mississippi in the district under consideration (Hennepin County) did not run in its present channel, but passed in a wide, deep valley by the way of the valley of Basset's Creek, and lakes Calhoun, Harriet, and others, along the western side of the Trenton area, and joined the Minnesota at some point above Fort Snelling. The country was then covered with the drift of an older glacial epoch. As the last glacial epoch approached, the Minnesota was much larger than the Mississippi, and the Mississippi was much larger than it is now.

"The ice of the Second Glacial Period," says Professor Winchell, "choked up the old valley of the Mississippi, filled it with the gray hardpan clay, and forced the river out of its channel over the Lower Trenton limestone rock, over which it passed, to reach the same valley again by plunging over the precipice at Fort Snelling, and thus originated the Falls of St. Anthony."

Since that time they have worn their way back, as we have said, eight miles; and the problem which Professor Winchell proposes to himself to solve is—How long they have been engaged in this operation?

Father Hennepin discovered the Falls in the year 1680, and describes them as divided in the middle by "a rocky island of pyramidal form" (Spirit Island).

Carver, in his Journal, describes them as he saw them in 1766.

Lieutenant Z. M. Pike visited them in 1805, and has

left a description of them in his Journal, published in London in 1811.

Major Stephen H. Long visited the spot in 1817, and left a yet fuller account of them as he saw them.

In 1823 they are described by Beltrami.

Mr. G. W. Featherstonhaugh describes them again in his "Report of a Geological Reconnaissance, &c.," in 1835.

Hennepin saw the falls in 1680, when Spirit Island divided them; Carver saw them in 1766, just as they were leaving Spirit Island and entering on Hennepin Island; Major Long saw them in 1817, when Hennepin Island divided them; in 1823 Beltrami saw them in pretty much the same condition; and in 1835 Featherstonhaugh repeats the same general description.

Professor Winchell does not consider the recession since 1856, in consequence of the construction since that time of a number of dams and mills, which have divided the water, and concentrated it at certain points. His calculation begins with 1680, and ends with 1856.

The entire calculation turns upon the accuracy of his observations, and his interpretation of the accounts of the position of the Falls as given at the several dates of their visits by the travellers who have been referred to.

We prefer to give his conclusions in his own words

Conclusion.

"Between Hennepin, 1680, and 1856, are 176 years. The recession in that time was 906 feet, or an average of 5.15 feet per year. The time needed at that rate to recede from Fort Snelling would be 8202 years.

"Between Hennepin and Carver are eighty-six years; the amount of recession was about 300 feet, or 3.49 feet per year. The time needed at that rate to recede from Fort Snelling would be 12,103 years.

"Between Carver in 1766, and 1856, were ninety years; the recession in that interval was 606 feet, or 6.73 feet per year; at that rate it would take 6276 years to recede from Fort Snelling.

"The average of these three results is 8859 years. Still the exactness of the datum between Carver and 1856 is such that the actual time of such recession is probably more nearly expressed by taking that only into the calculation. This brings the Glacial Period to a much more recent date than some other means of calculation; but it is probable that no other datum so exact for such a calculation has ever before been used."

Professor Winchell concludes with the remark, that "if the occurrence of our winter in aphelion, caused by the precession of the equinoxes, and the revolution of the line of the apsides, about 11,300 years ago, was the cause of our last glacial period, the greatest *effect* of those causes which had their greatest force at that time, was probably felt at a considerably later date, as suggested by Professor Rhame, in the same manner as the greatest heat of summer is not felt at the same time when the causes which produce it have their full activity."

There are two circumstances not adverted to by Professor Winchell, which it appears to us ought to be taken into account, and which we think would operate to retard the recession of the Falls since they entered upon Hennepin Island. This island is described as 100 yards broad, and 450 or 500 yards in length, and has lain as an obstruction to the current at the Falls since the time of Father Hennepin, and still divides the falls into two parts. The power of the stream, it seems to us, must have been weakened by this separation of the current.

The other fact which ought, we think, to be taken into account, is that between the Falls and Spirit Island (where Hennepin first saw them), the breadth of the river is twice as great as it is from Spirit Island to Fort Snelling; in other words, up to Hennepin's visit the river ran in a much narrower and deeper channel above the Falls than it has done since. The power of the stream to destroy the rock over which it falls has therefore been greatly weakened since 1680; and the work to be done by it has been greatly increased by the increased distance between the banks.

NOTE.—Professor Winchell replies to the first of these suggestions, that admitting the tendency of the obstruction offered by Hennepin Island to retard the recession of the Falls, there would in such case be less work to be done by the stream, as it would not have to cut across its whole breadth. But, as we state, the river has twice the width above Spirit Island that it has below; the amount of work to be performed is not diminished.

But here Professor Winchell replies again, that while the actual stream above Spirit Island has twice the width of the stream below, the *gorge* which the river has cut is as wide below as above.

On this we observe, that there must then have been formerly much more water in the stream than recently; and a greater volume of water would destroy the rock at a more rapid rate.

CHAPTER XXIV.

ST. NAZAIRE.

We have thus estimated the probable date of the close of the Glacial Age by three different methods:—1. By seizing upon the broad fact that the ice excluded the population of Europe from Denmark, Scandinavia, and Scotland until the Polished Stone Age had set in; 2. By the calculation of Dr. Andrews on the beaches of the North American Lakes; 3. By the calculation of Professor Winchell with regard to the Falls of St. Anthony.

In the present chapter we shall give a calculation based on yet different data, and on observations made in France during the past few years.

Calculations following this last method had been previously made by M. De Ferry and M. Arcelin from extended observations on the alluvium of the valley of the Saône. This river is gradually raising the plain through which it flows, and these archæologists, by independent observations, from the relics found at different depths, have undertaken to fix the dates of the Iron, Bronze, and Stone Ages. Comparing a number of observations, M. De Ferry fixes the accumulation of sediment since the Roman period at a thickness of

1.1m.; of the Bronze Age layer at 1.50m.; of the Stone Age layer at 1.50m. This would give for the Bronze Age an antiquity of 3000 years; for the Neolithic Age an antiquity of 4000 or 5000 years; and for the Palæolithic Age an antiquity of 9000 or 10,000 years. M. Arcelin adopts a somewhat different scale; assuming for the Roman layer a depth of one metre, deduced from twenty-four stations, he obtains for the Celtic Iron Age an antiquity of 1800 to 2700 years; for the Bronze Age an antiquity of 2700 to 3600 years; for the Neolithic Age an antiquity of 3600 to 6700 years; and for the Palæolithic Age an antiquity of 6700 to 8000 years.

Such calculations do not altogether secure our confidence, or at least only in a general way.

A most important consideration is, that both of these investigators assume the sedimentary deposits of the Palæolithic Period to have proceeded at the same rate as those of the succeeding periods, when, in fact, that was a period of unprecedented rains and floods, and, therefore, a period during which the deposits of one year might equal in amount the deposits of several centuries afterwards. The 7000 or 10,000 years of MM. Ferry and Arcelin is, therefore, *an extreme limit* for the date of the Palæolithic Age.

A more exact and cautious calculation seems to have been made by M. René Kerviler at St. Nazaire, at the mouth of the river Loire. This calculation has attracted the attention of the French Minister of Public Instruction, who has furnished means to M. Kerviler to continue his investigations, and seems to be regarded as reliable by the *Revue Archéologique*, which, after referring to the investigations of MM. Ferry and Arcelin in the valley of the Saône as not altogether satisfactory, speaks in the following terms of the investigations of M. Kerviler:—

"The twelfth chapter (*Epoque géologique actuelle*) of M. de Quatrefages' *L'Espèce humaine* is, on the contrary, a rapid and very substantial *resumé* of the efforts made to arrive at the establishment of a *Pre-historic chronology* by the aid of the study of the turbaries and alluvial deposits of different kinds. M. de Quatrefages shows very clearly the present position of this delicate problem. 'The results are still far from satisfactory; they are not the less interesting and fitted to encourage new researches. The method is good. It has only failed so far of sufficiently precise data, and we are permitted to hope that we shall realise them sooner or later.' Prophetic words. The readers of the *Review* have the proof of it. The solution is given to them at this very moment by the young engineer charged with the floating-dock of St. Nazaire, M. René Kerviler." (*Revue Archéologique*, Avril 1877, p. 286.)

M. Kerviler, as just mentioned, is engaged in the construction of an extensive floating-dock at St. Nazaire, and has made certain discoveries of human relics in the process of his diggings into the alluvial deposits of the river, which have been described by him in three papers contributed to the March, April, and May numbers of the *Revue Archéologique*.

In 1874 the workmen engaged in removing the beds of mud at the bottom of the basin of the Bay of Penhoüet encountered, at the depth of four metres below the level of low-tide, a dozen crania mingled with other human bones.

Farther excavations in the same basin in 1875 and in 1876, over a large surface at the same depth, revealed horns of the stag, potteries, bones of men and animals, worked stones, implements of bone and of bronze, trunks of trees, &c. All these objects were found in one and the same horizontal bed of sand and gravel, from five to twenty centimetres in thickness, and situated at a mean level of four metres below the present range of low-tide. This bed represented the bottom of the bay at the epoch when its banks were inhabited by the men and animals whose remains have been found, and the objects met with were either thrown upon the shore and swept into the sea by the tide, or thrown into the water from boats stationed in the bay.

Among the objects recovered were two leaf-shaped swords of bronze, a poniard of bronze, a bone needle eighteen centimetres long, an axe-socket in horn (*douille de hache en corne*), intended to receive a stone axe, implements of horn intended for lance-heads, plough-points, &c., rude pottery, stone anchors, bones of the *bos longifrons*, urus, aurochs, stag, roe, sheep, pig or wild-boar, &c.

M. Kerviler remarks that from this it incontestably results that when the bottom of the bay was at four metres below the present low-tide level, a people serving themselves with objects absolutely similar to those which are designated as characteristic of the Bronze Age, occupied this spot.

In August 1876 the workmen discovered in the same basin of the Penhoüet, at the depth of two and a half metres above the preceding bed, and therefore one and a half metres below the low-tide, some fragments of red pottery presenting the incontestable characters of the Gallo-Roman Period. Very soon they discovered also some amphoræ with ears or handles, and finally a bronze coin of the Emperor Tetricus.

From this M. Kerviler concludes that in the third century of our era the bottom of the bay of Penhoüet was situated at least one metre below the low-tide level, and that, as there are still six metres of mud above the point where these Gallo-Roman remains were found, which mud is stratified and presents regular horizontal layers, 1600 years have been required for the six metres of mud in question to form. This is the datum on which he rests his subsequent calculations. It is, he says, incontestable that the six metres corresponds with 1600 years, that is, the bed has formed at the rate of 0.37m. per century.

M. Kerviler starts a difficulty, however, as follows: Would the deposit of mud above the low-tide level be the same in a given time as that below it? He enters into an elaborate calculation on this point, and reaches the conclusion that the rate of deposit above ascertained needs to be somewhat increased.

M. Kerviler then starts a second difficulty: Does a certain thickness of mud at the lower depths represent the same lapse of time as a bed of equal thickness higher up? or must we not allow for the weight of the upper beds on the lower, and the compression of the lower beds, so as to destroy the value of our unit of measure? In order to determine this he makes a calculation based on a comparison of the weight of a cube of mud taken from the upper stratum and the weight of another cube taken at a depth of nine metres. It appeared that some compression had taken place, and a certain amount of error had to be allowed for. The two errors, however, were in opposite directions, and very nearly compensated one another, so that the original figure of 0.37m. per century remained substantially correct.

It will be remembered that the thickness of the deposit between the relics of the Bronze Period and those of the Gallo-Roman Period was 2.50m., and we ascertain that, at the rate of 0.37m. per century, seven centuries must have elapsed between the two periods, or in other words, the people of the Bronze Age here represented must have lived at the farthest 500 years before our era.

But, observes M. Kerviler, all this rests on the hypothesis, which may be contested, that the quantity of mud contained in suspension in the waters of the Loire has remained every century nearly the same for about 2000 years; and he was disposed to leave the matter here without farther inquiry, when "an accidental circumstance brought the absolute demonstration of the correctness of our (his) deductions."

It appears that his attention was called, while in company with M. Paul de Chastellier, whom he describes as an indefatigable archæologist, to a vertical section or cut in the alluvial mud, which had been exposed for some months to the weather. He was struck by observing that the section was not smooth and homogeneous like the sections at other points, but presented evident traces of regular and thin stratifications. Farther observation revealed the fact, that the action of the rain had disintegrated the parts interposed between the annual muddy deposits, and that the stratification thus exposed presented to them a striking image of the progressive march of the allusions; just as the concentric rings of the trunk of a tree indicate its successive development, and enable us to calculate its age. After a long series of observations, M. Kerviler ascertained that the horizontal stratified beds succeed regularly "from three to three" in the following order: sand, clay, vegetable debris, and so on. The beds of sand vary in thickness from one-fourth of a millimetre up to 0.002m. ordinarily; the beds of clay have a thickness varying from one-half of a millimetre up to 0.003m.; and the vegetable beds from a quarter of a millimetre up to 0.002m. and 0.003m. If a fresh section is attempted, all these diversities of structure disappear.

The conclusion is readily drawn, that the little vegetable beds which contain leaves and herbaceous remains indicate the annual deposit of the autumn; and the three successive beds of sand, clay, and vegetable matter represent the total annual deposit; the sand having without doubt been deposited during the winter, when the full waters of the Loire have a considerable velocity; and the clay having, on the contrary, been deposited during the summer from more tranquil waters.

The thickness of the whole of these three beds, which varies (at the depth of seven metres) from 0.001m. to 0.005m. (ordinarily), represents the regular annual deposit, and one may readily calculate the time required to form the entire depth of seven metres, which is at the rate of about 0.35m. in a century.

From this M. Kerviler concludes that the first calculation was substantially correct, and that the date of the Bronze Age at the mouth of the Loire must necessarily be fixed at 500 years (at the farthest) before our era.

He adds, that a farther calculation may be made to ascertain the age of the present Geologic Period, and the date of the commencement of the alluvial deposits of the Loire. This, by his calculation, amounts to a maximum of 6000 years, the sections in the mud having attained a depth of sixteen metres below the bed of bronze, before reaching the gravels which lie at its base.

We have no doubt, however, that here, as in the Saône Valley, the deposits during the Palæolithic Period were vastly greater than subsequently, and the time, therefore, should be reduced.

The only possible flaw in this calculation is, that the rate of deposit in the Bay of Penhoüet may have been affected by elevations and subsidences of the land. As on the south coasts of England, submerged forests have been observed on the [north ?] coast of Brittany. The North of France is being slightly lowered, while on the south the coast is slowly elevated. Such is the opinion of M. Bravais, who adds that the dividing line between these movements is through the peninsula of Brittany, and, therefore, near the mouth of the Loire.

It is evident that no serious change has occurred in the level of the Bay of Penhoüet since the Gallo-Roman or since the Bronze Period.

It is worthy of remark that all of these calculations arrive at about the same result. The beaches of the North American Lakes, the retreat of the cataract from Fort Snelling, the alluvions of the Saône, and the deposits at the mouth of the Loire, all indicate about 6000 years for the antiquity of the close of the Glacial Age. This is again strikingly in correspondence with the higher figures claimed for the early dynasties of Egypt and Babylonia, and with our own estimate of the date of this epoch based on its correlation in the North of Europe with the beginning of the Neolithic Age.

CHAPTER XXV.

THE ANTIQUITY OF MAN IN AMERICA.

Ruined cities of Central America—The mound-builders—Shell-mounds on the Gulf coast—The human skeleton found at New Orleans—Objects found at all depths in the mud of the Mississippi—Stone implements with the bones of the mastodon—The Calaveras skull, and the instances from California where stone mortars and weapons have been found at great depths in the auriferous gravel under the lava—Explanation of the position in which these objects have been found.

THERE is not a great deal to be said under this head: the evidences for the antiquity of man in America are comparatively meagre, and not well substantiated.

We shall briefly notice them, concluding with those which are assumed to correlate the antiquity of man in America with his remains of the Palæolithic Age in the River-Gravel of Europe.

THE RUINED CITIES OF CENTRAL AMERICA.

Captain Dupaix [1] regarded these as belonging to the Antediluvians, and Catlin remarks that the ocean rolled over them for thousands of years. There are no facts, however, on which to ground these opinions, and they are refuted by the declaration of Mr. Stephens, that he observed at Uxmal that the lintels of the doorways were formed of wood, which was still undecayed—

[1] Antiquités Mexicaines.

many of them being in a perfect state of preservation; while (as he observes) in 350 years structures described as existing at the time of the Spanish Conquest have crumbled in the dust. He found a specimen of wood also at Palenque, and wooden lintels at Orosingo.[1] This cannot be reconciled with any high antiquity in a climate like that of Central America, which, unlike the dry atmosphere of Egypt, is particularly unfavourable to the preservation of ruins of every sort.

THE MOUND-BUILDERS.

These mysterious people were probably a branch of the Village Indians of Yucatan and New Mexico. Their chronology is, of course, uncertain, but of their great antiquity there is no proof whatever. The only circumstance relied on in this connection is "the character of the arborescent vegetation covering their works."[2]

Trees are found growing on the mounds which are estimated to be 500 or 600 years old; and, reasoning from this, Schoolcraft fixes their date—"the period of active tumult among the tribes of the Mississippi valley"—in the twelfth or thirteenth century.

Dr. Foster, however, urges that there may have been several generations of trees of the same, or even different species, succeeding each other on the mounds.

This may have been the fact; there is no proof of it; but it is not unlikely.

The average life of the forest trees in Wisconsin, according to Dr. Lapham, is about 250 years. "In that

[1] Travels, vol. ii. pp. 313, 430.
[2] Pre-historic Races of United States, p. 372.

region it requires," he says, "a lapse of from 54 to 130 years for a tree to increase its diameter one foot; three or four feet is a large tree;" and hence we may infer that few of the trees now growing in Wisconsin can antedate the discovery of this continent by Columbus. "Farther south," he remarks, "where trees attain a larger size, they have had at the same time, owing to the genial climate and more fertile soil, a much more rapid growth, so that they probably do not exceed the trees of Wisconsin in age."[1]

If, therefore, we allow to the trees on the mounds of the Ohio valley an average life of 300 years, and suppose that four generations have succeeded each other, we go back 1200 years; and if we add a couple of centuries before the mounds were thrown up, we obtain 1400 years. The earliest relics of the Mound-Builders hardly exceed this age.

THE SHELL-MOUNDS ON THE GULF COAST.

There are shell-mounds on the North Atlantic coast, but these are recognised to belong to the Indians, and relics of European manufacture have been found in them.

On the Gulf coast they appear to be older. At Grand Lake, on the Tèche, the accumulations are from six to ten feet high, and three-fourths of a mile in length. Large live-oak trees are growing upon them. "This region," says Dr. Foster, "is now fifteen miles

[1] In the Smithsonian Report for 1863, there is an account of an old Indian fort and burial-ground, near Waterbury, New York, in which mention is made of a pine tree then growing on the embankment, and which was three and a half feet in diameter, p. 381.

inland, thus showing that marked changes in the sea-level have occurred in comparatively recent times."

It is sufficient to say that *glazed pottery* was found in these mounds, and we have, therefore, not an evidence for the antiquity of man, but an evidence that a great physical alteration in this coast has taken place within a very recent period.

Trees measuring 13 feet, 15 feet, 19 feet, 27 feet in circumference (the live-oak) were met with by Professor Wyman on the great shell-heap, which covers twenty acres, at Silver Spring, in Florida. The oldest of these trees he calculates to be 600 years old.

Dr. Foster assigns these mounds to the epoch of the Stone-Age Lake-Dwellings of Switzerland, though we do not see on what ground.

On the Pacific coast, near San Francisco, there is a shell-mound almost a mile long and half a mile broad. Several years ago, at a depth of twenty feet, numerous human skeletons were found, and "some bones of dogs and birds, and many implements of stone." "One baby had been rolled in a long piece of red silk, like the mummies, which had been covered with a coating of a sort of asphaltum." From the skulls, the skeletons were referred to a tribe of Indians. The burials were in a sitting posture. Dr. Foster considers the corpse in "the long piece of red silk" an "intrusive burial." But "intrusive burials" do not occur at the depth of twenty feet.

THE HUMAN SKELETON CITED BY DR. DOWLER.

This skeleton was found at the depth of sixteen feet

in the river mud, at New Orleans, "beneath (we are told) four successive tiers of cypress forests." Dr. Dowler estimates its age to be 57,000 years, and Lyell quotes the calculation with apparent approval, while Lubbock remarks that if the facts as stated can be relied on, "this skeleton must carry back the existence of man in America to a very early period." Dr. Andrews, commenting on the case in the "Chicago Advance," May 28, 1868, remarks that "Dr. Dowler is well known in the medical profession as an enthusiastic but unsound investigator, who is very prone to come to startling, but erroneous, conclusions; but that Lyell should be led astray by such enormous blunders may well excite astonishment. The accretion both of vegetable matter and of river-mud in the region of the Lower Mississippi is very rapid, and the United States Army Engineers have calculated that the whole ground on which New Orleans stands, down to the depth of forty feet, has been deposited within the period of 4400 years. Lyell himself states that he has seen many stumps of trees standing erect in the banks of the river, a fact which should have shown him that the accretion was rapid enough to cover these stumps to their summits before they had time to decay. I have myself seen in that region young cottonwood saplings only seven years old, around whose trunks the annual overflow of the river had deposited two or three feet of earth above their original roots. It is possible that the New Orleans man may be one or two thousand years of age; but to claim fifty thousand for him is provocative of laughter."

On the same Dr. Foster remarks: "Thus, then, with

these carefully-observed computations before us [of the United States Engineers, Humphreys and Abbot], we are not prepared to accept the antiquity assigned by Dr. Dowler to the human remains found beneath the surface at New Orleans. What he regards as four buried forests, which once flourished on the spot, may be nothing more than drift-wood brought down by the river in former times, which became imbedded in the silts and sediments which were deposited on what was then the floor of the Gulf." [1]

The Rev. Edward Fontaine, a geologist well acquainted with the valley of the Mississippi, speaking of these remains at New Orleans, remarks that similar specimens of antiquity, and probably in greater abundance, may be found between the present level and Tamaulipas Street, where the whole area, to the depth of more than one hundred feet, has certainly been deposited within the period of sixty years. He states that since the gas-works were constructed, the New Orleans Academy of Sciences was agitated by a report that in making some deep excavations at Port Jackson, at a considerable distance from the Mississippi River, and at a depth of fifteen or twenty feet, a piece of wood had been exhumed which had evidently been shaped by "human art," and dressed with tools which indicated the work of a highly civilised race of men. Several members of the Academy determined to examine the matter thoroughly. They found the facts to have been correctly stated. A

[1] Dr. Foster adds in a note, that since the above was written he had seen the remarks of Professor C. G. Forshey before the New Orleans Academy of Sciences, in which he discredits the observations of Humphreys and Abbot. See p. 76.

large piece of yellow poplar had been dug up at a great depth, and a considerable distance from the river —a distance as great as that occupied by the aboriginal mound in the graveyard at Point à la Hache above the forts. "It was squared with a broad axe, bored with an auger, cut with a hand-saw, and was unmistakably the gunwale of a Kentucky flat-boat!"[1]

"The age of no fossil," says Mr. Fontaine, "found in the alluvium of the present delta of Louisiana can be determined. The average depth of the river is about one hundred feet for the lower one hundred and twenty-five miles of its course, and its bottom current flows as swiftly as its surface, and the average velocity is about four miles per hour. Opposite New Orleans, the soundings of Harrison's map of 1847, in the New Orleans Academy of Sciences, showed a depth of from one hundred and sixty-two to one hundred and eighty-seven feet. Mr. Alfred Henson, who had lived in the city sixty years in 1867, told me that he recollected when the deep channel of the river flowed where Tchoupitoulas Street is now built, in the heart of the business part of it, a quarter of a mile from the present shore. By undermining and engulfing its bank, with everything upon them, logs tangled in vines and bedded in mud, cypress stumps, Indian graves, and modern works of art, are suddenly swallowed up and buried, at all depths, by its waters, from ten to one hundred and eighty-seven feet deep. The deep channel then works its way from them, and leaves them beneath a deep soil of inconceivable fertility, which quickly produces above them a dense

[1] How the World was Peopled, p. 86.

forest of rapid and short-lived growth; first of cypress remote from the shore, with willows and cottonwood next to its receding current; then of live-oak, hackberry, and elm, with a variety of other trees. But the restless and resistless giant soon returns with a sweeping curve, and invades the land of the oaks, and of the cypress also; and undoes quickly all the work of a quarter of a century, or of an age, to do it over again. In 1856, an Artesian auger penetrated a cedar log eighteen inches thick, which had been buried 157 feet beneath the pavement of Canal Street."[1]

STONE IMPLEMENTS WITH REMAINS OF THE MASTODON.

Cane-baskets and stone implements (already noticed) were found beneath the bones of the mastodon, on a layer of crystallised salt, in the island of Petite Anse, Louisiana: pottery and stone arrow-heads were found with bones of the same animal in the post-pliocene of Charleston, South Carolina; and stone weapons were said to have been found (by Dr. Koch) in Missouri, with mastodon bones. In all of these cases there is reason to doubt the contemporaneousness of the remains.

If they be of the same age, it would only prove that man in the United States was the contemporary of an animal whose remains are found in the peat-bogs and on the surface of the ground all over the country. We are inclined to think that this was the fact, as it surely

[1] All this throws light on Mr. Horner's researches in Egypt, in the mud of the Nile valley, which we have thought it hardly of sufficient importance to go into. The "Anthropological Review" regrets that Sir Charles Lyell "should have thought it worth while to notice such absurdities."

was if the "Big Elephant Mound" in Wisconsin represents, as is believed, the mastodon.

In California it has been stated that human skulls, and stone mortars, and weapons of stone have been found, along with bones of the mammoth and mastodon, in the auriferous gravel, 200 and 300 feet from the surface, and overlaid by thick beds of lava, and tufa, and gravel. The best known of these instances is the skull said to have been found in a shaft, near Angelos, Calaveras county, 150 feet deep. The shaft passed through five beds of lava and volcanic tufa. With regard to this particular case, it appears that Professor Whitney, who reported it (to the Chicago Academy of Sciences, we believe), was the victim of a hoax on the part of some miners. But Mr. Bancroft, in his "Native Races of the Pacific States,"[1] mentions various other cases of a similar character, which, although not the result of original scientific discovery, are, perhaps, to be relied on as reported with substantial accuracy. From the mining tunnels which penetrate Table Mountain, in Tuolumne County, we are told there was taken in 1858 a stone mortar holding two quarts, at a depth of 300 feet from the surface, lying in auriferous gravel under a thick stratum of lava. In 1862 another mortar was found at a depth of 340 feet, 104 of which were composed of lava, and 1800 feet from the mouth of the tunnel. Dr. Snell is said to have in his possession a pendant or shuttle of siliceous slate, spear-heads six or eight inches long, and a ladle of steatite, found under Table Mountain at the same depth as the preceding,

[1] Vol. iv. p. 698, *et seq.*

along with bones of the mastodon and other animals. At Gold Springs Gulch, in 1863, at a depth of sixteen feet in the auriferous gravel, a granite mortar and pestle were found, the former being twelve and a half inches in diameter, and weighing thirty pounds, and holding about two quarts. At Shaw's Flat, along with bones of the mastodon, a stone bead of calc-spar and a granite mortar, holding about a pint, were found at a point 300 feet from the mouth of the tunnel. At Gold Springs Gulch, above mentioned, "discoidal stones," three or four inches in diameter, both sides being concave, and perforated through the centre, were also found. "It has been suggested that these stones were used in certain hurling games." [1]

At the same place, with the usual bones, under from twenty to thirty feet of calcareous tufa, there was found, in 1862, a flat oval dish of granite, eighteen and a half inches in diameter, two or three inches thick, and weighing forty pounds.

At San Andrés, in 1864, large stone mortars were taken from a layer of cemented gravel six feet thick, lying under the following strata:—coarse sedimentary volcanic material, five feet; sand and gravel, one hun-

[1] These discoidal stones are found in the mounds of the Mississippi Valley. They are made of granite or some very hard stone. Schoolcraft's "Archives of Aboriginal Knowledge," &c., vol. i. p. 87. The same statement is made by Squier and Davis. We are told also by Colonel C. C. Jones, in his "Antiquities of the Southern Indians," that they were used by the Indians of Georgia, Tennessee, Alabama, &c., in their national game of *Chungke*. Numbers of them are found also in the plains and mountains of Chili—flat circular stones of granite or porphyry, about five or six inches in diameter, with a hole drilled through the centre. Those found in the North American mounds are often *concave* on both surfaces, like those described from Gold Springs Gulch. See "Antiquities of the Southern Indians," p. 352.

dred feet; brownish volcanic ash, three feet; cemented sand, four feet; bluish volcanic sand, fifteen feet.

At Kincaid's Flat, in clayey auriferous gravel, sixteen or twenty feet below the surface, a stone mortar and pestle, and many other stone implements, with bones of the elephant and mastodon, were found.

At Diamond Spring mortars were taken from a depth of 100 feet.

At Spanish Flat were found several polished stone hammers, with a groove around them, many mortars, and other stone implements, including two "pendants or shuttles," very well worked from greenstone, and similar to one obtained at the depth of 340 feet under Table Mountain.[1]

"These relics," we are told by Mr. Bancroft, "have been found in almost every instance by miners in their search for gold,"[2] and the relics in all the cases come from the "auriferous gravel."

Professor Whitney and Dr. Foster refer this auriferous gravel to the Pliocene Age, and Dr. Foster remarks that "since the introduction of man, the physical features of the country, as well as the climate of this region, have undergone great changes. The volcanic peaks of the Sierra Nevada have been lifted up, the glaciers have disappeared, the great cañons themselves have been excavated in the solid rock, and what were once the beds of streams now form the Table Mountains."[3]

[1] See Bancroft's Native Races of the Pacific States, vol. iv. pp. 697–709.

[2] See p. 698.

[3] Prehistoric Races of the United States, p. 54.

Dr. C. F. Winslow, in 1857, sent to the Boston Natural History Society the fragment of a human skull, which he represented as found in the "pay-dirt" (gold-gravel), in association with bones of the elephant and mastodon, 180 feet below the surface of Table Mountain. And in 1868, Professor Blake read before the American Association at Chicago an account of the finding of the teeth of extinct mammalia, two stone objects (of steatite) like shovels, some instruments resembling plummets, mortars, and polished spear-heads, beneath this same volcanic mountain, at the depth of 100 or 200 feet.

Professor Blake has, however, informed us that he entertains very great doubts as to the antiquity of these objects, and suggests that they may have been washed into their position through lateral fissures in the mountain. The spear-heads he stated to be polished implements, and "superior to anything produced by the present aborigines of the country."

Before expressing our views on the subject, we desire to mention some other cases of a similar character, in order to put the reader in possession of all the facts calculated to assist him in forming his conclusions.

Mr. Bancroft in a note mentions that at Don Pedro's Bar, in 1861, at the depth of thirty feet, and beneath a huge pine, the growth of centuries, there were found a figure of a deer's foot cut in slate, a slate tube five inches long, and an inch in diameter, and a small, flat, rounded piece of some very hard flinty rock, with a square hole in the centre, all highly polished, and black with age.

"An ancient skillet," says the "Grass Valley Sentinel," quoted by Mr. Bancroft, "made of lava, hard as iron, circular, with a spout and three legs, was washed out of a deep claim at Forest Hill a few days since. It

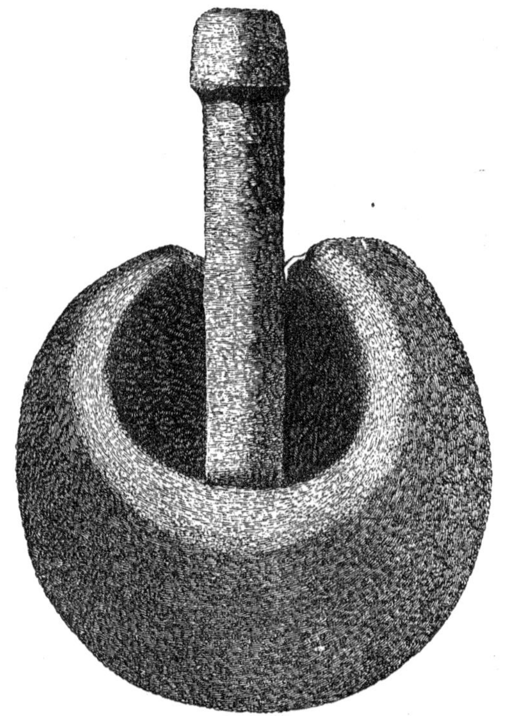

Stone Mortar—Kincaid's Flat.

will be sent to the State Fair as a specimen of crockery used in the mines several thousand years ago." A similar vessel was found at Coloma, in 1851, at a depth of fifteen feet, under an oak-tree not less than 1000 years old.

"Many stone mortars and mastodon bones," we are told, "have been found about Altaville[1] and Murphy's."

These relics, as we have stated, are referred by Professor Whitney and Dr. Foster to the Pliocene Epoch, and we are expected to believe that the region now

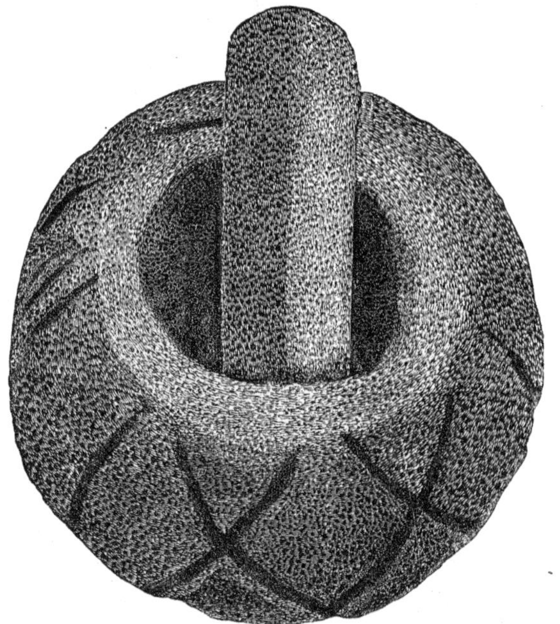

Granite Mortar—Gold Springs Gulch.

known as California was in its Polished Stone Age during what is geologically known as the Tertiary Age, and that the inhabitants made use of large granite mortars and skillets with spouts, and grooved stone hammers, and slate tubes, and ladles of steatite. The best com-

[1] It was at Altaville that the Calaveras skull was reported to have been found.

mentary on such a demand on our credulity is to give the annexed cuts (preceding pages) of some of the stone mortars which have been found, and which we take from Mr. Bancroft's work.

The following are representations of certain so-called "pendants" or "shuttles" from Spanish Flat, which are similar to others obtained from Kincaid's Flat and from Table Mountain.

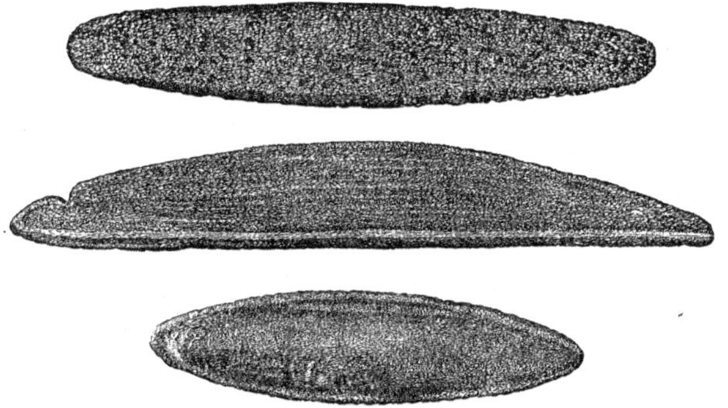

Stone Implements—Spanish Flat.

The following cut represents a relic from the San Joaquin Valley, which Dr. Foster pronounces "an exhibition of the lapidary's skill superior to anything yet furnished by the Stone Age of either continent." It is of sienite, and "is ground and polished so as to dis-

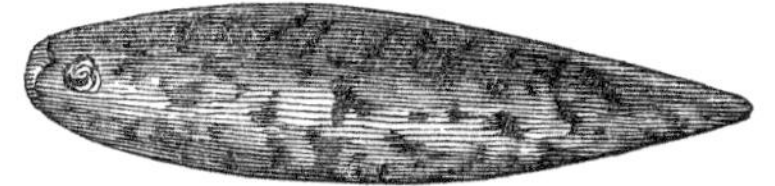

play in marked contrast the pure white of the feldspar and the dark-green or black of the hornblende." It was found, imbedded in gravel, at the depth of thirty feet.

With regard to Professor Whitney's idea of connecting these objects with the Pliocene Age, it may be observed that if their high antiquity were admitted we should have to refer them to the River-Gravel Epoch, and not to the Pliocene Age, as we find with them the bones of the mastodon and mammoth.

The volcanic matter which overlies them at Table Mountain (and elsewhere), moreover, is probably the result of by no means remote volcanic disturbances in this region. The whole chain of the Rocky Mountains and the Pacific slope have, as we have described elsewhere, at a *very* recent period been the theatre of physical convulsions unparalleled apparently in any other part of the world. Whole districts of country are covered with the basaltic outflow, and fire, ice, water, and tremendous subterraneous forces have together, or in succession, left the marks of a storm more terrible even than our conceptions of the DELUGE. These effects are visible in Montana, Idaho, Colorado, New Mexico, Utah, and California; and Professor Hayden tells us, as we have seen, that "this effusion of the basalt is a modern event, probably occurring, for the most part, near the commencement of our present period, after the entire surface reached nearly, or quite, the present elevation." "The lake-deposits" (to repeat what has been quoted elsewhere), he says, "are certainly of very moderate date, at least as late, and perhaps later, than the Pliocene. Upon this rests a huge bed of drift, which was deposited still later, and then comes the outflow of basalt"—in other words, it is post-glacial.

We saw, moreover, that these states and territories

are marked by numerous hot springs and geysers, which represent the expiring energies of the Volcanic Epoch—which has not yet closed—as Jorullo and numerous other instances in modern times have signally illustrated.[1]

We have no idea, however, that the implements found under Table Mountain and elsewhere are as old as this.

They were found, as we have stated, "in almost every instance *by miners in their search for gold.*"

Another noticeable feature is that they seem always to occur in the *auriferous gravel.*

We observe also the constant recurrence of *the granite mortars.*

It is obvious that these mortars have been left in these positions by the ancient inhabitants in their search for *gold.* Cortez, we know, found the Mexican palaces and temples resplendent with gold, and the work of their artisans in gold and silver is said to have surpassed the skill of the Spaniards. "The metallurgic arts," says Dr. Wilson, "were carried in some respects further by the Mexicans than by the Peruvians. Silver, lead, and tin were obtained from the mines of Tasco, and copper was wrought in the mountains of Zacotollan by means of galleries and shafts opened with persevering toil where the metallic veins were imbedded in the solid rock."[2] Both gold and copper, we are told by Mr. Bancroft, were mined in Mexico from veins in

[1] See United States Geological Survey of Territories, 1871, pp. 30, 42, 48; and 1872, pp. 35, 36, 43, 44, 50, 51, &c.

[2] Prehistoric Man, first edition, p. 193.

the solid rock, extensive galleries being opened for the purpose.[1]

They carried their excavations, we are told, to the depth of 200 feet or more, to procure the chalchiuite, so much worn for ornament, and so highly prized by them.[2] Obsidian they procured in the same way, the mines at the Cerro de las Navajas, near Monte Jacal, being described as openings three or four feet in diameter, and 110 to 140 in extent (horizontally), with side drifts where the material seemed abundant.

The Mound-Builders of the East, we know, were considerable miners, as the copper mines of Lake Superior and the mica mines of North Carolina testify.

The evidence, however, that the ancient population of California mined for gold in the region where the relics we have described have been found is not merely inferential. The proof is positive. "It was late in the month of August," says Schoolcraft, "in 1849, that the gold diggers at one of the mountain diggings called Murphy's,[3] were surprised, in examining a high barren district of mountain, to find the abandoned site of an antique mine. 'It is evidently,' says a writer, 'the work of ancient times.' The shaft discovered is 210 feet deep. Its mouth is situated on a high mountain. It was several days before preparations could be completed to descend and explore it. The bones of a human skeleton were found at the bottom. There were also found an altar for worship, and other evidences of

[1] Native Races of Pacific States, ii. 474.

[2] Ibid., iv. 673.

[3] Where, as we have mentioned, many mortars have been found. It seems to be at Table Mountain.

ancient labour. . . . No evidence has been discovered to denote the era of this ancient work. There has been nothing to determine whether it is to be regarded as the remains of the explorations of the first Spanish adventurers, or of a still earlier period. The occurrence of the remains of an altar looks like the period of Indian worship."[1]

This is the key which unlocks the whole mystery.

As regards the mortars, we suspect they were used for crushing the cemented gravel of the auriferous beds.

It is extremely to be regretted that eminent men of science, and writers like Mr. Bancroft, should deal in this shallow manner with a grave question like this.

The relics found under Table Mountain, and in other similar localities, might naturally excite the wonder of miners and magazine writers in California, and elicit from them extravagant speculations as to their antiquity; but it is inexcusable to have these crude suggestions repeated by Mr. Whitney or Mr. Bancroft, or (as at the late meeting of the American Association) by Professor O. C. Marsh.

If one finds a gold sovereign at the depth of 300 feet in one of the mountains of Scotland, is he to ascertain the age of the sovereign by proceeding to calculate the time which was required for the formation of all the geological strata above it? As well ascertain the age of a frog at the bottom of a well, by tracing the geological succession of events from the bottom to the top of the excavation.

[1] Schoolcraft's Archæology, vol. i. p. 105.

ADDENDA.

Page 77.

Pottery at Kent's Cavern.

The discovery of pottery in the "Bear's Den," at Kent's Cavern, is reported in the thirteenth annual report of the committee for the exploration of this cave, which was read at the late meeting of the British Association at Plymouth.

There are two floors of stalagmite at Kent's Cavern. Beneath the first, which is from one to three feet thick, is the cave-earth containing the palæolithic flints and the bones of the extinct animals. Below this cave-earth is another thicker floor of stalagmite, and under this is the "Bear's Den," so called from the great predominance of the bones of the cave-bear over those of the other palæolithic animals. In this, we are told, eleven flint implements have been found. And it was in "the excavated materials (from this den) left by M'Enery" (the first explorer) that the committee found remains of the cave-bear (two hundred specimens), mammoth, hyæna, fox, and deer, and "a few bits of coarse pottery." If this pottery got into this bed from above, it must have passed through two floors of stalagmite.

Page 93.

In a discussion (1874) on the Brixham Cavern, Mr. Whitley stated that in culverts which he had made he had seen stalagmite formed an inch in thickness, and stalactites six inches in length. Professor Tennant remarked that in the cave of Matlock birds' nests and chancellors' wigs were petrified by being put into the water. . . . In many districts in England, he said, spouts carrying water from mines were choked up in two or three years In the British Museum there was a table made from the four sides of a spout. The aperture of the spout was originally one foot square, but it was reduced to four inches by five years' deposits.—*Trans. Vict. Inst.*, part xxxi.

Page 115.

DOMESTICATED ANIMALS IN THE PALÆOLITHIC AGE.

There is strong ground for the belief that the palæolithic tribes were not unacquainted with the domesticated animals. The evidence for the domestication of the horse at Solutré has been laid before the reader in the chapter on that station. More than one of the domestic animals seem also to have existed at Veyrier and the Kesslerloch—the tame ox especially at the former, and the tame ox, the domestic pig, and probably the dog, as well as the horse, at the latter. There were found at the Kesslerloch not only bones which seem to belong to the domesticated pig, but an imperfect drawing (the fragment being mutilated) of the same animal. The head and neck are missing; but enough remains to make it nearly certain that it is a representation of the domestic pig (see pl. xi. fig. 67, in Merk's "Excavations at the Kesslerloch," translated by Mr. Lee, and "Matériaux," 1876, tome vii. p. 102). The presence of the dog, we are told in "Matériaux pour l'Histoire de l'Homme" (1876, tome vii. p. 102), has been ascertained in the cavern of Freundenthal (the neighbouring district) excavated by Professor Karsten of Schaffhausen. This cave is considered contemporary with the Kesslerloch, as is also probably the cave near Herblingen, where "a good deal of pottery" was found.

The remains of the dog have also been met with in one of the Swabian caves, and in the cavern of Nero in France, and, it may be, at Kent's Cavern (in the lowest bed). In the last case the bones, however, may belong to the wolf.

Page 131.

At 200 feet high the sea would have filled the valley up to the source of the Somme.

Page 157.

The whole argument so far as it is based on the reindeer.

The *close* of the palæolithic period seems to have been marked by considerable cold, at least so far as the winters are concerned.

It must always be remembered, however, in discussing this question of climate, that the bones of the hippopotamus and the hyæna are found side by side with those of the musk-sheep and the reindeer.

Page 159.

THE REINDEER.

In the United States the bones of the reindeer have been found on the surface of the ground in New York, and near the surface at Big Bone Lick, in Kentucky; but there was no means of ascertaining with any precision their age.

We find it stated now, however, that the bones of this animal (the caribou) have been recently found in an Indian mound in Lee County, Virginia, which is in the extreme south-western part of the State, on the Tennessee line.

The exploration of this mound is published in the Tenth Annual Report of the Peabody Museum of American Archæology (1877). The mound is 19 feet in height and 100 feet in diameter. In it were found human skeletons, pottery, arrowheads of stone, implements of horn, a quantity of Indian corn (some of it still on the cob), beads of shell, and bones of the black bear, deer, elk, caribou, turtle, crane, &c.

The mound is referred to the Indians; we think it more probable that it belonged to the Mound-Builders.

It may be added that it is mentioned in a Report made to the Hon. Lewis Cass (then Governor of this territory), in 1820, and published in the Wisconsin Historical Collections, vol. vii., that the reindeer was hunted at that time in Northern Wisconsin, on the southern shores of Lake Superior.

Page 161.

In Smith's "Cork," vol. i. p. 336, it is stated that the horns and teeth of a moose-deer were found in a bog, "in excellent marl," near Castle-Saffron, about a mile east of Doneraile; and with these remains were found, at the same time, a brass spur, a brass spoon, hazel-nuts, charcoal, &c.—See also vol. ii. p. 411.

As to the urus, which we have stated, on the authority of Baron Herberstein, to have been living in Germany in the sixteenth century, we may add that Bell, who travelled in Russia and Asia in the early part of the eighteenth century, remarks that "the uhr-ox is found near Kuznetsky (Siberia), and in the woods of Poland, and some other parts of Europe."—*Bell's Travels*, vol. i. p. 212.

Page 172.

In Siberia the mammoth and the tichorine rhinoceros belong unmistakably to the present fauna of the country. In the caves of the Altai examined by Professor Brandt, the bones of these animals, as well as those of the hyæna, were found, but associated with more than thirty other distinct species, all of which are now living near the same regions.—*Geographical Distribution of Animals*, vol. i. p. 111.

Page 173.

The lion survived in Europe later than the time of Aristotle. It is proved to have inhabited the mountains of Thrace by the concurrent testimony of Herodotus, Aristotle, Xenophon, Ælian, and Pausanias, "and probably," says Mr. Dawkins, "became extinct in Europe before the end of the first century after Christ."

And while "history" is silent as to the existence of the lion in Spain, his remains (the African lion) were found in the neolithic caves of Gibraltar, as were those of the hyæna, leopard, and other African animals.

We mention on p. 180 that the bones of the African elephant have been found in Spain.

It is stated also that the *Rhinoceros hemitœchus* was found at Gibraltar. Can this be a mistake? Mr. Wallace, in his "Geographical Distribution of Animals," makes no allusion to the statement, but does state that the *hippopotamus* was found here.

Page 174.

The bones of the spotted hyæna (as stated in note above) were found in the Gibraltar caves.

Page 181.

They bring also the white Syrian bear. The bear of Syria, as it grows old, becomes "nearly as white as the Arctic bear."—*Wood's Bible Animals*, p. 76.

Page 183.

The bones of horses, and sometimes elephants, with objects of gold, silver, &c., are found in the ancient graves of Siberia, near Tomsky.—See *Bell's Travels*, vol. i. p. 210.

Page 186.

Professor Dawkins identified, in the Oxford Museum, a last lower true molar of the pigmy hippopotamus, which Dr. Rolleston obtained from a Greek tomb at Megalopolis, in the Peloponese.—*Cave-Hunting*, p. 378.

Page 204.

Pottery has been found in a marine bed on the coast of South America, showing an elevation of 150 feet since it lay on the sea bottom.—*Encyclop. Britannica*, art. "America."

Page 336 (*note*).

No doubt the original migration of the Toltecs occurred much earlier than the time of Tscenghis Khan, perhaps in the fifth century.

Page 347.

NO EVIDENCE OF PRE-GLACIAL MAN.

Since the account of the Victoria Cave was written, Mr. Boyd Dawkins has come to the conclusion that "in England we have no evidence of pre-glacial man;" and that the fibula about which so much has been written, as found under glacial clay in the Victoria Cave, "seems to be ursine rather than human."—See *Proceedings of Geological Society of London*, April 11, 1877, and a report in "Nature," vol. xvi. No. 397, p. 106, of a discussion on the antiquity of man at the Anthropological Institute.

At the meeting of the Geological Society of London referred to, Mr. Evans remarked that, "for his own part, he had not met with any evidence of man's presence in glacial or pre-glacial times;" and "he was glad to find that the determination of the supposed human fibula from the Victoria Cave was so doubtful that it may safely be rejected."

Dr. Murie said: "With regard to the supposed human fibula

from Victoria Cave, he had, at Professor Busk's request, made a careful examination and comparison of it in the Museum of the Royal College of Surgeons, and come to the conclusion that it might be almost any bone; all ideas of the habits of the cave-dwellers founded upon it were therefore mere fictions."

Professor Hughes, at the Conference of the Anthropological Institute, reported in "Nature," remarked that "with regard to the Victoria Cave, he thought that the evidence was as yet decidedly against the pre-glacial age of any of the deposits containing even a suspicion of man."

This is another of these cases referred to in our chapter on "Premature Announcements of the Antiquity of Man." No longer ago than 1874, in his carefully prepared work on "Cave-Hunting," Professor Dawkins summed up his discussion of the Victoria Cave by remarking that "the pleistocene strata in the Victoria Cave may be considered pre-glacial;" and that "the small fragment of human bone found by the Settle Cave Exploration Committee in the former (the Victoria) cave, in 1872, establishes the fact that man lived in Yorkshire before the glacial period" (p. 411).

One of the latest evidences of "inter-glacial" man is based on some "sharpened" sticks found in an inter-glacial bed of lignite at Wetzikon, in Switzerland. We regard these beds in Switzerland as probably contemporary with the River-Gravel period in the Somme Valley, and should not be greatly surprised if traces of man should appear in them; but it appears to us that these two or three "sharpened sticks" constitute a rather weak foundation for pronouncing man inter-glacial, even in Switzerland. And, confirmatory of this, Professor Steenstrup writes to "Archiv für Anthropologie," that in several instances sticks have been found in the Danish peat which have been sharpened by beavers.

By the last report of Mr. R. H. Tiddeman, F.G.S., on the Victoria Cave, read at the late meeting of the British Association at Plymouth, it appears that a number of bones belonging to the goat (some of which seem to have been cut) and the Celtic short-horn ox (*Bos longifrons*) were found, during the past year, along with those of the grizzly bear, hyæna, rhinoceros, mammoth, &c.

This conjunction is so astonishing that some doubts seem to have been thrown over the carefulness of the explorations.

But on our theory that the ice lingered later in Scotland and the north of England than in the south of England and France, all these remains may have been found together, and all of them may even be "inter-glacial." The remains of the reindeer and mammoth have been found in the inter-glacial deposits of Scotland.

The ice lingered in these regions to the Polished Stone Age, and the last survivors of the palæolithic animals wandered occasionally farther north than their usual range, or were driven north as man advanced.

Page 365.

The question as to whether the Somme, the Thames, the Mississippi have excavated their valleys since the "high-level" gravels were deposited is put to rest by the existence of these old high-level beaches on Lakes Michigan and Huron. If the rivers have excavated their valleys since the palæolithic or post-glacial epoch set in, then the lakes likewise, during the same period, have excavated the basins in which they lie, beginning at the high-level beaches, and working down to their present levels. But this is absurd; and the true explanation in each case is that the rivers and the lakes were formerly larger than they are now, their beds being filled with a much larger body of water.

INDEX.

THE END.

PRINTED BY BALLANTYNE, HANSON AND CO.
EDINBURGH AND LONDON

www.ingramcontent.com/pod-product-compliance
Lightning Source LLC
LaVergne TN
LVHW021131110826
845150LV00005B/998

* 9 7 8 1 4 2 5 5 4 9 7 1 8 *